A Question of Intelligence

A Question of
INTELLIGENCE

The IQ Debate in America

Daniel Seligman

A Birch Lane Press Book
Published by Carol Publishing Group

A Birch Lane Press Book
Published by Carol Publishing Group
Birch Lane Press is a registered trademark of Carol
    Communications, Inc.
Editorial Offices: 600 Madison Avenue, New York, N.Y. 10022
Sales and Distribution Offices: 120 Enterprise Avenue, Secaucus,
    N.J. 07094
In Canada: Canadian Manda Group, P.O. Box 920, Station U, Toronto,
    Ontario M8Z 5P9
Queries regarding rights and permissions should be addressed to
Carol Publishing Group, 600 Madison Avenue, New York, N.Y. 10022

Carol Publishing Group books are available at special discounts for bulk purchases, for sales promotions, fund-raising, or educational purposes. Special editions can be created to specifications. For details, contact: Special Sales Department, Carol Publishing Group, 120 Enterprise Avenue, Secaucus, N.J. 07094

Manufactured in the United States of America
10 9 8 7 6 5 4 3 2 1

Library of Congress Cataloging-in-Publication Data

Seligman, Daniel.
    A question of intelligence : the IQ debate in America / Daniel
Seligman.
        p. cm.
    "A Birch Lane Press book."
    ISBN 1-55972-131-6 (hard)
    1. Intelligence levels—United States.   2. Intelligence tests—
United States.   3. Intellect.
    BF431.S4355   1992   92-24374
    153.9'3'0973—dc20   CIP

Contents

Preface

The "IQ debate" is really a cluster of debates. The controversy centers on these intertwined questions:

Do IQ tests really measure anything that might reasonably be thought of as "intelligence"?

Why do some people have higher IQs than others? Is it mainly because the high-IQ individuals have more privileged backgrounds, or does their advantage reside mainly in their genetic constitutions?

Why do some *groups*—socioeconomic and racial—score higher on average than others?

Are IQ tests culturally biased against the poor and minorities?

Why do some *countries* seem to have higher IQs than others?

To what extent can IQ be raised?

How much do IQ differences—at the individual, group, or national level—really matter? What advantages come with higher IQs?

Should IQ tests be abolished?

Or would we benefit from a lot more testing?

These are all highly charged questions, and people tend to get extremely emotional about the answers. Furthermore, many people who have never read much about IQ testing tend to have strong opinions about what the answers are. It is probably fair to say that most educated Americans—and a high fraction of the people picking up this volume—will be predisposed toward skepticism about IQ tests.

They are likely to doubt that the tests truly measure intelligence. They suspect that differences in IQ mainly reflect the social advantages of the high scorers and the disadvantages of the low scorers. They have been told repeatedly that the tests are biased against poor people and racial minorities and incline to accept this judgment as accurate. They would not be unhappy to have IQ testing abolished in the public schools. Because these sentiments are so pervasive in America, some school districts—most conspicuously in California—have in fact begun to bar IQ testing of children.

The perspective of this book is quite different. It will argue that IQ tests do indeed measure mental abilities that might collectively be thought of as intelligence. Also, that intelligence testing is a worthwhile enterprise and that data generated by the tests have enormous social value and explanatory power.

I hope and believe that I can persuade most readers about these matters. But I also believe that some of those persuaded will still find the message of the IQ data offensive and that most readers will find it deeply troubling.

It *is* a troubling message, on several different counts. The test data tell us that people are quite unequal in mental ability; that these inequalitites are in substantial measure heritable; that those who test low have substantially fewer options in life than those who test high; and—most troublesome of all—that population *groups* with low average scores are likely to lead lives of below-average social and economic achievement.

The connection between IQ and achievement has one positive implication: It tells us that people at the top in American life are probably there because they are more intelligent than others—which is doubtless the way most of us think it should be.

But the message of the IQ data is nevertheless saturated in pessimism. It is very much at odds with the American public style, which is upbeat and inspirational. We expect our commencement speakers to tell our kids, "You can be anything you want to be," and would be horrified by a speaker who added, "If your IQ is high enough." Plainly and understandably, most Americans do not wish to hear the IQ message spelled out, and many seem more than willing to take out their irritation on the messenger.

A "messenger" like me would seem to have a special problem. I have been following the IQ debate since 1969— that being the year when it was, in effect, precipitated by Arthur R. Jensen's famous article in the *Harvard Educational Review*. (See chapter 5 for a lot more on Jensen and the article.) I have, by now, read widely in the IQ literature and claim to have a handle on the debate's inner logic. Still, I am not an academic scholar, certainly not a psychometrician. I am a journalist (by background a *Fortune* writer and editor), here in the role of popularizer, not authority. Given the highly polarized arguments that have enveloped the subject, why should any nonexpert reader look to this book for guidance? Why should I expect its arguments to be persuasive?

Luckily, those questions have answers. The answers will unfold throughout this book but can be crisply summarized in three paragraphs here:

1. The debate is really rather one-sided. On just about all the main issues, scholars in the field are far more uni-

fied than you might suppose from exposure to the subject in the American media. Furthermore, the views of these experts more often than not turn out to be the *opposite* of those you encounter in the media. The experts overwhelmingly believe, for example, that the tests can be thought of as good measures of intelligence. They believe that genetic factors play a major role in explaining IQ differences between individuals.

2. The arguments put forward in this book are essentially those of most experts. Until a few years ago, it would have been impossible to speak categorically about what "most experts" believe about IQ-related issues. It became possible only with the emergence in 1988 of detailed survey data generated by psychometrician Mark Snyderman and political scientist Stanley Rothman. Their survey of IQ professionals is described at length in chapter 2 of this book; several other chapters rely on it, typically to make the reassuring point that my own rendering of the issue has a lot of scholarly support.

3. There is another good reason to be leery of those anti-IQ sentiments you keep bumping into in the media. Many of them, I shall be arguing at several points in this book, are manifestly driven by political agendas rather than empirical data.

I will also be arguing that the anti-IQ mind-set has had broadly perverse consequences. For one thing, it has left many humane and well-intentioned people predisposed to believe in panaceas—in programs that claim to lift the intelligence levels of low-scoring children. I do not want to deride the possibility of such gains. There is no theoretical barrier telling us that IQs cannot possibly be lifted by environmental intervention. Although there is dispute about the precise magnitudes, everybody agrees that variability in IQ is substantially affected by environmental differences, and there is every reason to keep searching for programs that work—that really do lift the intelligence levels of children from deprived environments now occupying the low end of the IQ distribution. The discovery of any such programs would be of enormous practical importance. It would mean that life's options could be broadened for millions of kids. Still, the record of intervention programs thus far is discouraging, and we should at least be clear about the present state of play: Psychologists today do not know how to effect permanent and significant increases in intelligence levels via programs of cultural enrichment.

Alfred Binet developed the first test in 1905 in an effort to help identify children who would benefit from remedial programs—children who had previously been expelled from French schools as unteachable. Banning the tests today only makes it harder to identify and help such children. I will be arguing, in any case, that the elimination of testing does not eliminate the need to make distinctions among people. With or without IQ tests, somebody will still have to decide which kids need help and which are candidates for scholarships. It is hard to argue that those decisions will be better and fairer if made without the unique, often surprising insights flowing from test scores.

So I also hope to persuade readers that, in the end, intelligence testing is fairer and more humane than the alternatives.

Statistics and the IQ Debate: A Handhold for the Daunted

This book is an effort to render the IQ debate in terms comprehensible to laymen. It is a "popularization" of the issues. One reason a popularization seems indicated is that much of the debate, over the years, has been conducted at a high level of statistical sophistication, rendering the arguments incomprehensible to most Americans. To those who never took even an elementary course in statistics—that is, to the huge majority of literate Americans—the thrust and parry of debate has ordinarily been impossible to follow.

It doesn't have to be that way. Two statistical concepts are required to understand the points at issue in the debate, and both of them can be assimilated fairly readily—even by readers who never strayed from the liberal-arts fold.

One is the concept of correlations. There will be endless references to them in this book—for example, to the correlation between IQ and income or between parents' and children's IQs.

Correlations express the degree of association between two sets of figures. The degree of association is quantified in the coefficient of correlation, a number in the range between 1.0 and −1.0. A coefficient of 1.0 would be a perfect positive correlation; it would mean that increases in one set of figures were always precisely matched by proportional increases in the other set. Example: For a worker paid on a piecework basis, the correlation between earnings and output would have a coefficient of 1.0. A coefficient of −1.0 would be a perfect negative correlation, that is, an increase in one variable implies a corresponding *decrease* in the other. Example: the correlation between the consumer price index and the purchasing power of the dollar.

You will observe that both these examples of correlational "perfection" are somewhat artificial—both depend on one variable's being neatly linked to the other by definition. In the much messier real world, correlations almost invariably turn out to be somewhere between 0.0 and 1.0 (or, if negative, between 0.0 and −1.0).

Suppose, for example, that a baseball fan wanted to know the relationship between players' pay and their "runs batted in"—RBIs being a major measure of batting performance. He could start out by creating a long column listing all major-league players except pitchers. Then, opposite each name, he could list each player's annual pay (published quite widely every spring). Finally, he could create a third column listing the number of RBIs by each player in the same year.

Eyeballing the two right-hand columns, he would doubtless be able to discern that higher pay did seem to be associated with more RBIs in most cases—but not all cases. Without the correlation coefficient, he would have some trouble quantifying the relationship. I will not undertake here to describe the procedure by which the coefficient is extracted from the two columns, but will note for the record that if the fan got the same results I obtained for the 1991 season, he would show a correlation of .51—a figure telling him that there is a significant relationship between RBIs and pay, but also telling him that something besides RBIs is involved in that pay.

Herewith a few random IQ-related correlations:

• IQ correlates about .65 with elementary-school grades and about .55 with high-school grades.[1] The coefficient is somewhat lower in high school because a certain number of poor students drop out, narrowing the IQ range, which works to depress the correlation.

• IQ and myopia (i.e., nearsightedness) have long been known to be positively correlated. The relationship is not terribly strong (about .20 to .25) but it turns up persistently. For many years, it was assumed that this persistence reflected the heavier reading habits of high-IQ students, but recent studies have rejected this view in favor of a "pleiotropic" connection—meaning that some set of genes is thought to be affecting both IQ and eyes.[2]

• The IQs of husbands and wives have a correlation of about .45.[3] As is well known, husbands and wives select each other for a lot of different reasons, but it appears that the IQ correlation is higher than that for just about any other measurable trait. The correlation of husband-wife height, for example, is .30.[4]

• Facial features correlate weakly but positively with IQ. In one experiment, judges were asked to estimate the IQs of eighty-four women students merely by looking at photographs of their faces. The judges' estimates correlated about .20 with the students' actual IQs.[5]

• Contrary to certain stereotypes attached to athletes and intellectuals, physical coordination is positively correlated with IQ. Technical studies done by the U.S. Department of Labor report a correlation of .35 between coordination and cognitive ability.[6]

In measuring the degree of association between two sets of data, the correlation coefficient is not purporting to measure the extent to which one causes or "explains" the other. It is merely measuring the extent to which the two variables tend to rise or fall together. In principle, they may rise together without one's causing the other (as in the pleiotropic explanation of IQ and myopia). If there clearly is a causal connection, as in the correlation between IQ and school grades, it is still not measured by the correlation coefficient but by the *square* of this number, the so-called coefficient of determination. That is, a coefficient of .65 for IQ and elementary-school grades implies that 42 percent of the variablity in grades is attributable to IQ (because $.65^2$ is .42). How do you tell which variable is the causative one and which the one being caused? Mainly by using the brains God gave you, which would in most cases leave you able to envision how a high IQ could lead to high grades and to reject as implausible the possibility that the grades themselves were causing the high IQ. To be sure, there are plenty of cases in which it is much less clear which way the causation flows.

The other statistical concept required for following the debate is the standard deviation. The standard deviation (SD) is a measure of dispersion. Specifically, it measures the extent to which data are clustered around their average.

Why are such measures important? Because in thinking about the data pertaining to groups, you typically want to know more than their average performance. Suppose—to start out with an example unrelated to IQ—you wanted to know how much reporters earned on metropolitan newspapers. Suppose that somebody told you their average salary was $50,000. Your logical next question would be about the SD. You would want to know whether that salary figure meant most reporters made around $50,000 or, alternatively, that this figure just happened to be the average of a group containing a wide range of salaries. A low SD would tell you that most of the reporters were indeed bunched around $50,000; a high SD would suggest that this average reflected a lot of diversity in salaries.

When data are *normally* arrayed in the ubiquitous bell-shaped distribution curve, the SD has certain arresting properties. It turns out that just about 68 percent of the data are within one SD of the average. If, say, the SD for the newspaper reporters was $15,000, you could infer that something like 68 percent of them earned between $35,000 and $65,000. The other 32 percent would be evenly divided between 16 percent under $35,000 and 16 percent above $65,000. In other words, you could calculate that a reporter earning $65,000 would be around the eighty-fourth percentile.

For adult Americans tested on the Wechsler Adult Intelligence Scale (see chapter 1), the average score is 100, and the SD is 15 points. This means that 68 percent of the population has an IQ between 85 and 115. The SD is lower for some other nations that have more homogeneous populations. Japanese, for example, have a somewhat higher IQ than Americans but a somewhat lower SD—about 12 points instead of 15. The implications of these transnational comparisons are elaborated in chapter 9.

1

What It's Like to Take an IQ Test

The IQ debate to be rendered in these pages is heavily political, and succeeding chapters will track a succession of social and political controversies swirling up out of the IQ data. This chapter is much more mundane. It describes your author taking an IQ test.

Soon after I began outlining this book, I somewhat nervously decided that it was mandatory for me to take an IQ test. I had not confronted one in over forty years—not since I was in an undergraduate psychology course at New York University. Our instructor suggested, plausibly enough, that we would all have a better sense of intelligence testing if we had our own IQs measured. (He took the same line with a broad range of personality and aptitude tests, so we came out of the course with few secrets from the NYU psychology department.) Four decades later, I remember my IQ score, which I will coyly not disclose, but not a whole lot else about the event.

Most testees are young children or teenagers. The

usual reason for testing them is to get a line on the level at which they should be studying and to check on whether there might be a need for any special remedial efforts. But adult tests are very much available. The one I wanted to take was the Wechsler Adult Intelligence Scale, or WAIS, commonly pronounced "wayce." (There is also a Wechsler Intelligence Scale for Children, or WISC, pronounced "wisk.")

The WAIS, originally developed by psychologist David Wechsler in the 1950s, was substantially revised in 1981; the revised version is usually described as the WAIS-R. It is far and away the most widely administered adult test today. (The WISC also dominates child testing.) I went looking for somebody who routinely administered the WAIS-R and ended up in the office of Yaakov Stern, a psychologist based at the Neurological Institute at Columbia-Presbyterian Medical Center in New York City.

Stern proved to be a youthful (thirty-five), amiable, lanky, red-bearded professional wearing a colorful patterned sweater. In years past, he told me, his testing had mostly been of children. Nowadays, however, his practice is mostly with adults who have known or suspected medical problems. The most common case would be somebody who felt his memory slipping and feared the onset of Alzheimer's. On three of the eleven subtests that collectively make up the WAIS-R, scores are influenced by various kinds of memory skills; however, Alzheimer's is also associated with losses of other cognitive functions, so it would be reasonable for a suspected victim to take the entire test (along with quite a few other tests).

Chatting with Stern before the test began, I learned something that in years of studying IQ-related issues I had somehow never heard before. It turns out that the test questions, in addition to being copyrighted, are closely guarded—*very* closely guarded. Even if you were willing to shell out the $350 or so required to buy the Wechsler test kit, it would not be sold to you unless you were a licensed psychologist (like Stern) or had other professional credentials. The restriction is reasonable enough, when you think about it, the point being, of course, to keep the questions out of the hands of prospective testees and their mothers. Unfortunately, the secrecy will impose some limits on the description of my own test adventures. Before turning on my reporter's tape recorder, I had to agree not to be too precise in characterizing the test questions. So I have either invented questions that seem similar to those actually asked or else described the questions only in general terms.

The WAIS consists of eleven subtests, each consisting of questions or problems that tend to be easy at first, then grow progressively more difficult. The first subtest, labeled Information, checks out your fund of general information and your ability to retrieve it in a reasonable time. (This is one of the subtests bearing on memory.) I turned out to be mortifyingly slow responding to Stern's first two questions. The first, which concerned the position of the sun in the sky, could have been answered instantly by a neolithic four-year-old, but I found myself suddenly caught up in confusion trying to envisage shadows falling on New York City streets at different times of day; the tape shows that it took me about three seconds to answer (correctly). After the first two questions, we moved along more rapidly. However, two of my answers (out of twenty-nine) were wrong. Like the question about the sun in the sky, both involved physical phenomena and reminded me that I was a dumbbell in seventh-grade science.

The next exercise, Picture Completion, was one of the so-called "performance tests." (The performance tests require you to *do* something, not just answer questions.) Picture Completion also tests memory; in addition, it gauges your visual alertness and attention to detail. You get to look at a succession of twenty cards, each of which shows a drawing of some familiar scene or object. You have to say what's missing from the drawing. I knew I would be terrible at this one, and I was. On the cards Stern thrust at me, I failed to see what was missing in pictures of a frog, some pliers, a violin, a pair of eyeglasses, and several more. Dismal score: only twelve right out of twenty.

In the middle of the exercise, I found myself thinking back glumly to a chronic professional problem during my years as an editor of *Fortune*. The magazine has always placed a lot of emphasis on its artwork. My problem as an editor was a curious inability to think critically about the illustrations being proposed. They all looked fine to me. I could look at a page of text and instantly catch a typographical error, but flaws in the art were somehow invisible to me.

I did much better on the next exercise: the Digit Span. This is a test of short-term memory in which the examiner reads off a string of digits and asks you to repeat them. He begins with three digits and proceeds incrementally to nine. If you miss twice at any level, you are judged to have scored at the next-lower level. I made it to nine with no special difficulty.

But there is a fiendish round two to Digit Span. Beginning with two digits and proceeding on to eight, the examiner asks you to repeat the digits *backward*. This was a lot tougher. I found that once we were up to six or seven digits, it helped me to "chunk" them into groups of three or four. Of course, you still have to hold the first chunk in your head while focusing on the second, and twice during the exercise I lost that first chunk. On the other hand, I batted a solid .500 on the eight-digit span backward—accomplishing it once in two attempts—and found my morale somewhat restored.

Footnote to the above: Sometime after taking the WAIS-R, I read an account by Arthur Jensen (see chapter 5) of some tests he had adminstered to Mrs. Shakuntala Devi, an Indian calculating prodigy. Devi is in the *Guinness Book of World Records* for having multiplied two 13-digit numbers (randomly selected by a computer) in only twenty-eight seconds, her correct answer being 18,947,668,177,995,-426,462,773,730. Jensen reported on a performance he witnessed himself at Stanford University, where she repeatedly managed similar unbelievable feats, for example, giving the eighth root of a fourteen-digit number in ten seconds, never making an error.

Which brings us to a stunning detail: When tested on the WAIS, Devi could not get beyond four digits backward (which is roughly normal for adults).[1]

Next Stern threw another performance test at me. In Picture Arrangement, you get to look at several cards—at least three, sometimes as many as seven—each of which shows a drawing. The drawings look like panels in comic strips. You are asked to arrange the cards from left to right so that the drawings tell some kind of meaningful story; in some cases, more than one sequence is allowed to be meaningful. Picture Arrangement measures, among other things, your ability to anticipate and to engage in "social planning." (I am quoting a psychology textbook.)[2] Possibly evidencing his weakness in social planning, the tape at this point records a frustrated sixty-four-year-old mumbling to himself in anguish and occasionally expressing delight at a solution. His final score was nothing to boast about.

Stern then moved on to the Vocabulary subtest. If you have spent your professional life as an editor of a first-rate magazine, you ought to have a pretty good vocabulary, and the WAIS confirmed that I do. The drill in this subtest is as follows. Your examiner reads off a list of words—thirty-five in my case—and asks you to define them. If you give a superior answer, going to the heart of the meaning, you get two points; if your answer seems to show only some general understanding of the context in which the word might be used, you get one point; if the answer totally misses the point, you get a goose egg. I got two points on thirty-three of the definitions and one point twice. When Stern and I sat down after the test and went over the results, I found myself sadly agreeing that the two one-pointers had in fact reflected somewhat wobbly answers.

Many people do not quite see why vocabulary should be tested in an exercise that is supposed to be measuring mental *ability*. Their objection: that vocabulary mainly reflects acquired knowledge rather than an ability to learn. In fact, vocabulary is a pretty good proxy for overall IQ; if a professional tester had to make do with just one of the subtests, he would probably land on Vocabulary. The reason it correlates so powerfully with IQ is that you build a vocabulary in a process that requires a lot of reasoning. In your reading and listening, you are endlessly making inferences about different shades of meaning and the different contexts in which words are used. A somewhat similar point might be made about the Information subtest (which many people also view as unrelated to intelligence). You acquire a fund of information not by absorbing data in isolation but by noting the connections between different data. Both Vocabulary and Information correlate about .80 with overall IQ—a figure that is higher than those for any other subtests.[3]

Stern and I next moved on to Block Designs, another performance test. Again I could see art problems coming. Block Designs requires you to work with plastic blocks, all cubical in shape. Each has two red sides, two white sides, and two sides divided diagonally between red and white. The examiner first shows you a design pattern, then scrambles the blocks on the table and asks you to assemble them so as to re-create the pattern. Some of the patterns require you to manipulate nine blocks, some only four. Anybody, even I, can do the design if given enough time; unfortunately, the time you take is factored into your score. On the first eight efforts, I did finally manage to replicate the designs, but my times were generally terrible. On the ninth effort, I gave up in frustration, even though I clearly had eight of the nine blocks in place. Block Designs tests your ability to see the component parts of visual patterns. The tape again has a lot of morose muttering.

The subtest called Arithmetic proved to be a breeze and morale restorer. The questions were what we used to call "problems" in the sixth grade, generally taking this form: If a car averages forty miles an hour, how far will it travel in forty-five minutes? Evidencing possible updating needs for the WAIS, one of the questions concerned the change you might get upon purchasing a certain number of two-cent stamps.

By this time—we were now a little past the one-hour mark—a pattern had emerged. Although I was not being told my scores on the subtests, it was fairly obvious that I was doing well on the verbal-arithmetic front, not so well when confronted with spatial-visual problems. So I blanched again when confronted with Object Assembly, still another performance test. In Object Assembly, you are given a series of odd-shaped cardboard cutouts and asked to fit them together. Except for not having much of a clue as to what the finished product will look like, you are essentially doing a jigsaw puzzle. I managed to complete each of the puzzles, but once again my times were not too great.

Next Stern brought on a subtest that, I later learned, is called Comprehension. It gauges your ability to organize information about the world you live in and arrive at some commonsense understanding of various social phenomena. Most of the questions seemed sensible, but I found myself suddenly rebelling against one question on ideological grounds. The question assumed a need for certain laws bearing on labor relations and asked *why* they were needed. My instant answer, which would have been backed by many eminent economists, was that the laws are not needed and are in fact counterproductive. Obviously uninterested in debating social policy, Stern cheerfully restated the question so that all you needed to produce was the theory behind the laws. I got scored correct for the theory (and generally did quite well on Comprehension); however, I found myself still muttering about David Wechsler's grasp of economics.

Marching toward the end of the test, we now reached Digit Symbol, a performance test that involved some more memory skills. What you had to remember this time were visual symbols, so I approached the test with minimal confidence. You begin by inspecting a table that shows nine simple symbols—a circle, a plus sign, etc.—and are told that each represents a digit from 1 through 9. Then you are shown several rows of the digits, arranged in random order. The object is to draw the appropriate visual symbol in a box under each digit and to complete as many boxes as you can in the allotted ninety seconds. If you can memorize the symbols as you are doing the exercise, you will of course go much faster, and complete more boxes, than if you have to keep referring back to the table. I found that I had to keep referring back to it; at least I knew I would make a fair number of mistakes if I tried to rely on memory. It struck me, midway through Digit Symbol, that it would have been nice to know something about the scoring tradeoffs between accuracy and speed. Possibly I was overconcerned about accuracy; anyway, I ended up with a so-so total of fifty-four symbols. The subtest is designed to measure attentiveness and quickness, and, not surprisingly, it is tough for us old folks. Of all the subtests (I later discovered), it shows the greatest age-based decline in raw scores.

The final subtest, Similarities, is a measure of abstract reasoning ability. It all seemed very easy. The examiner mentions two nouns—like, say, chicken and pigeon—and the testee responds by saying what they have in common. (In this made-up example, the answer would be that they're both birds.) Nothing to it.

When the test ended, after about ninety minutes, I went over my answers with Stern and watched him convert them into an IQ score. Actually, you walk away with three scores: one covering the overall verbal portions of the test (where I did quite well), one covering the performance tests (where the results were mediocre), and a weighted average that becomes your IQ. Being still coy, I decline to state the number on the bottom line. I do insist on mentioning, however, that the scores were adversely affected by my age.

IQ tests are of course normed for age. Anybody taking the test is in effect compared only with people around his own age. This arrangement seems obvious and natural when you are thinking of children; after all, it would make no sense to hold a five-year-old child to the same standards as a six-year-old. It should be, but possibly isn't, equally obvious that you shouldn't hold a sixty-four-year-old to the same standards as a younger adult. As we shall sadly see in chapter 6, many of the mental skills measured by the test decline sharply with age. So the testers' procedure is to take the average raw score at every age and assign it a value of 100—the norm for that age. Reflecting the bell-shaped distribution of results, around two-thirds of all the testees in the age bracket get an IQ somewhere between 85 and 115; around 95 percent get scores between 70 and 130.

In talking with Yaakov Stern about the norming process for people my own age, I discovered with some annoyance that the WAIS data are not extensive enough to make possible a precise fit for sixty-four-year-olds. It seems that in calculating my score he had to think of me as belonging to the whole cohort aged fifty-five to sixty-four. This means I was being compared with sharp-witted folks in their fifties, whereas if I had taken the test six months later, after my sixty-fifth birthday, I would have been normed against dotards ranging up to sixty-nine—and my IQ would have been five points higher. I may go back for a replay.

Postscript: I had promised Stern a look at my draft of this chapter and sent it on to him a week or so after the test. He pointed to a few factual flaws in my description of the test. These have been corrected, as has my characterization of his sweater, which—inept to the end at handling visual details—I had confidently described as plaid.

2

Searching for Intelligence

In June 1923, Prof. Edward Boring of Harvard wrote in the *New Republic*: "Intelligence as a measurable capacity must at the start be defined as the capacity to do well in an intelligence test. Intelligence is what the tests test."[1]

That statement has been quoted a lot over the years. Among those quoting it liberally have been critics of IQ tests eager to make a point: that the whole testing enterprise is driven by circular reasoning.[2] David Wechsler, perhaps the world's most successful developer of IQ tests, seems to have been nettled by the circularity argument; in any case, he mentioned it back in 1939 as a reason for proposing a definition of intelligence that went beyond "what the tests test." His definiton: "Intelligence is the aggregate or global capacity of the individual to act purposefully, to think rationally, and to deal effectively with his environment."[3] Wechsler later modified the definition somewhat; in a 1975 version, intelligence was the "capacity of an individual to understand the world about him and his resourcefulness to cope with its challenges"[4] But even if he had been perfectly consistent and even if his tests perfectly measured the capacities he described, the critics would not have been mollified. For who was to say that Wechsler's definition was "right"? And if it was wrong, why should anybody think IQ tests measured intelligence?

Critics pushing this line of argument can in fact point to eminent psychologists who deny that IQ tests measure intelligence. Some argue that intelligence is not one attribute but a lot of different ones. Howard Gardner of Harvard has promoted the idea of mutiple "intelligences" and denies that they can be meaningfully combined in a unitary score like an IQ.[5] Prof. Robert J. Sternberg of Yale, also a critic of IQ tests, has proposed a "triarchic theory" in which intelligence is broken down into conceptual, creative, and contextual modes of thinking.[6] Contextual thinking, the third member of the triarchy, is also known as "practical intelligence," or PI, which nowadays has quite a few fans besides Sternberg. PI is typically identified by the fans as "street smarts," said to be far more important in the real world than the "school smarts" measured by IQ tests.[7] (The next chapter will consider practical intelligence at some length.)

These familiar objections to IQ testing are less formidable than they might appear. Most scholars believe that IQ tests measure skills it is reasonable to think of as intelligence.

In support of this answer, I now bring onstage a survey that will also be cited at several other points in this volume—usually because I will be trying to get a line on what "most experts" believe about some controversial matter. The survey was an extraordinary event. It was run by Mark Snyderman, a Harvard-trained psychologist who has since pursued a career in law, and Stanley Rothman, professor of government at Smith College. In 1988 they published the survey results in a book called *The IQ Controversy: The Media and Public Policy.*[8] The book was written, say the authors, because of a concern "that the views of the relevant expert community are reported inaccurately to the attentive public by the elite media." By way of addressing this concern, Snyderman and Rothman (a) did a massive content analysis of IQ-related reporting over the years and (b) surveyed the experts for their views on various controversial issues. The experts were 661 scholars—a random sample of members of academic and other professional organizations— who responded to detailed questionnaires about intelligence testing (but were told not to answer questions outside their own areas of competence). I should hastily add that in citing the experts, I am not mindlessly assuming that experts are always right; obviously, they are not. The point of citing them here is only to do a little counterpunching: to weigh in against the widespread perception that experts are contemptuous of IQ tests as a valid measure of intelligence.

Snyderman and Rothman began by asking the experts which attributes they considered "important elements of intelligence." The resulting list was headed by an ability to reason abstractly (included by 99.3 percent of the respondents), to solve problems (97.7 percent), and to learn (96 percent).[9] How well were these and other important abilities represented in existing IQ tests? The answers collectively registered a few concerns—a major one was that creativity is not represented strongly enough—but, overall, provided a strong endorsement of the tests. The authors' summary: "On the whole, respondents seem to believe that intelligence tests are doing a good job measuring intelligence, as they would define it."[10]

What about the thought that intelligence comes in many varieties and that, as Howard Gardner says, these cannot be captured in a numerical score like the IQ? There is no doubt that diverse flowers bloom in the garden of intelligence. I write this passage a day after having read Paul Johnson's portrait of Bertrand Russell in *Intellectuals*.

Russell was a titan of modern philosophy and arguably the most intelligent man of the twentieth century, but Johnson notes that he was totally detached from physical reality. He could not make his hearing aid work, and he never learned how to make a pot of tea. His wife kept leaving him detailed instructions, for example, "Pour water from kettle into teapot"—but he never got the hang of it.[11]

The fact of diverse mental abilities is not exactly a secret to IQ testers. Or to testees. My own test experience shows all too plainly that many different abilities are tapped in the tests—also, that you emerge with more than one score. Analysis of subtest scoring patterns and efforts to extract diagnostic insights from the patterns represent a flourishing minor industry. I learn from *Assessment of Intellectual Functioning,* a textbook written by Lewis R. Aiken of Pepperdine College, that many studies have attempted to explain people like me who score much higher on the verbal than on the performance scales. Not making my day, Aiken notes that some studies relate this pattern to right hemisphere brain damage and others suggest the pattern is to be expected among "emotionally disturbed individuals."[12]

But if people have diverse mental abilities, why should anyone think of intelligence as singular rather than plural? And how can a single number like an IQ score be used as a gauge of intelligence? An answer to those questions might begin by conceding that the IQ score is a rough-and-ready measure, not a finely honed report. In some circumstances, you would indeed want to know a lot more about an individual's intelligence than his IQ score. But most of the time that score would tell you all you need to know. Richard J. Herrnstein of Harvard has put the case this way (in *IQ in the Meritocracy,* published in 1973): "The IQ cuts across the fine structure of the various theories, coming up with what is a weighted average of a set of abilities.... And since the abilities themselves tend to be intercorrelated, an omission here and there will have little effect.... When the task is to get a single number measuring a person's intellectual power, the IQ still does the job, even with the proliferation of theories and tests."[13]

Herrnstein, it happens, worked with Boring during the latter's last years at Harvard. (Boring died in 1968.) I asked him a while ago what Boring had meant by his often-quoted statement "Intelligence is what the tests test." Herrnstein said it was not at all intended as a put-down of IQ tests, certainly not as a complaint about circularity. It represented, rather, the perspective of a psychologist who believed (a) that "intelligence" needed to be anchored to some unambiguous operational definition and (b) that the cluster of abilities measured by IQ tests constituted a reasonable anchor. Fast analogy: You could define length (as my *Webster's Third New International Dictionary* does) as "a distance or dimension expressed in units of linear measure." You could also define it as the thing that tape measures measure.

The intercorrelation of all those subtest scores has another important implication. It has led most scholars to a belief in "general intelligence," or *g*. In the Snyderman-Rothman survey, two-thirds of the experts responding to the question supported a *g*-based model of intelligence, 15 percent preferred a model based on separate abilities, and the rest said they were unsure.[14]

During the past two decades or so, the case for the *g*-based model has been tirelessly argued by Arthur R. Jensen, professor of educational psychology at the University of California at Berkeley (see chapter 5). But the idea of general intelligence—and the habit of labeling it *g*—have deep roots in the history of psychology. Both are traceable to Charles Edward Spearman, a pioneering English psychologist who died in 1945.

Spearman got to *g* via studies of many different tests of mental ability. The studies led him to a stunning insight: *all* tests of mental ability are positively correlated.[15] In other words, people who score above (or below) average on any one test will in general score above (or below) average on any other. It is true that anything is possible in an individual case. It is also true that the positive correlations between tests are not of equal strength. But in large samples of randomly selected testees, the correlations are always positive, no matter how different the tests appear. Despite Bertrand Russell, you would find in the average case a positive correlation between skills in advanced mathematical logic and in learning to make tea. The persistence of these correlations—which imply that some general factor is at work—is the foundation beneath the idea of g.

Some mental processes plainly require much more general intelligence than others. The inter-test correlations, while invariably positive, are not equally strong in all cases. In the WAIS-R, for example, the Information subtest correlates .80 with Vocabulary but only .45 with Object Assembly (the jigsaw-puzzle-like subtest).[16] Using a statistical technique called factor analysis—basically invented by Spearman—scholars can take the intercorrelations for any group of tests and extract the general factor common to them all. You could then rank the tests by the extent to which they exhibit this general factor, which is also the extent to which they call upon general intelligence. Tests of simple addition do not call upon it heavily; they have only a modest correlation (about .40) with g. The correlations are much higher for questions requiring some reasoning. This one, for example, correlates about .80 with g. Question: *Bob is twice as old as his sister, who is now seven. How old will Bob be when his sister is forty?* (About one-quarter of American adults give the wrong answer. They usually say 80 instead of 47.)[17]

As the foregoing suggests, g involves the more complex, higher-level mental functions. Tests of abstract reasoning ability tend to be the most highly "g loaded" of all, and in the IQ literature you sometimes see references to g as basically synonymous with reasoning ability.[18] Many psychologists who emphasize its centrality have in their heads a "hierarchical" model of intelligence in which g sits at the top. In a second layer, general intelligence is divided into two primary abilities, sometimes roughly characterized as verbal and mathematical. In the third layer is a long list—it gets longer every year—of specific abilities. Some of these are thought of as particular forms of the second-layer talents, but some others, like a memory for musical rhythms, are viewed as entirely separate.[19]

Another message in the correlations is that many tests not formally labeled IQ tests—as are the WAIS-R and the Stanford-Binet—nevertheless give you a pretty good measure of IQ. The Scholastic Aptitude Test (SAT), the U.S. Employment Service's General Aptitude Test Battery (see chapter 11), and the Armed Services Vocational Aptitude Battery are all heavily g loaded and highly correlated with formal IQ tests.[20] While a sizable majority of psychometricians support a g-based model of intelligence, nonspecialists tend to have trouble getting their hands on g. This is possibly not surprising, as the concept is entirely a product of mathematical manipulations—and fairly rugged math at that. The existence of g is known solely from its correlates.

These correlates, however, are all over the place. Several years ago, Christopher Brand of the University of Edinburgh pointed to studies in which g had been positively correlated with—among many other attributes—altruism, anorexia nervosa, height, sense of humor, rank in the U.S. military, the ability to benefit from psychotherapy, and speed of talking. It was negatively correlated with alcoholism, dogmatism, impulsivity, and smoking.[21] And, as we shall see in chapter 11, variability in g is a powerful predictor of job performance.

Futhermore, g is highly heritable. In any large group, variation in g will be attributable mainly to genetic factors and only secondarily to environmental factors. We defer to chapter 7 the explanation of how these distinctions are made. Meanwhile, the fact of high heritability has a strong implication. It tells us forcefully that g is a neurophysiological phenomenon.[22]

Meaning that g, and IQ, will ultimately have to be explained by researchers into the human brain.

3

How Much Do "Street Smarts" Matter?

A familiar rap on intelligence testing is that it is useful enough for measuring academic intelligence (the mental skills that enable one to earn good grades in school) but quite inadequate as a guide to real-world intelligence (the kind you need in adult life). A number of scholars, perhaps the most insistent being Robert J. Sternberg of Yale University, have stressed the distinction between academic and "practical" intelligence, also known as "street smarts." A compact statement of their case appears in a 1986 volume edited by Sternberg and Richard K. Wagner of Florida State University. The book, *Practical Intelligence: Nature and Origins of Competence in the Everyday World*,[1] has fifteen chapters, most of them quite absorbing. Contributors to the volume represent a broad range of scholars united mainly, it seems, by a conviction that IQ tests are somehow bypassing the mental abilities needed in the real world.

Belief in the primacy of street smarts (and the inadequacy of IQ) also seems to be widespread on the street. In talking about the distinction with friends, I note that many, perhaps most, of them instantly spark to the idea. They will often serve up examples: the uneducated carpenter who (they assume) would do poorly on an IQ test but makes quite dazzling calculations about the best way to build a boat; the entrepreneur who spouts nonsense when talking about literature or art or politics but who has an uncanny knack for making money; the presumably low-IQ bartenders and taxi drivers who can instantly sense which customers are going to be trouble, even though outsiders watching them at work might detect nothing untoward going on. To be sure, my friends never turn out to actually possess IQ test results for the street-smart folks they are confidently casting as low scorers.

The view to be argued here is that the case for practical intelligence is ultimately less compelling than the examples above may suggest. The idea is useful in reminding us that intelligence is applied in many different realms; it really is a trait possessed by carpenters and bartenders, and not just by students and teachers. But in the end it is unclear that the concept of practical intelligence is adding much to our understanding of the practical world.

Proponents of the concept begin, almost invariably, by criticizing the broad irrelevance and artificiality of the problems addressed in standard IQ tests. Here, for example, is Norman Frederiksen of the Educational Testing Service, writing in the Sternberg-Wagner anthology on the limits of IQ-like tests:

> There are two ways in which paper-and-pencil tests fail to represent the whole domain of intelligent behavior. One has to do with the nature of the tests themselves. Most real-life problems cannot be posed in the form of conventional test items without seriously distorting the problem; even a "what would you do?" question about how to deal with, say, disruptive behavior in a classroom cannot possibly capture the

complexity and immediacy of the real-life situation.
... Furthermore, the use of the multiple-choice format
tends to limit the kinds of items that are written and
in some instances the nature of the cognitive processes involved in taking a test....

The other major limitation of conventional testing
is that there is very little variation in the situations in
which data are collected. Tests are typically administered in academic settings where the expectation is
that one should strive for as many "right" answers as
possible, following specified time limits and procedures.... In real life, one might decide to settle for an
approximation or a probability that satifies his or her
own needs rather than strive for an optimal solution;
or one might postpone the problem until he or she
can talk to someone or get a book off the shelf.... [2]

In their own contribution to the anthology, Sternberg
and Wagner also lean hard on the proposition that IQ tests
measure skills suitable only for dealing with the "artificial"
world of the schools. They note the following limitations of
the problems posed in IQ tests:[3]

• *They are problems formulated by other people.* In the real
world, of course, the problem solver is frequently obliged
to begin by figuring out that there is a problem needing to
be solved and then identifying it.

• *The problems are often of no intrinsic interest.*

• *The problems as presented contain all the information
needed for a solution*—obviously not always the case in the
real world.

• *The problem is "disembedded from" the individual's experience.* In the real world, of course, most problems involve
matters related to our own lives.

• *The problems are well defined.* Many real-world problems are of course somewhat elusive.

• *They have but one correct answer* (which helps the tester
decide what's right and what's wrong). In the real world,

many problems can be successfully addressed in more than one way.

So the case for practical intelligence is heavily centered on the presumed shortcomings and artificiality of IQ-based intelligence, the kind you use in school. The case seems intuitively very plausible. All of us can think of children who seemed like stars in school but somehow never amounted to much in later life—the mirror image of the cases noted above, wherein individuals presumed to have low IQs nevertheless turn out to have important practical skills. Clearly there are limits to the predictive power of IQ tests. To be sure, nobody ever denied this.

But if proponents of street smarts are to make their case convincingly, they must at some point get beyond criticizing IQ tests. It is not enough for them to keep saying that practical intelligence *isn't* academic intelligence. At some point, they need to state crisply just what it *is*. On the evidence of the Sternberg-Wagner book and some others I have looked at—especially *Practical Intelligence: Working Smarter in Business and the Professions,* by Roger Peters[4]—this is the point at which they become less convincing. (Peters is a cognitive psychologist at Fort Lewis College.)

How do the Sternberg-Wagner authors define practical intelligence? The first thing a reader will note is that they are a long way from agreeing among themselves. The volume offers us many different versions of practical intelligence. Taking all the authors together, you would have to conclude that practical intelligence is not just one way of thinking; it is a whole lot of ways. Some of the authors themselves seem bothered by the definitional problems they are confronting. In one essay, which focuses on intelligence among the elderly, Sherry L. Willis and K. Warner Schaie (both of Penn State's College of Human Development) bemoan the fact that researchers have so much trouble getting beyond all the statements about what practical intelligence isn't.[5]

Indeed, a major point being made by many of the con-tributors is that practical intelligence comes in many dif-ferent guises—as, they insistently argue, intelligence itself does. The case for practical intelligence frequently turns out to be another variant of the idea of "multiple intelli-gences," a phrase generally associated with Howard Gardner of Harvard. Gardner is in fact a contributor to the Sternberg-Wagner volume, and his essay (coauthored with Joseph M. Walters, also of Harvard) is one of a number that turns the case for practical intelligence into an attack on *g*—on the idea of general intelligence. The basic thought behind *g*, you will recall, is that all mental abilities are in some measure an expression of general intelligence, that is, they are all "*g* loaded" to some extent. Gardner's view, in contrast, is that the multiple intelligences he has identified are essentially independent of one another.[6] As noted in chapter 2, this is a minority view: Only 13 percent of the experts polled by Snyderman and Rothman believed that measured intelligence is best described in terms of "sepa-rate faculties."

At this point, let us pause and catalog some of the principal points made about practical intelligence by its adherents (represented mainly by the Sternberg-Wagner authors but to some extent also by various formulations in other volumes). Three themes recur in their statements about practical intelligence:

1. *The importance of task-specific knowledge, or "know-how."* Many of the examples of practical intelligence depend on the problem solver's being extremely knowledgeable about the task he or she is undertaking. The chapter by Sylvia Scribner, a psychologist based at the graduate center of the City University of New York, looks closely at some drivers whose job is to deliver different types and quantities of milk to different customers and calculate the amount that should be billed to each customer. The drivers could, of course, look up the price of each type of milk and multiply it by the number of units being dropped off; most of them,

however, found it tedious and time-consuming to keep referring back to the company price list, and so they used different algorithms to come up with the dollar total. The drivers seem to have been quite good at devising solutions that minimized their own time and effort.[7]

The chapter by Sternberg and Wagner also offers many examples of practical intelligence that seem to depend on specific knowledge. Their chapter emphasizes the importance of "tacit knowledge," said to be (a) practical rather than academic, (b) informal rather than formal, and (c) usually not directly taught. Most of the examples offered seem to involve knowledge of the kind one would naturally pick up in the workplace after being on the job for a while. In one close-to-home example, they say, "Deciding which journal to submit a manuscript to is an example of a task that requires tacit knowledge."[8]

2. *The importance of distinguishing between thinking skills and actual performance.* A number of the essays make the obvious but important point that problems do not get solved by thinking ability alone: that outcomes all too often depend on traits enabling one to implement the thought successfully. In their own contribution, for example, Sternberg and Wagner refer to the sometimes decisive importance of motivation.

In a similar vein, the essay by G. O. Klemp, Jr. (a Boston-based management consultant) and David C. McClelland of Harvard is a quite fascinating report on the characteristics of successful managers. A high fraction of those being studied were senior managers in "Fortune 100" companies (all of which would have had multi-billion-dollar sales figures). What makes a superior manager? Klemp and McClelland lean heavily on the distinction between intellectual competencies and what the authors call "influence competencies"; the latter include the determination to translate ideas into action, a trait not exhibited by all managers. Bottom line: "The difference between capacity to act and disposition to act forms the distinction between average and outstanding senior managerial performance. Any theory of managerial intelligence must take this important difference into account."[9]

3. *The importance of social skills.* Several of the contributors to the Sternberg-Wagner volume come down hard on social skills as a particularly important dimension of practical intelligence. A contribution by Jane R. Mercer of the University of California at Riverside, Margarita Gomez-Palacio of Mexico's Department of Education, and Eligio Padilla of the University of New Mexico—much of their essay deals with the measurement of academic and practical intelligence in Mexico—goes a long way toward equating practical intelligence with "social-behavioral" skills. Although offered in overdense "sociologese," the authors' view of these skills seems at first blush quite reasonable. Their basic statement: "The social-behavioral approach to conceptualizing intelligence has focused on the individual's ability to deal with the external world of social structures and social interactions, to play a variety of roles in various social systems, to establish and maintain interpersonal relationships and ties, to interpret the intentions and meanings of the acts of others accurately, and so forth."[10]

Despite Mercer et al., the view of social intelligence as a major dimension of practical intelligence is somewhat underrepresented in the Sternberg-Wagner volume. Sternberg himself has elsewhere written extensively about the importance of social skills, including the ability to "read" other people. "One important aspect of your everday life," he wrote in *Intelligence Applied* (1986), "is the ability to decode the nonverbal messages that people send you. Such messages, transmitted during the course of a conversation, may in some cases correspond to what a person is saying, but in other cases, they may not. Often the nonverbal messages are a better indication of a person's true feelings than the verbal messages they accompany. It is therefore quite important to be able to decode such messages."[11]

The passage seems straightforward and persuasive, and Sternberg accompanied it with a couple of interesting tests. One test consisted of twenty photographs of men and women stated to be heterosexual couples. You are told that half the photographs depict couples actually involved in romantic relationships; the other half are uninvolved couples. The reader is asked to guess which is which. I instantly submitted to the test and found I got ten right out of twenty—the median expectation for an individual utterly lacking social skills and obliged to guess every time.

Sternberg's second test consisted of ten photographs, each showing two individuals at work. One is an ordinary worker of some kind; the other is the worker's supervisor. You are asked to guess which is which. Again evidencing no more social skills than a coin flipper, I got five of the ten right.

Roger Peters's *Practical Intelligence* also lays considerable emphasis on the importance of social skills and mentions a number of research findings pertaining thereto. One finding—supported, Peters says, in seventy-five different research projects—is that women rather consistently do better than men in tests of social skills.[12] They appear to be far better than men in picking up on nonverbal cues to emotion and in judging the intentions of others. Given the abundance of psychological research showing that women are more "empathetic" than men, these findings seem quite plausible.[13]

All three of the themes delineated in the Sternberg-Wagner volume are worth taking seriously. But all have serious limitations, too.

1. As to the "task-specific knowledge"—the "know-how"—on which practical intelligence often depends: It seems entirely persuasive that dairy delivery men, bartenders, and other ordinary workers depicted in the volume have mastered a lot of detailed information about their jobs and have also worked out some useful algorithms

enabling them to solve task-related problems. But does one need a new theory of intelligence to make this unsurprising point?

The maestros of practical intelligence would have advanced the ball quite a way if they had demonstrated the existence of, and clearly delineated, a version of intelligence that somehow makes it easier for people to assimilate and manipulate this know-how. But the relationship between the know-how and the practical intelligence remains fuzzy throughout the discussion. In a summary essay in the Wagner-Sternberg volume, Wagner notes that "an important task for those who study practical knowledge is to provide an explicit account of the relation between practical *know-how* and practical *intelligence*."[14] This comment led Raymond S. Nickerson, who reviewed the volume in the *American Journal of Psychology*, to remark in apparent exasperation that the account is indeed needed and that in its absence the whole idea of practical intelligence is hard to defend.[15] (Nickerson, now retired, was a psychologist at BBN Laboratories, Inc., a management-consulting firm in Cambridge, Massachusetts.)

A question not adequately dealt with by the Sternberg-Wagner authors is whether, for all their lengthy put-downs of academic intelligence, the practical know-how and mental skills they are describing might in fact have been captured fairly well in standard IQ tests. It would have been interesting, for example, to ascertain the IQs of those milk delivery men and observe the relationship between test-score differences and variability in their on-job performance.

2. I found myself puzzled by the repeated invocation in the Sternberg-Wagner volume of the distinction between thinking ability and actual performance. The latter is of course heavily affected by noncognitive traits, which can be of decisive importance in many situations, as the Klemp-McClelland essay makes apparent. Clearly their es-

say is onto something: We all know individuals who are, in the vernacular, "all talk"—superior thinkers eternally unable to translate their ideas into action. The authors' finding about what differentiates superior managers from average managers—the disposition to act—is utterly persuasive.

Still, it seems odd to identify the deficiencies of the poorer managers as a want of *intelligence*. The term "intelligence" has been stretched a lot in the literature of modern psychology, but surely there remains a distinction between intelligence and motivation. Efforts to make a case for "practical intelligence" by identifying it with noncognitive personality traits leave me with an uneasy sense that the dealer is switching the deck.

3. Of all the efforts to distinguish practical intelligence from tested IQ, the most promising seem to be those emphasizing the importance of social skills. We can presumably all agree that social skills affect people's ability to cope with their environments. We can possibly agree that this coping ability is an important element of intelligence. Remember David Wechsler's 1939 definition: "Intelligence is the aggregate or global capacity of the individual to act purposefully, to think rationally, and to deal effectively with his environment."

Dealing with it is plainly easier if you can sense which kinds of appeals will be most effective in winning others to your point of view, if you can sense how others view you, or if you know how to "fit in" with groups that can be helpful to you. Someone who goes through life paralyzed by shyness, who is unable to remember names or faces or basic information about people he deals with constantly, who is eternally oblivious to such matters as the romance under way between two friends, or who would be alone in not noticing that his boss has a drinking problem—someone who in general is just not "with it"—is presumably at a certain disadvantage in life.

But even with social skills, conceptual problems surface when you try to establish what it is about such skills that ought to be thought of as "intelligence." Take the problem of shyness. Shy people are, almost by definition, lacking in social skills. But shyness is ordinarily presumed to reflect psychological disturbances of some kind, not a want of cognitive ability. It would seem somehow wrong to equate shyness with a lack of intelligence.

Another conceptual problem is built into the idea of "with-it-ness," a term I first came across in "A Search for Tests of Practical Intelligence," by Bernard Rimland of the Naval Personnel and Training Research Laboratory in San Diego. (His essay appears in *Mental Tests and Cultural Adaptation,* a 1972 volume.) One figure said to be not with it was Isaac Newton, of whom Rimland tells the following story:

> Once, while entertaining a houseful of guests, Newton left for his wine cellar to replenish the wine. When he did not return after a lengthy absence, the guests went down to the cellar to try to find him, thinking that perhaps he had stumbled in the dark and injured himself. They found him sitting by a dusty barrelhead scribbling mathematical formulas in the dust atop the barrels. He had become engrossed with an abstract problem while on the errand.[16]

The story certainly does suggest that Newton was weak in social skills. But given the lifetime accomplishments that flowed from his deep absorption in mathematical formulas, does the story deserve to be taken as evidence of a failure to deal with his environment? An alternative reading would be that Newton went through life dealing quite effectively with his environment, even if he was defining its challenges quite differently from the way his wine-starved dinner guests might have wished.

Most of us, to be sure, are not Newtons and would have to rate any comparable behavior on our parts as unvarnished foolishness. Social skills surely matter a lot to most of us. It does indeed seem reasonable to accept that many of the skills being talked about by practical-intelligence adherents represent environmental adaptation of the kind David Wechsler was talking about in his definition of intelligence. I am assuming here that qualities like motivation should not be thought of as a form of intelligence; also, that neurotic traits like shyness do not betoken a want of intelligence. But that still leaves us looking at a broad range of social skills and wondering whether they do indeed represent a form of practical intelligence not adequately measured by standard psychometric tests.

Scholars attempting to identify social skills have produced a broad range of findings. One study that seems typical was generated by Ronald Riggio, Jack Messamer, and Barbara Throckmorton, all of the California State University at Fullerton. Their data are based on studies of 171 undergraduates, all of whom were tested on standard measures of academic ability (e.g., the Wechsler Adult Intelligence Scale—Revised) and also on several measures of social skills (e.g., a Social Etiquette/Tacit Knowledge Test, designed to measure awareness of appropriate social behavior). The authors end up concluding that it is possible to identify social skills that are different from academic intelligence; they concede, however, that there are sizable overlaps between the two domains. Their bottom line: "Correlational and factor analysis indicated that although social and academic intelligence may be conceptually distinct, there is considerable measurement overlap between the constructs."[17]

What about the possibility that practical intelligence, including even the social skills, *is* measured quite adequately by IQ tests? At first glance, this seems intuitively implausible. Certainly the kinds of problems thrown at you in standard IQ tests seem a long way from the issues being addressed in the Sternberg-Wagner volume. Before they are home free, however, the practical-intelligence adherents must deal with another possibility: that the mental abilities they are talking about, including the social skills, are something more than a reflection of *g*—general intelligence.

Many eminent scholars believe that practical intelligence is not a whole lot more than "*g* applied." Richard Herrnstein of Harvard, for example, says he suspects that most of what is called social skill is simply common sense applied to social situations; along with many others, he also believes that common sense is more or less synonymous with *g*.[18] The underlying proposition here is that the ability to think straight will manifest itself in social situations, just as it also does in academic situations, and that the dichotomy between the two is essentially false.

There is no doubt that *g* represents the major difficulty for the idea of practical intelligence. It directly challenges the notion that we are getting anyplace, or adding to our explanatory powers, by postulating endless new categories of intelligence. The claim for *g* is that it suffices to explain differences in thinking ability in all the realms of human activity. It explains not only social skills but also the skills of dairy delivery men calculating their customers' charges and all the other forms of "task-specific knowledge" represented in the literature on practical intelligence. Arthur Jensen is among those who believe that the simplest way to think of practical intelligence is to view it as *g* being applied to the practical concerns of everyday life.[19] Given the broad support for *g* among scholars—the concept of a general factor being favored by about two-thirds of the Snyderman-Rothman experts who answered this question—this somewhat dismissive vision of practical intelligence is itself hard to dismiss.

The fact is that *g* has enormous predictive power in real-world situations. Jensen has demonstrated that it is what overwhelmingly accounts for the predictive validity of personnel tests like the General Aptitude Test Battery (GATB). When you separately examine the nine subtests of the GATB, you find that their ability to accurately predict on-the-job performance correlates .65 with their g loadings.[20] In other words, g is a powerful link between the test and the subsequent real-world performance. If the challenge is to find models of intelligence applicable to the real world, it is far from clear that any variant of the practical-intelligence model explains more than "g applied."

Which brings us to another weakness of the idea of practical intelligence: the proposition that IQ test scores measure abilities irrelevant to real-world problems. As we are observing at numerous points in this volume (see especially chapters 4 and 11), IQ scores are positively correlated with numerous desirable outcomes in life. They predict not only higher grades in school but an ability to get and hold the better and more prestigious jobs, not to mention greater productiveness on the job—desiderata that all seem ultimately quite "practical." So proponents of practical intelligence have an instant large problem in seeming to represent that the mental abilities measured by IQ scores are somehow "impractical."

It is a problem they have not yet solved.

4

The Roots of the Controversy

There was a time when IQ testing was not controversial. It was perceived as an exercise obviously useful to school administrators obliged to educate children who had different levels of ability. It became controversial for several reasons.

One is that Americans increasingly came to see education as the path to success, and in many educational contexts IQ scores became "gatekeepers"; they were involved in determinations about which children got into the best nursery schools, the best academic programs, and Harvard. Against this background, it could be guaranteed that millions of American parents would perceive the tests as unfair to their own children. Parents, being naturally ambitious for their children's advancement, often tend to overrate their mental ability. A number of studies have shown that teachers make better guesses about children's IQs than do the kids' own parents.[1]

The IQ controversy was also broadened by mounting

evidence that test data have considerable relevance for the careers of adults. In hundreds of occupations, the tests are superior predictors of job performance. Indeed, they are predictors of "life performance." IQ is positively corre-lated with just about all major measures of success and well-being: occupational status, socioeconomic status, in-come, marital stability, even good health and life expect-ancy. The correlations tell us the United States is very much a meritocracy, and the kind of "merit" that matters most is intelligence.

IQ matters in most, perhaps all, developed societies. While working on this book, I started collecting the IQs of miscellaneous famous people and soon bumped into the striking fact that all the major Nazi war criminals had high IQs. (Before going on trial at Nuremberg, they were sub-jected to a broad range of tests.) Hermann Goering tested at 138; Franz von Papen, at 134; and Albert Speer, at 128. The lowest of the Nuremberg defendants was Julius Strei-cher, the gauleiter of Franconia, and even he was somewhat above average with an IQ of 106.[2] As the figures forcefully remind us, it is a mistake to confuse IQ with human worth.

Among some other IQ sightings: Muhammad Ali's armed-services exam turned up an IQ-equivalent score of 78, reminding us that some low-IQ people do attain occu-pational success.[3] Thomas Reeves, a recent biographer of John F. Kennedy, has established that JFK tested at 119 just before entering Choate Academy.[4] Roger Morris, a bi-ographer of Richard M. Nixon, reports that Nixon scored 143 when tested at Fullerton High School in California.[5] You might think Nixon would have done better in those famous debates with Kennedy during the 1960 presidential campaign.

Before and after Desert Storm, the media repeatedly reported that Gen. Norman Schwarzkopf had an IQ of 170, a truly prodigious figure, and reporters I have spoken to claim to have got it from the general's staff; however, it has never been solidly confirmed. Gangster John Gotti, who long headed the Gambino organized crime family, tested at 110 in Franklin K. Lane High School in Brooklyn, a figure that seems quite plausible.[6] In *Crime and Human Nature,* published in 1985, James Q. Wilson and Richard J. Herrnstein present data indicating that criminals tend to have IQs clustered around 90.[7] In a sense, then, you can think of Gotti's rise to mob stardom as basically concordant with the general rule that smart people get to the top.

The single most important reason for hostility to IQ testing in America today is the country's commitment to the idea of equality. For all their utility and explanatory power, IQ scores insistently convey a message that egalitarian America does not want to hear. The message: that people are unequal in mental ability.

That message has several unsettling implications. In a modern industrial society, most jobs require some level of mental ability, and the IQ tests tell us who can, and cannot, function at that level. They tell us that ambition, hard work, and good character are not enough: you also need the brains. Most people are no more capable of making it as, say corporate executives than they are of making themselves into major-league pitchers. Many are incapable of making it even in modestly demanding white-collar jobs.

At some level of consciousness, most Americans doubtless accept all of the above. They possibly also realize that in the absence of mental-ability tests like the IQ, somebody would still have to make differentiating decisions among the claimants for life's plums; somebody would still have to decide who gets into the top school and who gets the big job. And it is hard to argue that the decisions would be better and fairer if uninformed by test results.

But the message of the IQ tests incorporates another thought that is harder still to live with: the thought that not only individuals but *groups* differ. The IQ tests tell us that the rich, on average, are more intelligent than the poor.

(See chapter 11.) The average white tests substantially higher than the average black. Furthermore, the "structure" of mental abilities is different in the two races, that is, their patterns of strengths and weaknesses are quite dissimilar. (See chapter 12.) East Asians, too, have a distinctive structure of intelligence, and on average they test somewhat higher than whites. Jews on average test higher than gentiles and also have an IQ structure of their own. (See chapter 10 for data on East Asians and Jews.) Men and women also turn out to test differently. While both sexes have average scores of 100, the men's scores include more extreme cases. Men are overrepresented among the super smart—above IQ 140 there appear to be at least 20 percent more men than women[8]—and also among those with severe mental disabilities. Men and women also have somewhat different intellectual structures: At any given IQ level, men will do substantially better at quantitative tasks, women somewhat better at verbal tasks.[9] (Their IQs and g scores are equivalent because verbal abilities are more g-loaded and therefore weighted more heavily.[10]

Testing has become unpopular for still another reason: The tests unambiguously identify a population with limited mental abilities—and the country has evolved no satisfactory solution for dealing with this group. The schools, which confront the problem most directly, have taken several different tacks. One is to replace "mainstreaming" (everyone takes the same courses) with some form of "ability tracking." Tracking systems typically involve a two- or three-layer division of the kids into better and worse students, possibly using labels ("red birds" and "blue birds") intended to blur distinctions as much as possible. A recent RAND Corporation study found that tracking was widely used in all grades, including kindergarten, and was pervasive in the higher grades and tougher courses. Citing data from the Second International Math Study, the Rand scholars concluded: "U.S. middle schools and junior high schools routinely sort eighth graders into four types of mathematics classes (remedial, typical, enriched, and algebra); this ability grouping was more extensive than that practiced in any other country studied."[11]

There is broad agreement that ability tracking helps the best students, who are enabled to advance more rapidly, but no agreement at all about the effects on poorly performing students. An educator defending separate tracks for weak students could argue that they encounter less frustration when proceeding at a slower pace and/or handling less demanding, vocationally oriented material; and that it is counterproductive, if not cruel, to impose college-preparatory standards on low-IQ kids who will have enough trouble graduating from high school. The opposing view is that slow-track children are cheated of a real education. "Kids at the top are reading Socrates, and kids at the bottom are reading Superman," complained Mary Futrell, then head of the largest teachers' union, the National Education Association, in a 1988 interview.[12] Whether children with IQs around, say, 75 would benefit from reading Socrates was an issue she prudently did not pursue.

The case against tracking weak students also incorporates some evidence that they get the least experienced teachers and inadequate shares of school resources—a fact extensively documented in the RAND study. Since weak students are often minority students, the argument has also taken on civil-rights overtones.[13]

The U.S. educational establishment remains utterly divided on ways to help the low-scoring kids, and the air is filled with assorted revolutionary manifestos. One of the most publicized has been a 1989 proposal by the Carnegie Corporation of New York. It would transform the country's middle schools into quasi-welfare agencies that would deliver a lot of health care, counseling, and family-planning education—while also somehow providing a superior academic program for all kids. Tracking would be abolished.

In its place, the schools would set up "cooperative learning" groups, each with kids at all levels. Superior students would devote time to tutoring underperformers. It is hard to believe America is ready for so large a revolution in its public schools, but the attention paid the Carnegie report surely reflects the country's uneasiness over present arrangements. And its bafflement about handling the low-scoring population targeted by the tests.[14]

Because the message of the tests is so broadly unsettling, many Americans have responded to it with massive denials. This has been notoriously true of the American media. When the subject of testing arises in the press and on television, certain themes recur endlessly. The tests do not truly measure intelligence; they reflect only environmental differences (and are therefore biased against the poor); they stigmatize and otherwise work against racial minorities and other groups that score low on average.[15] In some versions of the indictment, the tests are *intended* to put down the poor and minorities. This was the central message of, for example, a popular 1981 book called *The Mismeasure of Man,* by Stephen Jay Gould, a Marxist professor of geology at Harvard. Gould views IQ tests as instruments of class oppression. In *Mismeasure,* he spun a long argument endeavoring to prove that the IQ has long served the American ruling class by putting down the poor and minorities.[16] The book elaborating this wild proposition was reviewed enthusiastically. The *Saturday Review* said Gould had produced "a rare book—at once of great importance and wonderful to read...a fascinating historical study of scientific racism." Gushing about the author, the *New York Times* said, "He can hit us in the social conscience." *Newsweek* called the book "a splendid new case study of biased science." The *Boston Globe* speculated hopefully that this book might "lay the beast to rest once and for all"—the beast being IQ tests.[17]

While they have been relentlessly skeptical of all claims made for the IQ's utility and validity, the American media have persistently fallen uncritically for another kind of story: the one in which some new educational program is found to be dramatically raising IQs. The media are attracted to such stories because they seem to support the cultural-bias argument (and to discredit the idea of heritable intelligence). A book called *The Raising of Intelligence,* by Herman H. Spitz (a scholar based at the Edward R. Johnstone Training and Research Center in Bordentown, New Jersey), is a treasure trove of reports on failed programs—and on media gullibility in accepting the initial claims made for them.

In the seventies and early eighties, there was a flood of favorable news stories about the so-called Milwaukee Project, said to be doing wonders for the IQs of underprivileged black children from the city's slums. The *New York Times* cheered the news: The children, who had undergone intensive programs of early intervention, had IQs some 30 points higher than a matching control group at age 6.[18] The *Washington Post* stated breathlessly that the success of the project has "settled once and for all" the question of whether deprived kids were being held back by heredity or environment.[19] Indeed, the project is still occasionally cited by writers committed to a belief in mental plasticity; however, the number of mentions went down substantially when Rick Heber, the project's director, was convicted and sent to prison for embezzling government money.[20]

You could argue that the embezzlement was irrelevant, since it did not involve funds for the Milwaukee Project itself (which received some $14 million[21] in federal support), but for another program in which Heber was involved. You could also argue that the director's sticky fingers are not ultimately what matter; what matters is the performance of the kids. In any case, this performance constitutes the real bad news about the Milwaukee Project.

In 1988, Howard L. Garber, a long-time associate of Heber, finally provided a detailed report on the project.[22] It cast a new light on the IQ gains. The 30 points appeared to represent largely a "practice effect"—a result of years of intensive drilling on problems very much like those in the Stanford-Binet test. The IQ gains declined steadily in the years after the children left the program to enter school. And the gains never did carry over to academic achievement: Results for the first four grades indicate that the kids' reading skills were low (at the nineteenth percentile by the fourth grade) and that the differences between their skills and those of the control group were not statistically significant.[23]

Some serious students of intelligence testing have grumbled extensively about media coverage of the issue, and one of them—Richard Herrnstein, a Harvard-based psychologist—wrote an article in the *Atlantic* in 1982 detailing his own maddening experiences with editors and TV producers inflexibly committed to anti-IQ positions.[24] But the case against the media was never spelled out systematically until 1988, with the publication of *The IQ Controversy: The Media and Public Policy*, by Snyderman and Rothman.[25] The book documented the existence of a gulf between the media and the experts on just about all the big questions: Are IQ differences largely attributable to environmental factors? Are the tests biased against minorities? Are they mainly an expression of middle-class culture? The media have answered yes to all those questions, while the experts keep saying no.

The book was devastating, but in a sense the media had the last laugh. The Snyderman-Rothman book, a work of meticulous scholarship bearing on questions of enormous public interest, was largely unreviewed (although I put in some kind words for it in *Commentary*).[26]

In its early years, intelligence testing was commonly viewed as something rather "progressive"—a measure of mental ability that was at once fairer and more accurate than subjective judgments. One might make the case that the first intelligence tests to affect significant numbers of people were the civil service examinations given in the Chinese Empire for perhaps 2,000 years (ending in 1905). The tests represented efforts to gauge the educational attainments of prospective bureaucrats and were initially employed by emperors wishing to run the civil service on a "merit" basis.[27]

The roots of modern IQ testing can be traced back to the work of Sir Francis Galton (1822–1911), a brilliant and pioneering student of human nature. Galton set up a laboratory in London to measure mental abilities. Since these were viewed at the time as largely a function of sensory discrimination, much of his work was devoted to testing sight, hearing, nerve-end sensitivity, etc. His work was nevertheless enormously prescient, foreshadowing modern IQ research in many different ways. He was fascinated by twins, for example, and was the first scholar to sense that twin studies had the potential for illuminating "nature and nurture." Like most modern scholars, he believed that nature was the more important determinant of differences in intelligence. "There is no escape," he once wrote, "from the conclusion that nature prevails enormously over nurture when the differences of nurture do not exceed what is commonly found among persons of the same rank of society and in the same country. My only fear is that my evidence seems to prove too much and may be discredited on that account, as it seems contrary to all experience that nurture should go for so little."[28] Note that Galton also was a pioneer in sensing that his views on nature-nurture would be unpopular.

Galton's studies anticipated twentieth-century IQ testing in other ways. He worked hard at checking out his subjects' short-term memory, and he foreshadowed the work of Arthur R. Jensen (see chapter 5) in identifying reaction time as an indicator of intelligence. Unfortunately, Jensen observes, Galton's world did not yet have the statistical

techniques required to distinguish different degrees of intelligence with reaction-time data.[29]

The first modern, successful intelligence test was developed by Alfred Binet (1857–1911), a distinguished
French psychologist. In turn-of-the-century France, children of substantially subnormal mental ability were typically expelled from school as unteachable. But then a law
was passed requiring special programs for such children—
which meant, of course, that they had to be identified. It
was in this context that the first IQ tests were developed.[30]

Binet's first effort was a 1905 test, designed for children up to the age of eleven and consisting of thirty items.
Called the Binet-Simon Scale (his collaborator was Theo-
dore Simon), it had a few items designed to test sensory
discrimination, in the Galton tradition. Most of the items,
however, called for a certain amount of judgment or reasoning, which Binet viewed as central to intelligence. One
item required the child to take sentences in which words
were missing and supply the words—he was offered several choices—that made sense in context. Sentence-com-
pletion tests are still widely used today, and they correlate
powerfully with overall IQ scores. As in today's IQ tests, the
Binet-Simon test items were arranged in order of increasing difficulty (with the difficulty levels established by experiments on children aged three to eleven). A child's
intelligence was determined basically by the point in the
test at which he was no longer able to handle the items.

The 1905 test was revised and expanded a few years
later. A 1908 version had more test items, now subdivided
into groups that corresponded to different "mental levels"—defined by Binet as the levels at which 80–90 percent
of children of a given age passed the test. By now the Binet-
Simon had norms for every age from three to thirteen. In
effect, the child's score was the highest mental level he was
able to pass at. In a further 1911 revision, the age levels for

children were pushed upward to fifteen, and an adult level appeared for the first time.[31]

The term *IQ* came out of adaptations of the Binet-Simon by psychologists in other countries. A German psychologist, Wilhelm Stern (1877–1938), picked up on the concept of mental age as a basic measuring rod but went a step further. He proposed dividing each child's mental age (MA) by his chronological age (CA) to create a good basic indicator of the child's intelligence. A five-year-old with a mental age of six would have a distinctly superior "quotient" of MA/CA = 1.2.[32] In 1916, this was renamed IQ by the American psychologist Lewis M. Terman (1877–1956), who also thought to multiply the fraction by 100 to get rid of the decimal. More important, Terman reworked the Simon-Binet to develop what became known as the Stanford-Binet, which during much of this century was the world's most widely used IQ test.[33]

As indicated in the chapter on my own test adventures, the most widely used IQ tests today are those developed by the late David Wechsler. (He died in 1981). One change associated with the Wechsler tests has been the abandonment of all references to "mental age," a concept that made no sense in adult testing. In place of mental age, Wechsler introduced the concept of a "deviation IQ," which simply related any individual's raw score to the norm for his age.[34]

Up to this point, you will observe, there has been nothing in twentieth-century intelligence testing that looks particularly controversial. The tests had been designed to identify schoolchildren who would benefit from remedial-education programs and for many years were used largely for that purpose. The roots of the present IQ wars go back to some ideas of Terman, who had a somewhat broader focus on the tests. He had a shrewd instinct that intelligence had many more correlates than schooling, and he actively promoted research to prove it.[35]

Some part of the proof was delivered via the so-called Terman Gifted Group, one of the truly great social-science research projects of the twentieth century. The project took shape in the early 1920s, long before government money was available for such research. In its absence, Terman talked a number of private foundations into backing his creation of the group. (In a further stunning contrast with modern academic procedures, he also put a fair amount of his own professor's salary into the project.) His idea, brilliantly implemented over the past seventy years and still on display, was to assemble a large group of intellectually gifted—meaning high-IQ—children and follow them through life.

He began by asking California public-school teachers to nominate the three brightest kids in their classes and testing those nominated. Terman's only selection criterion was IQ. He had specified a score of at least 140 for membership in the group, but for various reasons, he ended up also including a few (less than 5 percent) with IQs in the 135–139 range. As finally constituted, the group included 857 boys and 671 girls—a total of 1,528. Some of the kids were related to one another: 182 families contributed more than one member to the group, and two families actually contributed five apiece. The group was mostly white, but it included some Asians, Mexicans, and blacks.

The mean IQ of the Gifted Group was 151. It included seventy-seven children with scores over 170 and a few over 200. If you think of the typical bell-shaped curve as representing the entire distribution of American children's IQs in 1921, you can imagine the Gifted Group as occupying a minuscule sliver of space off at the right tail of the curve.[36] (An IQ of 140 is above the ninety-ninth percentile for the population as a whole.)

When the group was assembled in 1921, its average age was eleven. Terman himself was forty-four. Exhaustive physical and psychological reports on the kids demonstrated early on that they were superior by many different measures. At birth they had been above average in weight.[37] As infants, they had walked about one month earlier than average children and talked about 3-1/2 months earlier.[38] Nearly half had learned to read before entering school; 6 percent could read before their fourth birthday.[39] At eleven, the group's general health was above average, and the incidence of physical abnormalities was well below average.[40] They also had superior character traits: Elaborate psychological tests of propensity to cheat showed they were less likely to do so than average children.[41] They were more likely than other kids to wear eyeglasses,[42] but otherwise they deviated rather dramatically from stereotypes of child prodigies.

Terman died in 1956, when his Gifted Group was in mid-life. The report issued on the group a couple of years after his death affords abundant clues to the blessings flowing to high-IQ people in the United States:

• For openers, somewhat more of them were alive than would have been expected from normal actuarial calculations. Less than 7 percent had died by the mid-1950s, versus an average 8 percent among all Americans in their age cohort.[43]

• By the mid-1950s, 93 percent of the men and almost 90 percent of the women had married. That was about average for men and women of their age in that era;[44] in addition, those in the Gifted Group were distinctly less likely to show a history of divorce. Around one-fifth of them had been divorced, versus estimates of one-third to one-fourth for others in their age group.[45]

• Among the men in the group, 86 percent were in the highest-status occupations: professional, proprietor, manager, executive.[46] Among the women, about half were housewives[47]—the standard career for women of that era. Of the women who worked, most seem to have accepted undemanding jobs, but a significant minority had risen far in a man's world. About one out of nine had high-level professional jobs,[48] and another 8 percent were business executives.[49] Seven of the women were listed in *American Men of Science*.[50]

- The men had above-average incomes. In the mid-1950s, when the median earnings of American professionals and managers was around $6,000,[51] the men in the Gifted Group made $9,640 on average.[52] (In 1992 dollars, that would be around $50,000.) They were, of course, still awaiting their peak earnings years.

The Terman study of the gifted was not, of course, the only research being done on the correlates of intelligence, but it was probably the most publicized. In any case, it helped to plant in Americans' minds the thought that IQ and "success" were powerfully linked. When this thought was combined with several others—including those pertaining to racial differences and to the heritability of intelligence—it produced a rather explosive mixture. In the egalitarian 1960s, the mixture exploded.

5

Jensenism

Arguments about intelligence testing are as old as the tests, that is, more than eighty-five years old. But when you talk about the "IQ debate" nowadays, you are mainly referring to some ideas put forward by Arthur R. Jensen, a professor of educational psychology at the University of California at Berkeley. Jensen launched the debate a quarter century ago, and he has been at the center of it ever since.

Jensen, now in his late sixties, does not come across as argumentative. His style is understated, his manner a bit diffident. I am told that he is an effective debater, but he is plainly not a natural polemicist. In talking about IQ-related controversies, he does not gravitate to put-downs or killer arguments. I had a rambling five-hour conversation with him in April 1989, in the course of which we touched on dozens of scholarly disputes he has been involved in over the years; listening to my tapes afterward,[1] it struck me that he had not spoken rancorously of any of his adversaries. I had learned much earlier that reporters who ask him uninformed questions invariably get answers that are courteous and helpful.

But the low-key style is in some ways deceptive. Jensen is a steely, determined, and formidable proselytizer of his ideas. He has pressed them in lectures, five books, a blizzard of scholarly papers (over 350 at last count), and endless high-level debates with other scholars; he has also supported them in years of laboratory research. Obviously possessed of plenty of nerve, he has remained unflappable when eggs have been thrown at him in lecture halls, when demonstrators have invaded his Berkeley classrooms, even when a tear-gas canister was lobbed into one of them. (Luckily, nobody was hurt.) During a period in the late sixties and early seventies, he had plainclothesmen sitting in on his classes, bodyguards as he moved around the campus, and a beeper enabling him to contact the campus police wherever he was. At one point, the administration at the University of California at Berkeley suggested that perhaps he would prefer to stop teaching and stay out of sight for a while. Jensen declined the offer and went on arguing his ideas.

These first reached a wide audience via an instantly famous essay he produced for the winter 1969 issue of the *Harvard Educational Review*. Entitled "How Much Can We Boost IQ and Scholastic Achievement?"[2] the essay served as my own introduction to the debate, as indeed it did for thousands of Americans who had not previously paid much attention to the study of intelligence.

The essay, which ran around sixty thousand words (almost the length of this book), touched a number of exposed nerves. To the question posed in the title, it basically answered: Not much. That answer was exactly what the country did not want to hear. Richard Nixon was president when the essay was published, but in the world of ideas, Great Society activism was still riding high. Americans in the "idea business"—academics, think-tank researchers, editors, government officials—were overwhelmingly committed to social programs built on the assumption that you *could* substantially boost the intelligence of people from deprived backgrounds. They saw Head Start, affirmative action, open enrollment, compensatory education, and other such programs as offering the country a way out of the boundless social problems associated with black poverty. Arguing that they were not a way out, Jensen found himself received as the skunk at the garden party.

The more so because his case was formidable. His essay pointed first to the track record of compensatory-education programs up to that time. The record was one of repeated failure. This judgment itself was not controversial, and as Jensen noted, it was shared by the U.S. Commission on Civil Rights (which had exhaustively reviewed efforts to raise the performance of disadvantaged children).[3] What set the fur flying was Jensen's attack on the programs' fundamental assumptions. In a much-quoted passage early in the essay, he wrote: "In other fields, when bridges do not stand, when aircraft do not fly, when machines do not work, when treatments do not cure, despite all conscientious efforts on the part of many persons to make them do so, one begins to question the basic assumptions, principles, theories, and hypotheses that guide one's efforts."[4] The time had come, Jensen wrote, to reexamine the assumptions of those trying to boost the performance of the disadvantaged children.

Their unexamined core assumption was that, except for an unfortunate few born with neurological defects, all children have the same potential intelligence. Which implied that low intelligence levels must reflect only environmental deprivation. Which implied in turn that the levels could be lifted by environmental enrichment.

None of this was true, said Jensen: Variability in IQ was mainly attributable to genetic factors. Only where environmental deprivation was extreme—in, say, the rare pathological cases involving children who had spent years locked in attics and deprived of sensory stimulation—was it possible to improve performance significantly and permanently by changing the child's world. Where the problem was simply a lack of middle-class culture and amenities, environmental changes would do little or nothing for the child's intelligence level. "Children reared in rather average circumstances," Jensen wrote, "do not show an appreciable IQ gain as a result of being placed in a more culturally enriched environment."[5] In any case, the main problem in compensatory programs was children whose potential was low to begin with. And since genetic potential represented an insurmountable barrier, those kids could not be turned into good students.

Oddly enough—at least it seems odd, given the furor over the essay—the link betwen genes and IQ was far from a new idea. It was, in fact, one of the best-documented findings of the science of psychology. In the thirties and forties, you could have read about it in numerous psychology textbooks, not to mention the *Encyclopaedia Britannica* article on intelligence.[6] To be sure, the genetic case had become less popular in the postwar years, in part because Nazi racial theories had discredited hereditarian ideas in many people's minds, in part because the social activism of the sixties had given new life to environmentalism. Still, the data cited by Jensen continued to have broad acceptance among psychologists specializing in intelligence studies; indeed, they were being reinforced by new studies every year. The data showed heritability estimates mostly clustering in the zone between 50 percent and 80 percent (meaning that half to four-fifths of the variability in IQ was attributable to genetic factors).[7]

Perhaps the most explosive thought in the essay was one that Jensen put forward rather tentatively. Was it possible, he asked, that the black-white IQ gap (about 15 points) had a genetic component? This was his answer:

The fact that a reasonable hypothesis has not been rigorously proved does not mean that it should be summarily dismissed. It only means that we need more appropriate research for putting it to the test. I believe such definitive research is possible but has not yet been done. So all we are left with are various lines of evidence, no one of which is definitive alone, but which, viewed all together, make it a not unreasonable hypothesis that genetic factors are strongly implicated in the average Negro-white intelligence difference. The preponderance of the evidence is, in my opinion, less consistent with a strictly environmental hypothesis than with a genetic hypothesis, which, of course, does not exclude the influence of environment or its interaction with genetic factors.[8]

These are still Jensen's views. As elaborated in chapter 12 (see page 162), they now appear also to be the views of around half of the scholars working on IQ-related studies. To be sure, this support for Jensen surfaced rather discreetly. It turned up in the Snyderman-Rothman survey of experts—who in this instance could venture their opinions without disclosing their identity. To this day, not a whole lot of experts want to get out front with Jensen.

The 1969 essay did a lot more than just make the case for heritable intelligence. What gave the essay its force was a wide-ranging argument, buttressed by an avalanche of citations from the empirical record. Jensen linked the case for high heritability to a theory of intelligence centered on *g* (general intelligence); explained how intelligence is captured in the IQ data; argued persuasively that IQ tests are valid and unbiased measures of intelligence; also elaborated the central role played by intelligence in determining where people end up in our society; and—the bottom line—argued against the utopian visions of educators determined to make all kids "succeed" by middle-class educational standards. Those standards, Jensen argued, guaranteed years of frustration and defeat for low-potential students. He suggested, without getting terribly specific, that such students needed different kinds of schooling, geared to their different and more limited talents.[9]

People tended to have quite extreme reactions to the essay. My own reaction was to be bowled over. I was among those who saw the essay as having enormous explanatory power. In addition to explaining the failure of all those compensatory programs, it cast a new light on some familiar old questions about who gets ahead in America, and why.

Not surprisingly, a lot of Americans instantly lined up on the other side of the argument. A newsletter published by the American Anthropological Association contained a proposal, apparently quite serious, that the offending issue of the *Harvard Educational Review* be burned.[10] The first round of comments in the *Review,* featuring exchanges between Jensen and a number of eminent psychologists and geneticists, indicated that they generally supported his central idea—the emphasis on a strongly heritable IQ.[11] But reports in the press, including all the major newsmagazines, made it appear that Jensen was somehow being put in his place by some real scientists.[12] Meanwhile, the editors of the *Review* were evidently taking flak for having let him off too easily. In any case, the journal soon published a second round of criticism that was much more hostile; this time, furthermore, Jensen was not allowed to answer (an incredible breach of protocol for a scholarly journal).[13]

Later that year, the *New York Times Magazine* published an article on "Jensenism," defined in a headline as "the theory that IQ is largely determined by the genes."[14] The article itself was reasonably well balanced, but it drew a flood of letters furiously attacking Jensen. A *Times Magazine* editor later told Jensen that it had received more letters about the article than about any other in its history.[15] Those it published were overwhelmingly hostile to Jensen and to intelligence testing generally. It was in this period that the campus police provided him with his beeper, which he retained for several years.

Jensen got to IQ studies, and for that matter psychology, after a fair amount of youthful experimenting with other interests. He grew up in San Diego, in a comfortable middle-class family—his father was a local businessman—that seems to have had a broadly indulgent view of child rearing. Once, at around age nine, responding to something learned at school, he formed the daffy ambition of becoming a full-time tree dweller. His parents helped him build a platform on a large pepper tree in their yard, and his mother actually brought food up to him during the two or three days he lived in the tree. A year later, he was being allowed to create his own minizoo populated by snakes and lizards. Says Jensen today: "I've got to say that my wife and I haven't been that indulgent with our own daughter."

His first serious interest was music. He mastered the clarinet and piano, was good enough to play clarinet with the San Diego Symphony while still a teenager, and seriously considered building this talent into a career. "I finally decided this wasn't the best bet for me," he recalled recently. "I knew too many people who were just as talented as I was, and I wasn't impressed by where they had got to."

Jensen was more deeply attracted by the idea of becoming a conductor. At fourteen, he conducted a San Diego band that won a nationwide contest held in San Francisco and ended up leading his charges through some Sousa marches in the mayor's office. Over the years he has done a fair amount of amateur and semipro conducting of serious orchestras, and for a while he studied conducting in a seminar given by Nikolai Sokoloff (who had earlier led the Cleveland Symphony). "I can conduct," Jensen states firmly.

Even after finishing his undergraduate years at Berkeley, where he had majored in psychology, he seems to have continued flirting with the idea of conducting. Soon after graduating, he took a year and a half off and moved to New

York City, mainly to be near his idol Arturo Toscanini, then in his seventies and obviously close to retirement. "I didn't want to die without seeing him in the flesh," Jensen recalled recently. He supported himself with a job in Columbia University's zoology department but spent much of the eighteen months going to concerts. ("I practically lived in Carnegie Hall.") He wangled permission to attend Toscanini's rehearsals of the NBC Symphony Orchestra and spent as much time as possible at the rehearsals, score in hand, raptly watching the maestro's technique. To this day Jensen remains a close student of conducting. When he buys recordings of some symphonic work, he still makes a point of obtaining the score. "It's interesting to follow along with the score," he says, "and see the different conductors' ideas about how it should be exploited." Jensen views conductors as men of high intelligence. "The musicians in symphony orchestras are kind of average," he observes. "They're at about the level of an average B.A. graduate. But the conductors—now they're something else again."

In his early years, Jensen was being pulled in still another direction. While in high school, he developed an enthusiasm for Gandhi and, incredibly, found time to produce a book-length manuscript about the Mahatma. Under Gandhi's influence, he also became a vegetarian. That did not last too long, but Jensen retains an interest in Indian culture and customs—and food. When he bought a lakeside vacation home several years ago, he put in a second kitchen so that he could prepare Indian dishes without getting in his wife's way.

I asked Jensen what it was about Gandhi that had attracted him. Was it, for example, the pacifist message? "No," Jensen said, "I can't say I was ever really a pacifist." (He expected to serve during World War II but ended up with a medical exemption.) Given his determined advocacy of unpopular ideas during much of his life, the reason he gives for gravitating to Gandhi seems significant. The main reason: "Gandhi's willingness to go wherever his convictions took him."

Jensen seems to have been somewhat adrift in the five years or so after he left New York. He returned to San Diego and for a while became, of all things, a social worker. (All you needed was a B.A. in psychology, which he had, to get a job with the San Diego Department of Public Welfare.) He also wrote a novel, suffering rejections by several publishers. He went back to work on his Gandhi biography but ultimately grew discouraged about the competition from world-class journalists like Louis Fischer and Vincent Sheean; Jensen sought out both of them, evidently hoping for more encouragement than he got. Then he tried, unsuccessfully, to get a publisher for a collection of Gandhi's writings that he had put together.

Jensen says he is glad he spent time as a social worker. "It showed me a side of the world I'd never seen before," he recalls. "Going into the homes of people who had nothing, who had to be taken care of—it was a real eye-opener." But he also determined that it wasn't the right career for him, and after a year or so, he entered San Diego State College to do graduate work in psychology. To make a little money on the side, he also got himself certified as a high school substitute teacher. His thought was that he could teach biology, but somehow he ended up more often in demand as a conductor. "I pretty much guest-conducted every high-school orchestra in San Diego County," he reminisced recently.

Despite these agreeable diversions, his career in psychology was now on track. After getting a master's degree at San Diego State, Jensen moved on to Columbia University for his Ph.D. (This move to New York possibly had something to do with the fact that Toscanini was still conducting the NBC Symphony.) His interest in psychology during this period was centered on personality studies, and his doctoral thesis was on the Thematic Apperception

Test (TAT)—a "projective" test designed to elicit information about people's mind-sets and basic values. Testees are
asked to react to various ambiguous scenes depicted in
black-and-white drawings, and the responses can turn up
clues to their ambitiousness, say, or need for social ap-
proval, or concern with material wealth.

Working as a research assistant to Columbia psychologist Percival Symonds, Jensen got deeply involved in a project involving the TAT. His assignment was to track down a
sizable group of men in their late twenties who had taken
the TAT fifteen years earlier, retest them, interview them
about their careers and personal lives, and in general help
to evaluate the predictions based on those earlier tests.
Traveling around the country with a ponderous 1950s-era
tape recorder, Jensen did in fact unearth most of the testees. The results of this exercise are described in a 1961
volume, *From Adolescent to Adult,* that he coauthored with
Symonds.[16] It indicated that the predictions based on the
TAT were pretty good.

Columbia was followed by a year interning at the University of Maryland's Psychiatric Institute. Jensen recalls
his work that year as being not terribly satisfying. Mostly it
consisted of interpreting and writing up diagnostic reports
on patients. Jensen says he got to be quite expert at this
work but increasingly came to feel it was not really science.
"Especially as I became more skilled at it," he wrote in a
self-portrait years later, "it all came more and more to seem
...a kind of literary rather than scientific activity."[17]

In this frame of mind, he was instantly receptive to a
book he came across: *The Scientific Study of Personality,* by H.
J. Eysenck.[18] It led him to read much more of Eysenck's
work and to form an enthusiasm for the man's quantitative
and experimental approach to psychology. "This, I felt
sure, was the kind of psychology for me," Jensen wrote in
the self-portrait. When his internship at Maryland was finished, he applied for—and got—a position as a postdoc-

toral fellow in Eysenck's London research center.

Eysenck is today well known as a heavyweight in the IQ debate—one who generally shares Jensen's perspective—but he was then famous mainly for his research on human personality differences. Jensen himself was less interested in personality than in problems of human learning; however, he did seem to acquire from Eysenck a commitment to "differential psychology." The thought behind that phrase is that psychological studies are most fruitful when they try to explain human differences (the alternative view being that psychologists should seek laws of mental functioning applicable to everybody). During his two years in Eysenck's laboratories at the University of London, Jensen finally got his career into focus: "I saw the career before me as being devoted to the study of individual differences in basic learning processes."

The call to Berkeley came in 1958, when an assistant-professor slot opened up in the university's educational psychology department and Jensen got enthusiastic recommendations from London, Maryland, and Columbia. Unlike academics who perish because they fail to publish, he rapidly became a prodigious producer of scholarly papers—most of them in this period on the psychology of learning—and kept getting accelerated promotions. He had tenure by 1962. He got his first sabbatical in 1964, which turned out to be a good year for sabbaticals at Berkeley. Jensen was in London, watching it all on TV, when Mario Savio and the New Left took over the campus, initiating months of pandemonium at Berkeley and the long time of troubles for American higher education.

In the years leading up to 1969 and his sudden national fame, Jensen continued to write and publish at a prodigious rate. The *Harvard Educational Review* essay that made him famous was, in fact, his seventy-sixth scholarly publication. Until that essay came along, however, most of Jensen's papers were concerned only marginally with IQ tests. His central preoccupation continued to be human learning, not intelligence. He broadened his focus, and began moving more deeply into IQ studies, in response to some perplexities encountered in studying childhood learning.

The perplexities centered on the relationship between what he called Level I abilities (mostly rote learning and memory) and Level II abilities (the higher reasoning functions). Jensen was then studying EMR children—the "educable mentally retarded." Some of the children came from middle-class white families, but most were poor and culturally disadvantaged, and many were Mexican-American. All had IQs below 75. (Such scores were then required in California for admission to EMR programs.) All had done poorly in school.

What was puzzling was that many of the disadvantaged Mexican-American kids did *not* do badly on the rote-learning tests. Indeed, they did as well on such tests as many children of average ability (IQ around 100) and in some cases as well as those of superior ability (IQ over 130). Making matters even more mysterious was the fact that no such patterns were demonstrated by the middle-class EMR kids, who rather consistently performed as poorly on the low-level tasks as on those involving reasoning.

Pondering these data, Jensen believed for a while that the disadvantaged Mexican-American children might be more intelligent than supposed. Perhaps the pattern they exhibited—low IQs but high scores on a simple memory test—reflected cultural biases in the IQ test (and the absence of bias in the memory test). But this hypothesis did not pan out. When he tested Mexican-American children who had scored fairly well on IQ tests, he found that they did less well in rote learning. In other words, they did best on the test hypothesized to be biased.

It was in trying to make sense of such puzzling data that Jensen increasingly moved into broader studies of intelligence. With the help of several research assistants, he tested over fifteen thousand California schoolchildren, representing every race and socioeconomic level. A main objective of the tests: to gain a greater understanding of the relationship between Level I abilities and Level II abilities. The results were fascinating on several counts.

For one thing, they undermined the idea that Level II abilities were functionally dependent on Level I abilities. A fair number of psychologists, including Jensen himself, had assumed this to be true; they believed, in other words, that you could not develop superior reasoning ability unless you had a strong rote-learning foundation. The California test showed that this presumption was false. They kept turning up children who scored high at one level but not the other.

The tests also showed that the relationship between Level I and Level II was quite different for different subgroups in the population. Among middle-class whites, children who performed well (or poorly) on one level were likely to perform well (or poorly) on the other. Among minority-group members, however, these correlations were much weaker. Which explains why a Mexican-American child with a low IQ might still do well at rote learning. Looking at these large population differences, Jensen deduced that Level II skills are unlikely to depend on Level I skills; at least it was hard to see why that dependency should be so much stronger for one group than another.

In any case, the studies turned up plenty of examples of children who tested high at one of the levels and not the other. The child who is poor at Level I but superior at Level II is the classic "late bloomer" who has trouble in school so long as the assignments are centered on memory-related tasks but who flourishes in the later grades, where problem solving is more important. The opposite case—strong on Level I, weak on Level II—involves children who may star in the lower grades, turning in strong performances in penmanship, spelling, and learning the multiplication table, but who are doomed to frustration as the curriculum comes to demand more analytic skills.[19]

The "levels theory" was a major theme in academic psychology during much of the seventies and eighties. Jensen promoted it vigorously and seems to have hoped for a while that it might lead to major educational reforms (in which there would be different curricula for children who performed well, and those who performed poorly, at Level II). If this was his hope, it has proved vain. Egalitarian America appears to be a long way from any educational concepts explicitly based on different ability levels among students.

In any case, Jensen has shown less interest in Level I and Level II in recent years. His current view is that the levels concept is valid but ultimately superfluous. The mysteries illuminated by the levels theory, he now believes, can be explained more parsimoniously by focusing on g—general intelligence—which is essentially synonymous with Level II thinking. Jensen has probably done more than any other scholar to convert the world of educational testing to a belief in the centrality of g.

When he first began arguing the importance of g a quarter century ago, he was probably in a minority in taking it seriously. Today a substantial majority of psychologists agree with him. The experts surveyed by Snyderman and Rothman (see chapter 2) were asked whether they thought "intelligence" was better described as a general factor or in terms of separate faculties. Among those who answered this question, two-thirds favored the "general" solution, while only around one scholar in six squarely endorsed the "separate faculties" solution.

Jensen's major experimental research at Berkeley has been in a field called "reaction time" (RT). Here again the studies have been controversial, and again, Jensen and his allies seem to be winning the argument.

The RT studies have produced findings of extraordinary interest and significance from experiments of almost childish simplicity. In a typical experiment, the subject sits in front of a console looking at a number of small green light bulbs. At random intervals, a few seconds apart, one of the green lights goes on. The subject then moves his finger, as rapidly as he can, to a button just below the light; when he hits the button, the light goes off, and he waits for the next green light to go on. Electronic timers measure (in milliseconds) the time it takes the subject (a) to move after the light goes on and (b) to hit the "off" button.

The first major finding is a consistent negative correlation between reaction time and IQ. (The correlation on the experiment described above is around −.35.)[21] The smarter subjects, in other words, react more rapidly. This finding seems intuitively implausible to many people, whose exemplar of high intelligence is the slow-speaking, reflective, thoughtful individual, not the fast talker. Jensen observes, however, that the individual who comes across as reflective is not really slow; he is probably just processing a lot more data before delivering his judgment.

When I first heard of these findings several years ago, I told Jensen that the data seemed hard to square with the incredible RT performances of some athletes. A major-league baseball player, for example, has to be able to make split-second decisions about whether pitches traveling at ninety miles an hour are an inch or so off the plate; yet we all take it for granted that many major leaguers lack high IQs. In response, Jensen made two main points: (1) The skills I was describing involve a lot more than reaction time; they also depend heavily on physical coordination and endless practice. (2) It was, however, undoubtedly true that there was some IQ requirement—Jensen guessed it might be around IQ 85—below which you could never recruit for major-league baseball. (About one-sixth of Americans fall below 85.)

A second finding of the RT studies is that the *variabil-*

ity of RT has an even larger negative correlation with IQ than does speed. The smarter subjects, in other words, are not only faster but more consistent. On the test described above, the correlation between IQ and the standard deviation of subjects' reaction times becomes about .50. The likeliest interpretation of these data is that individuals with good, preferably redundant, "wiring" in their heads will consistently get the message rapidly. Those who are poorly wired have problems somewhat comparable to those afflicting users of a weak telephone line with a lot of static; the message will sometimes get through right away, but at other times it may have to be repeated once or twice. So their RT speeds will vary all over the lot.

A third intriguing finding is that both the RTs and IQs are correlated with certain measurable physical processes in the brain. These correlations emerged from experiments in which the RT subjects had electrodes gummed to their scalps, making possible analysis of their "brain waves" on an oscilloscope. Basic finding: Those with high IQs (and low reaction times) require fewer and smaller electrical discharges in the cortex in order to react—another indication that their neural systems are more efficient than those with low IQs. Correlations of −.10 to −.35 have been reported between IQ and "average evoked potential."[22] (The AEP can be thought of as a measure of cumulative electrical discharges in the brain.)

Along with many other scholars, Jensen has recently been excited about the possibility of linking *g* and IQ to physical activity in still another way, via the so-called PET scan. His excitement reflects some preliminary results using positron emission tomography, a technology that affords unparalleled and "noninvasive" looks inside the human brain. The data again point up the importance of neural efficiency. They show, for example, that high-IQ subjects taking tests heavy in *g* metabolize less glucose (the basic food of the brain) in the process than do testees who score lower.[23]

The RT tests have a number of powerful implications. (1) The correlations between reaction time and IQ demonstrate rather conclusively that IQ scores reflect real human abilities, not just acquired knowledge and skills. (2) In linking IQ scores to physical processes in the brain, the RT data provide another powerful argument for the heritability of IQ and *g*. (3) The data also afford some intriguing clues to the kinds of neural structures that may be required for intelligence. It pays, apparently, to have dense networks with plenty of backup—which might seem unsurprising except that it is incompatible with strong environmental interpretations of IQ differences.

I once asked Jensen if he knew his own IQ. It turned out that he had never taken any of the standard tests, like the WAIS. The question of testing him first arose during the year of his Maryland internship, but by then he could not take the WAIS because he was too familiar with it (having administered it to others perhaps a hundred times). Of the various mental tests he has taken over the years, the Terman Concept Mastery Test (CMT)—a high-level measure of verbal skills—probably provides the best approximation of an IQ test. Jensen took it when he was forty-three. He declined to tell me the score—and seemed distinctly unhappy at my interest in the subject—but did finally mention that his CMT score was about at the average for those members of Terman's Gifted Group who had gone on to earn Ph.D.s.

Poking my nose into volume 5 of Terman's *Genetic Studies of Genius*, I learn that this subgroup of the gifted had Stanford-Binet IQ equivalents of 156,[24] well into the 99.9 percentile. Which possibly helps to explain why Jensen has been such a dominant figure in the IQ debate.

6

Slipping: How Intelligence Declines With Age

It is no secret that physical and athletic skills decline with age. Every sports fan knows that a baseball, football, or tennis player is "old" at thirty-five. It is also well known that people slip mentally as they grow older; however, this decline is often mistakenly conceived as exclusively a phenomenon of senior citizenship. In fact, some kinds of brainpower begin declining in the twenties. In most occupations, this "aptitude" decline is at once masked and offset by "achievement" gains, that is, by gains associated with increased knowledge and experience. But there are some kinds of work in which experience is relatively unimportant and other skills—abstract reasoning ability, imagination, creativity—are totally dominant. A theoretical physicist capable of making breakthroughs at forty-five is about as unlikely as an NFL linebacker at forty-five.

In the average case, the neural power and efficiency of the human brain appear to reach a peak around age twenty or twenty-five.[1] This is roughly the age at which brain size and weight are maximized. As you grow older, your skull thickens and your brain shrinks. In a famous essay called "The Problem of Mental Deterioration," psychologist David Wechsler (developer of the WAIS and the WISC) published a chart that crisply summarized the effect of this shrinkage. One line in the chart showed IQ raw scores declining with age; the other line showed brain weight declining. By age sixty-five, the brain has typically lost about 6 percent of its weight at twenty, and raw scores are perhaps 15 percent lower.[2] The age-norming scales used to derive IQs from WAIS raw scores tell us that peak performance is attained in the zone around ages twenty-five to thirty-four.[3] WAIS raw scores average 103 at age 16, 114 at age 25, 103 at age 40, and 93 at age 60.[4]

As in all such generalizations about large groups, it is important to keep reminding yourself that we are talking here about the average case—and not about all cases. Even some geezers in their eighties will be capable of generating WAIS raw scores comparable to those of thirty-year-olds. Timothy A. Salthouse, recently a visiting scholar at the Max Planck Institute for Human Development and Education in Berlin, has observed that in a group representative of the population as a whole, you would expect less than 16 percent of the total variability in test scores to be attributable to age differences.[5] On the other hand, Salthouse notes, age-based differences are better predictors of mental ability than just about any other variable: "An individual's age may be the most valuable piece of information about that individual for the purpose of predicting his or her level of cognitive performance."[6]

Mental ability does not decline across the board as one grows older. Some kinds of skills hold up pretty well into the sixties and seventies, while others go into a long, steady decline much earlier. In the average case, scores hold up well in the WAIS subtests for Information, Comprehension, Vocabulary, and Arithmetic. These subtests generally measure what has been called "crystallized" intelligence—

the ability to perform familiar mental tasks one has practiced for years. Most job skills depend on crystallized
intelligence, which is why most workers remain competent
into their sixties. If you have been driving a car all your
adult life and are otherwise healthy, you can presumably
continue driving without mishap well into your seventies
or even eighties.

Declines in mental ability are much more substantial
for Digit Symbol, Block Design, and Picture Arrangement.[7]
This latter group—the subtests that pose the greatest problems for old folks—lean heavily on what has been called
"fluid" intelligence. Fluid intelligence involves the ability
to learn new tasks, which is why otherwise healthy sixty-
year-olds would have trouble learning to drive a car.

Research performed over several generations tells us
that elderly people have more difficulty than young adults
in following instructions about matters not familiar to
them. The Army Alpha test, developed during World War I
and later used in various civilian contexts, included a subtest called Following Directions, on which correlations between age and scores were negative at significant levels.[8]
Here is Salthouse describing another test of ability to follow instructions: "One set of directions concerned details
about the delivery of a parcel, including when and where it
was to be delivered, what to do if no one was home, and
how to obtain a receipt for the delivery." When a sizable
sample of adult testees, aged twenty-five to ninety, was
asked to recall the directions after an interval, their scores
showed a powerful negative correlation (−.51) with age.[9]

Fluid intelligence involves the ability to learn, to see
things in new ways, to devise inventive solutions to unfa-
miliar problems. Above all, it involves abstract reasoning
ability. Fluid intelligence, and especially fluid g (i.e., the
general factor in fluid intelligence), are essentially synonymous with raw brainpower and generally dependent on
the physical brain. In the IQ literature, you sometimes

come across the thought that fluid *g* is "real" intelligence, while crystallized intelligence is mainly a reflection of experience.

The young-old gap in fluid intelligence is quite substantial. It turns up dramatically in, for example, Arthur Jensen's reaction-time studies. "If you're over 30, you're over the hill," Jensen has said about the studies.[10] On the Wechsler subtests measuring fluid intelligence, differences between twenty-year-olds and sixty-five-year-olds range between .5 and 1.5 standard deviations. With a difference of 1 SD (i.e., the midpoint of that range), you would expect the average sixty-five-year-old to register fluid-intelligence scores placing him around the fifteenth percentile among twenty-year-olds.[11]

The fluid-crystallized distinction was proposed a half century ago by Raymond B. Cattell, an eminent British psychologist and the originator of a devastating insight about old age. Cattell observed that elderly people were forever complaining about their memory lapses but could never be heard to gripe about declining judgment.[12] In fact, judgment collapses a lot faster than memory.

Can it be? Yes, quite definitely. Wise judgments can be improved by knowledge and experience, which older folks may have in abundance, but judgment depends most of all on reasoning skill: the ability to think through the implications of various possible solutions to the problem at hand. In the end, there is no getting around the need for raw processing power in forming judgments about matters of any complexity. And processing power clearly declines with age.

Elderly people naturally wish not to acknowledge that their judgment is declining and may in fact be unaware of any slippage. But the decline of their memory is a fact of life that is hard to escape. If you need your eyeglasses to read newspapers or watch television, it is impossible not to notice that you are recurrently unable to find the glasses (not to mention the newspapers), to cite a detail that brings your author uncomfortably close to home.

The process of remembering is often broken down into three categories: (1) instant recall—the kind of skill involved in holding a seven-digit telephone number in your head for the brief interval between the time you get it from an operator and the time it takes to dial the number; (2) short-term recall—the ability to retain information learned in recent weeks; and (3) long-term recall—remembrance of the events of years ago.

IQ tests do fairly well at measuring instant recall. In the WAIS-R (see chapter 1), both the Digit Span and Digit Symbol tests offer straightforward evidence on recall. On Digit Span (the test in which you repeat back from three to nine digits after hearing them read aloud), David Wechsler has published data showing that performance peaks in the age zone between twenty and thirty-four, then tails off slowly through about age sixty-five, after which it drops more sharply.[13] On Digit Symbol, the decline with age is greater. This subtest is the one in which you try to remember which of nine visual symbols goes with which digit and write down as many digits as you can in a minute and a half when presented with random arrays of the symbols. Because it calls for more mental processing, this test of memory produces a sharper and earlier falloff with age. On a scale where teenagers and young adults score around 10, adults between fifty-five and sixty-four average only about 6 1/4 and could look forward to further sharp declines after sixty-four.[14]

Memory of events or details learned in the distant past, or even several weeks ago, are harder to gauge—if only because the tester has no way of verifying what the testee knew in the past. It does seem clear from various tests that older people have more trouble than younger adults in supplying details about what they were doing when John F. Kennedy was assassinated or in reeling off the names of their teachers in school;[15] but in the absence of any verification of answers, these tests always seem less than satisfactory.

A partial solution to the challenge of gauging long-term memory is the Wechsler Information subtest. Information can be viewed as in some measure testing long-term memory because you are being asked to rapidly retrieve an assortment of facts, many or most of which you presumably once knew. The Wechsler data show no falloff at all in this subtest; in fact, those aged fifty-five to sixty-four do slightly better than any of the younger cohorts.[16] To be sure, the subtest results reflect the added knowledge that comes with age, which in considerable measure masks a decline in pure retrieval power.

Old folks are just about always prepared to groan about their memory lapses. Among normal (i.e., not institutionalized) elderly people, the single most common complaint, by a landslide, is the inability to recall the names of people. Dana J. Plude and Lisa Murphy, two psychologists based at the University of Maryland, who often lecture to elderly audiences on memory problems, are my authorities for that statement.[17] They add that in second place is the inability to recall whether you have performed some routine task, like turning off the stove before you left the house—the classic "absentmindedness" problem.[18]

Why are the elderly more absentminded? Plude and Murphy suggest that part of the answer, at least, is the lower level of analysis performed by older people in thinking about events in their lives. You are most likely to remember something if you thought about it seriously while it was happening—if you focused on its meaning to you—and much less likely to remember it if your thoughts never went beyond surface appearances. Say Plude and Murphy: "In general, it has been found that elderly adults tend to engage a shallower level of analysis compared with younger adults, which impairs the older adult's performance in laboratory-based memory tasks."[19]

The explanation seems persuasive: The key to remembering something is thinking about it. One familiar but still incredible-seeming stunt performed by chess grand masters is playing twenty or so simultaneous games, then recalling every move in every game. The stunt is made possible not by superiority in rote memory but by deep immersion in the logic that governs every move. If the grand master were Russian, let us say, and you took him to a baseball game without his knowing the rules, he would do far worse than an ordinary American baseball fan in reconstructing later what he had seen.

There is some evidence to suggest that as you approach the end of life, your fate can be foretold via IQ testing. A sharp decline in IQ predicts impending death. Data supporting this arresting thought come partly from studies of elderly patients who lived in a retirement community and were repeatedly tested on the WAIS. The most detailed evidence, however, comes from a study of male veterans in a VA hospital. A sizable group of the vets were tested in the 1960s and then retested after intervals of five to ten years. It turned out that the veterans who died within a year of the retest tended to be those whose scores had fallen most sharply during that five-to-ten-year interval; on average, their test-retest decline was 15 1/2 IQ points. In contrast, the veterans who died between one and two years of the retest had suffered a decline of only 9 points. What about those who were still alive two years after the retest? Their scores, on average, had declined by only 5.67 points.[20]

The meaning of these data are not entirely clear. Possibly the sharper declines associated with earlier deaths reflected mounting deficiencies in blood flows to the brain, which might in turn increase risks from strokes. It does at least seem clear that declining judgment is bad for you.

7

Behind Nature and Nurture

Passions are regularly torn to tatters in the endless row over the heritability of IQs. Before plunging into the row, it will pay to state precisely the point at issue. The question: How much of the observed variability in people's IQs is attributable to genetic factors? Note that the question is about variability—about differences between people—and not about the respective contributions of genes and environment to an individual's own IQ. The latter question, frequently asked by newcomers to the debate, is unanswerable. It is somewhat like asking an expert to quantify the respective contributions to Joe DiMaggio's success in baseball of (a) natural ability and (b) training and practice. All the expert could say is that the two were inextricably intertwined and inseparable, which is also all that can be said about an individual's genes and environment.

In responding to the question about IQ variability, the only answers allowed are in the range from 0.0 to 1.0. If you answer that heritability is, say, .60, you are stating that

60 percent of the variability is genetically based (leaving 40 percent for environmental factors).

Another question *not* at issue in the debate is the existence of "an intelligence gene." No serious scholar believes in a single gene that shapes intelligence. The substantial majority of scholars who believe in some genetic contribution to IQ differences have in mind a "polygenic" model— that is, they assume that the genetic factors are expressed in infinitely complex interactions among some uncertain number of the 100,000[1] or so genes in the human system. On some estimates, 50,000 or more of these genes may be involved in the shaping of intelligence.[2]

Why is nature versus nurture, aka heredity versus environment, so emotionally charged? Why do so many educated Americans feel a deep, instinctive commitment to the "environmentalist" side of the argument? (In the IQ context, you will observe, that term is applied to people who are *against* nature.) Why is it that after furiously resisting the idea that IQ test scores matter at all and finally being persuaded that maybe they do, so many of these educated Americans get furious all over again at being told that variability in scores is powerfully affected by genetic factors?

An answer might begin by observing that, for many Americans, the ideal of equality has always gone well beyond equality of rights. Deeply embedded in the national psyche is the idea that people are truly born equal in *ability.* A few scholars believe that in composing the memorable sentence about all men being created equal, Thomas Jefferson intended to impart the thought that they were indeed equal at birth, or at least equal in their potential. In *Inventing America: Jefferson's Declaration of Independence,* Gary Wills argues that such formulations were common enough among the Enlightenment philosophers who influenced Jefferson and other Founding Fathers.[3] Even conservative icon Adam Smith believed men to be equal in ability—or, more precisely, potentially equal at birth. In *The Wealth of Nations,* Smith wrote: "The difference between the most dissimilar characters, between a philosopher and a common street porter, for example, seems to arise not so much from nature as from habit, custom, and education."[4] His travels in the United States left Alexis de Tocqueville marveling at American egalitarianism: "They have all a lively faith in the perfectibility of man."[5]

The idea that humans are equal in ability implies that the manifest inequalities observable in everyday life are unfair—also that they are reversible. For some, this lively faith is combined with a more politicized thought: that the nurtural side of the argument is the "progressive" side. It is deemed progressive because it implies that the right social programs can change people for the better (and not only with respect to intelligence).

This reasoning was pushed to fantastic extremes in the Soviet Union under Stalin, when it was hard doctrine that communism *was* changing people for the better. In the Stalin era, many scholars were shot for positing that human differences might have some genetic basis. In 1936, the Soviet Medicogenetical Institute was dissolved, accused of exalting heredity over environment. In 1948, the Communist Party Central Committee officially repudiated the entire science of genetics. Soviet academics were obliged to teach the pre-Darwinian doctrine that acquired characteristics can be transmitted to one's heirs. A pseudoscientist named Trofim Lysenko, who had done some minor work in plant breeding, became with Stalin's backing the overlord of the biological sciences and arranged for the arrest and execution of numerous scholars deemed insufficiently attentive to the new orthodoxy.[6] It was not until the mid-sixties that Lysenko's scientific nonsense was formally repudiated by Soviet authorities.[7]

To be sure, it was always logically fallacious to argue that the environmentalist side of the argument is the progressive side. As the late philosopher Sidney Hook observed,[8] environmentalism implies not only that intelligent social programs can make people better; it also suggests that government can change people for the worse. The nightmare totalitarian world envisioned in Orwell's *1984*—featuring a dictatorship that had systematically brainwashed its subjects and left them utterly unable to think critically—is also an expression of the environmental model.

Still, it is harder by far to make a progressive case for the "nature" side of the argument. A belief in substantial heritability of IQ leads one, logically and inescapably, to a conclusion from which egalitarian America reflexively shrinks. The problems for egalitarians were expressed forcefully in *IQ in the Meritocracy*, an influential book published in 1973. Its author, Prof. Richard J. Herrnstein of Harvard, expressed the implications of heritability in this compact syllogism:

1. If differences in mental abilities are inherited, and
2. If success requires those abilities, and
3. If earnings and prestige depend on success,
4. Then social standing (which reflects earnings and prestige) will be based to some extent on inherited differences among people.[9]

To be sure, nobody participating in the IQ debate would argue that variability in intelligence is *entirely* genetic. Herrnstein himself estimates heritability around .60 to .70[10]—meaning that 60 percent to 70 percent of the variability in IQ has genetic origins. Among serious scholars, the debate about heritability takes two forms nowadays. First, there are never-ending disputes about the "right" heritability estimate. Among such scholars, the range of estimates is from .50 to .80. Second, mainstream scholars continue to argue with a few of their colleagues, heavily overrepresented in media presentations of the issue, who keep trying to prove that heritability might be 0—meaning that variation in IQ could be entirely explained by environmental factors.

Note that heritability estimates of .50–.80 still leave a certain amount of running room for environmentally driven explanations (assumed to explain 20–50 percent of IQ differences). These environmental effects are well documented. One famous study, reported by L. R. Wheeler in 1942, compared the IQs of Tennessee mountain kids in 1930 and again in 1940. The 1940 group tested about 10 points higher. It seems clear that the environment of such children was dramatically tranformed during the intervening years; indeed, you could argue that rural electrification and the Tennessee Valley Authority were suddenly bringing the mountain population into the twentieth century. Most scholars seem inclined to link these changes to the IQ gain, or at least much of it.[11]

Two other points need to be made about environmental effects. First, it will pay to zero in a bit on the term "environment." Most people one talks to about nature and nurture seem to think of the latter as synonymous with "culture." They think of a good environment as one that is, above all, strong on education. They believe it matters to have teachers and parents who lead children to view education as their top priority, who stimulate children intellectually, who encourage them to read widely and make it possible for them to do so. Nobody would deny that all these cultural influences are important.

But environmental influences affecting test scores embrace a lot more than culture. You really have to think of nurture more broadly—as encompassing *everything not captured in the child's genetic heritage*. Some part of the environment is prenatal, for example. Twins test a bit lower on average than singletons (see the next chapter), and there is some evidence that the disparity reflects crowding and a

resultant loss of oxygen in the womb. Another environmental effect that may show up in test-score differentials is
nutrition. It is well established that prolonged periods of
malnutrition work to depress IQ and that scores can be
raised by rescuing children from severe undernourish-
ment. Improved nutrition surely played some role in the
gains made by those Tennessee mountain kids. And as we
shall see in chapter 13, some scholars believe that IQs have
risen substantially during the past half century or so
mainly because of superior nutrition. For many poor families, it seems clear, the IQ gains from improved nutrition
have outweighed the gains from increased spending on
schools.

A second point worth reflecting on: It is wrong to
think of nature as "passive" and nurture as "active." Many
people seem predisposed to think of it this way, that is, they
view the individual's genetic constitution as a kind of blank
slate on which active environmental influences will do
their writing. But this model is much too simple. The genes
themselves will affect the environment. Teachers will
shower more attention on children who learn more rapidly, and even the most loving parents will be more apt to
spend time talking and reading to children when they get
some intelligent responses from the kids.

To the same point: Arthur Jensen once told me a grip-
ping story about a child in India who was denied a formal
education because, as a low-caste "untouchable," he was
not allowed to attend the only school in his region. The
child nevertheless managed to learn a lot by spending
hours peering through the schoolroom windows and, ultimately, figuring out what the teacher was explaining at the
blackboard. He learned to read this way, which enabled
him to pursue an education on his own and qualify for the
University of Bombay. Eventually, he became a distinguished Indian lawyer. It is hard to believe that he would
ever have made these heroic efforts to transform his environment without some genetic head start.

A distinction that recurs endlessly in the IQ literature is that between genotype and phenotype. Your genotype is your genetic constitution. Your phenotype is the trait or characteristic resulting from the genotype, for example, your height or IQ score. Bearing these terms in mind, consider the following statement about genotype-phenotype relationships, put forward in 1983 by Sandra Scarr (University of Virginia) and Kathleen McCartney (Yale University):

> Both genes and environments are constituents in the developmental system, but they have different roles. Genes determine much of human experience, but experiential opportunities are also necessary for development to occur. Individual differences can arise from restrictions in environmental opportunities to experience what the genotype would find compatible. With a rich array of opportunities, however, most differences among people arise from genetically determined differences in the experiences to which they are attracted and which they evoke from their environments.[12]

Scholars who point to significant environmental effects while still insisting on high heritabilities enjoy a commanding majority these days. It is nevertheless worth pausing to focus on the thought that heritability may be zero or trivial, if only because of the play this proposition has long received in the American media.

The case for zero heritability—for a totally environmental explanation of IQ differences—is hard to sustain. From the avalanche of correlations generated by IQ studies, there has emerged one set of data that would appear to clinch the argument against zero heritability. The data contrast the IQs of identical twins reared apart and fraternal twins growing up together. The former are genetically indistinguishable but have grown up in diverse environments. The latter share only half their genes in common but have grown up together. Yet the separated identical twins are more similiar in IQ than the raised-together fraternal twins. Correlation coefficient for the identical twins raised separately: .72. For the fraternal twins raised together: .58.[13] The hypothesis that IQ differences are entirely environmental cannot, or at least should not, survive those data.

Indeed, the case for zero heritability seems nonsensical even before you approach such data. The zero hypothesis would require you to believe either or both of two hard-to-swallow propositions: (1) that of all the human organs bestowed on children at birth, only the brain has been unaffected by the parents' genes; and (2) that brain function does not govern intelligence.

Both propositions are of course absurd. Like other human organs, brains are inherited and dissimilar from one individual to another. In *The Human Brain,* a textbook by neuroanatomist Paul Glees, the brain is said to represent the "signature of a genetically unique person."[14] Brain size has roughly tripled in the 5 million years of human evolution, and it is widely accepted that larger brains evolved precisely because they made possible learning and problem-solving abilities that increased survival rates.

In recent years, we have been learning a lot about the link between IQ and the physical brain. The link has often been derided by scholars seeking to minimize genetic factors in IQ variation. In *The Mismeasure of Man,* his wide-ranging polemic against mental testing, Stephen Jay Gould of Harvard devotes many pages to quarreling with writers who have linked brain size to intelligence or, indeed, who have been so impolite as to look for such links.

For example, he attacks Arthur Jensen for having mentioned a correlation of .30 between brain size (adjusted for body size) and IQ. Along the way, Gould points to the numerous practical difficulties in measuring brains, an exercise traditionally performed only on corpses. He notes that the data are inconsistent about such matters as the point on the spinal cord where the brain was severed, the temperature at which the brain was preserved after death, and whether the meninges (membranes covering the brain) were removed before weighing. In addition, data on corpses have often been confounded by incomplete information on the cause of death, since some diseases would be expected to result in shrunken brains.

A number of recent technologies have transformed the whole argument about the IQ/brain-size nexus. With magnetic resonance imaging (MRI), it is now possible to develop very precise measurements of *living* individuals' brains. An article in the journal *Intelligence*[15] describes an experiment at the University of Texas in which forty young (average age: 18.9 years) students were divided into two groups. One group consisted entirely of young men and women with IQs above 130, the other with IQs below 103. After a statistical correction to adjust for the "extremeness" of the sample IQs, the correlation between IQ and brain size was given as .35—not a whole lot different from Jensen's .30.

Scholars arguing for the possibility of a zero heritability (most of them seem to be Marxists) have not done well in dealing with the evidence for high heritability. To some extent, they have dodged the issue, using up most of their firepower in detailed critiques of studies arguing a case for substantial heritability (and seldom explicitly making an affirmative case of their own for zero). They have also leaned hard on a proposition that has, in fact, some validity: that the brain's development in infancy is affected by the child's environment. You will observe, however, that the case for zero heritability requires them to go further—to argue that environmental effects account for the *entire* developmental difference between the brains of two children. Unfortunately for the argument, no neuroscientist would give credence to any such claim.

And when you look closely, the claim is ultimately not made, not even by R. C. Lewontin, Steven Rose, and Leon J. Kamin, authors of *Not in Our Genes,* perhaps the most detailed expression of the extreme environmental case. (Lewontin and Rose are biologists, Kamin a psychologist now based at Northeastern University.) The book was written, said its authors in the preface, to rebut the views of other scholars whom they saw as "acting to preserve the interests of the dominant class, gender, and race."[16] In a passage on the brain's development, they write: "The human infant is born with relatively few of its neural pathways already committed. During its long infancy, connections between nerve cells are formed on the basis not merely of specific epigenetic programming but in the light of experience."[17] The acknowledgment that "epigenetic programming" plays a role can be read as a muffled concession to reality. Your brain does indeed reflect your genetic heritage.

In effect, then, you can throw out the case for zero heritability. You can also throw out the case for 100 percent heritability—or, rather, there is no such case. (You cannot find a psychometrician or behavioral geneticist arguing that differences in IQ are explained entirely by genes.) So the question on the table is not really an either/or question: nature or nurture. The only question that makes sense is about the relative strengths of the two effects. The scholars polled by Snyderman and Rothman, asked to estimate heritability (the "nature" effect), turned in answers averaging around .60.[18] That is, the scholars' collective judgment was that genes account for 60 percent of the variability in IQ. Studies in recent years have generated answers ranging from .50 to .80. In other words, genes are thought to account for half to four-fifths of the variability in IQ.

Where do such figures come from? How do you measure the relative strengths of the two effects? Basically by designing experiments in which you try to hold one of the effects constant while varying the other.

In describing these experiments, we shall now slide into the psychometricians' habit of referring to identical, or monozygotic, twins as MZs and dizygotic, or fraternal, twins as DZs. (Identical twins come from a single cell, or zygote; fraternal twins, from paired cells.) We shall also follow the professionals in referring to twins raised apart as MZAs or DZAs and twins raised together as MZTs or DZTs. The science of psychometrics is believed to have saved carloads of ink over the years as a result of these notational conventions.

Most studies over the years have fallen into one of three categories.

1. Studies Comparing the IQs of MZTs and DZTs.

This method leaves you looking at sets of twins, all of which are presumed to have similar environments, that is, because in each case they have grown up together in the same household. (To ensure maximum environmental similarity, many of the studies have limited the DZs in their samples to those of the same sex.[19]) Some of the twin sets (the MZTs) also have identical genes; the others (the DZTs), however, are genetically different from one another, since fraternal twins, like ordinary siblings, share only about half their genes. In effect, then, the MZT-DZT studies are one way of holding environment steady while varying heredity.

When you examine the IQs of the two kinds of twins, you will find that those for the MZTs are much more strongly correlated than those for the DZTs. A typical result would be correlations of around .85 for the MZTs and .60 for the DZTs.[20] In calculating heritabilities from such data, you would subtract the lower figure from the higher and double the result. Using the figures in our example, you would get a heritability of .50 (because .85 − .60 = .25 x 2 = .50).[21] As the example suggests, this method has generally yielded results at the low end of the range.

The method has one large advantage over most other

kinds of heritability studies: American twins who have grown up together are abundant. (There are more than 2 million sets of them.[22]) The method also has some disadvantages. There continue to be fierce arguments about the meaning of some data generated by such studies.

One cluster of arguments concerns the degree of similarity in the upbringings of identical and fraternal twins. Prof. Leon Kamin, for example, has argued that identical twins inevitably have far more similar environments than fraternal twins, if only because their parents are more predisposed to treat them as equivalents. Kamin adds that the environmental "supersimilarity" (not his term) for MZTs might by itself explain why their IQs correlate more powerfully than those of DZTs.[23]

This argument seems wobbly, however. In an effort to evaluate the environmental effect of being treated as an MZ, one scholar—Sandra Scarr, now based at the University of Virginia—put together a sizable group of DZs who had been mistaken for MZs in their early years. Basic finding: The DZs in question had IQ correlations much like those of other DZs, not like those of MZs. In other words, the effects of supersimilar treatment seem not to carry over to IQ scores.[24]

A difficulty that seems more bothersome is the possibility of bias in the selection of twins—especially the DZs—who get to participate in such studies. Ordinarily, you would get to the twins through their parents, whose permission you typically need. Psychologists who do twin studies have often observed that the parents of twins tend to be enormously cooperative: They rightly regard their kids as special and find it natural that professionals would want to test them. But there are exceptions. Parents are thought to be much less cooperative when they have reason to believe that one of the fraternal twins will test significantly higher than the other; in such families, the tests can begin to look like a source of anguish and embarrassment.[25]

If it is true that DZ twins of unequal ability are under-represented in the studies, then the data are indeed flawed. The implication of any such bias would be that the correlations for the DZTs have been artifically raised. Which would imply in turn that the bottom line—the heritability estimates—have been artifically lowered. In the example above, for example, note that if the DZT correlation were suddenly discovered to be .52 instead of .60, the derived heritability would become .66 instead of .50.

2. *Studies of Adopted Children*

Adoptions afford a unique opportunity to sort out the effects on children of nature and nurture. Most children, of course, get both their genes and their home environments from their natural parents, which makes it impossible to separate the two effects. But adopted children grow up in households that are giving them only "nurture." One familiar kind of adoption study tries to measure the nurtural effect by relating the adopted kids' IQs to a broad range of environmental variables (including the adoptive parents' education, income, and IQs).

In another version, the study contrasts adopted children and those growing up with their natural parents. It would typically show that adopted children's IQs correlate about .20 with the average of their adoptive parents' IQs, versus about .50 for children growing up with their own parents.[26] As in the studies of MZTs and DZTs, we derive a heritability estimate by subtracting the lower figure from the higher and doubling the result. So—the adoption studies typically yield heritabilities in the neighborhood of .60 (because .50 − .20 = .30 x 2 = .60). As the numbers in these examples suggest, adoption studies often yield heritabilities higher than do the MZT-DZT studies.

Like the studies of MZTs and DZTs, the adoption research has given analysts plenty to argue about. In principle, the kinds of studies described here should be based on IQ samples representative of the population as a whole. Unfortunately, the researchers collecting twin data have trouble meeting that standard. "Adoptions are not arranged for the purpose of scientific studies," Arthur Jensen has dryly observed;[27] and because adoption agencies do persist in putting the interests of children above those of psychometricians, the logic of the studies often gets a bit mucked up by various statistical biases. Perhaps the most serious bias—in any event, it seems to be the one most discussed—resides in the broad social and intellectual superiority of adoptive parents. These parents are "upscale" by many different measures, mainly because adoption agencies tend to screen out candidates deemed deficient in education, income, or intelligence. To the extent that adoptive kids grow up in superior environments, the calculations contrasting them with other children will inevitably be imperfect.

3. Studies of Identical Twins Reared Apart

Studies of MZAs have long had a special appeal for psychological researchers. The appeal resides in the stark simplicity of the experiment. The correlation coefficient for MZs' genetic traits is, of course, 1.0. If they were separated at birth and assigned to foster parents broadly representative of the population, then the coefficient for environmental effects would be 0—that is, differences between the twins would on average be unaffected by their environments. With environmental effects wiped out, you could assume that the IQ correlation for MZAs was itself a good measure of heritability.

To be sure, MZAs who meet the criteria are hard to find. Until quite recently, most scholars interested in twin studies were focused on three classic studies, covering a total of only sixty-five pairs of twins.[28] One of the studies was performed by an American team in the thirties, another was reported by a British researcher in 1962, and the third was reported by a Danish team in 1965.[29] The weighted average of the three studies shows a heritability of .72.[30]

Until the late seventies, most scholars would also have included the twin studies prepared by Sir Cyril Burt, long the dean of British psychologists. But after his death, anomalies in Burt's research led to charges of fraud against him, and during the eighties virtually nobody cited his work. Two recent volumes, written by British scholars but also published in the United States—*The Burt Affair,* by Robert B. Joynson, and *Science, Ideology and the Media: The Cyril Burt Scandal,* by Ronald Fletcher—argue persuasively that the fraud was nonexistent and that Sir Cyril was railroaded (see chapter 9). Still, there remain enough doubts about his twin studies to preclude their use in current analyses of the data.

The three classic studies of twins reared apart had a number of imperfections. Most of the twins had not really been separated at birth, but sometime later. (Average age at separation in the three studies: about 16 months.[31]) In addition, the data generated by the studies were contaminated by some of the same problems besetting other twin researchers, especially the tendency of adoption agencies to place the children in similar and in any case superior environments.

Still, most students of the subject have found the conclusions of the twin studies persuasive. In the Snyderman-Rothman survey, 84.4 percent of "the experts" cite these studies as a reason for believing in some heritability. Comparable figure for adoption studies: 63.4 percent. For MZT-DZT studies: 70.3 percent.[32]

Since the Snyderman-Rothman survey was published, still another twin study has been reported. It is by far the largest of any MZA study ever performed. Based on fifty-two sets of identical twins plus a few sets of triplets, its findings are the product of the enormously ambitious Minnesota Study of Twins Reared Apart, a venture run by Prof. Thomas Bouchard and several of his colleagues in the University of Minnesota's Department of Psychology. In just about all major respects, the study is qualitatively superior to its predecessors. For example, the average age of its MZAs at separation is only five months.[33]

The Minnesota twin studies are endlessly fascinating, and I have dealt with them at greater length in chapter 8. Here it needs to be said that the IQ data reported by Bouchard and his colleagues are generally in line with those of the earlier twin studies. When the data reflected scores on the WAIS, the Bouchard MZAs generated a coefficient of .69. When the data reflected combined scores on the Raven Progressive Matrices and the Mill Hill Test—which together measure verbal and reasoning skills—the coefficients rose to .78. A third measure also yielded .78. Bouchard thinks it is reasonable to average the three data sets, giving you a bottom line of .75.[34]

Unlike the earlier MZA studies, those at the University of Minnesota have been designed to explicitly account for two possible sources of bias. One is the possibility that the separated twins grew up in rather similar circumstances and that this similarity, rather than shared genes, is what mainly accounts for the high IQ correlations. In addressing this possibility, Bouchard and his colleagues performed exhaustive interviews to ascertain each adoptive household's physical facilities and intellectual resources (e.g., books). In addition, each twin was tested on the Moos Family Environment Scale, a test that measures the individual's retrospective impressions of his treatment during childhood and adolescence. Bottom line: Similarities in the adoptive environments contributed only about .03 to MZA correlations.[35]

A second possibility of bias was that the twins' similarities reflected the time they spent together either before separation or after being reunited. Here the Minnesota researchers concluded that similarities between the twins was more likely to be a reason for contacts between them than a result of the contacts, and the extent of that contact had just about no effect on the degree of similarity in test scores. ("Degree of social contact between two members of a reared-apart twin pair accounts for virtually none of their similarity.")[36]

Which means the heritability estimates above are hard to challenge. The most exhaustive recent twin studies of predominantly American and British subjects are telling us that genes appear to account for about 75 percent of the variability in IQ.

That Bouchard's data are recent is significant. An idea that surfaced early in the eighties, and still has a fair number of adherents, is that heritabilities may be in a process of secular decline—that even if Jensen was correct in estimating correlations of around .80 in his *Harvard Educational Review* article, they have been falling since then. Robert Plomin, a respected behavioral geneticist, did a major search of the literature in 1980 and concluded that the later studies showed lower heritabilities. "The older data are compatible with a heritability of .70 or higher," Plomin wrote, "whereas the newer data suggest a heritability closer to .50."[37]

Why might heritability change over time? In principle, it could do so because of environmental changes. Heritability, remember, is defined as the portion of variability in intelligence that can be attributed to genetic factors. If the environmental factors somehow became more important, the heritable portion would perforce decline. But for environmental variance to rise, you would need an increase in environmental inequality—in other words, a more heterogeneous, less egalitarian society. It is hard to think of any major currents in American life that might be described in these terms. By most of the obvious measures, the kids being tested since the sixties were living in a much *more* egalitarian world than those from earlier decades.

So the Plomin data look to be something of a puzzle, and efforts to explain them are very much on the agenda of participants in the IQ debates. The arguments about these numbers will possibly never end, and since the numbers might indeed change over time, they probably never should.

I close this chapter on a more practical note. An old friend of mine, a chap very much interested in IQ, recently fathered a baby boy. Reflecting his long-standing interest in the heritability of IQ, no doubt reinforced by the fact that he was now personally transmitting genes to a son, he asked how you go about calculating the probability of a child's ending up with IQs at various levels. Given the known IQs of the parents, in other words, how do you go about creating a "probability distribution"—a chart or table that shows the range of possible IQs and the probability assigned to each?

The first datum we require in creating any such chart is, of course, the parent's own IQ—or, better yet, the scores of both parents. The correlation between one parent's IQ and the teenage IQ of a child who has grown up with both parents is generally put at around .4. But if you start out knowing the IQs of both those parents, the correlation rises a bit higher, perhaps to .5 (i.e., using the midpoint of the parents' scores).[38] For purposes of this explanation, let us hypothesize a bright couple whose midpoint IQ is 120. What sort of possibilities are they looking at for their child?

The calculation of these possibilities begins with a statistical phenomenon hitherto unmentioned in these pages: the so-called regression to the mean. This phenomenon tells us that the single most likely IQ for the child of above-average parents is a figure somewhat below theirs but still above the population mean of 100. In other words, the child's IQ will have "regressed" some distance toward the mean. If we were writing about below-average parents, we would similarly look for the child's IQ to be *above* theirs, but still below 100. In either case, you would be telling yourself that the single best bet for the child's IQ is a figure between his parents' average and the population average of 100.

Regression toward the mean is a subject that often comes up in discussions of parent-child IQ differences and seldom arises in other contexts. Over the years, it seems safe to say, many readers have come away with a mistaken impression about what is involved in the phenomenon: They believe there is some biological or psychological imperative requiring that smart parents have somewhat less smart children (with the same rules operating in reverse in below-average families). So they are stunned to discover that regression toward the mean also works from child to parents: If you start out knowing that a child is well above (or below) average, your best bet for his parents is that they, too, will be above (or below) average, but less so.

Regression toward the mean is not a biological imperative. It is merely reflecting the fact that the correlations we are working with here are less than perfect. If they were perfect—if the correlation between parents' and children's IQs were 1.0—then there would be no regression, and the child would always be expected to have the same IQ as his parents. At the other extreme, if there were no association at all between the IQs of parents and children—if the coefficient were 0—then the single best bet for the child would be an IQ of 100, that is, the population average.

With a coefficient of .5, the single most likely result for a couple whose IQ midpoint was 20 points above average would be a child 10 points about average, that is, with an IQ of 110. The figure is derived by going to the mean of 100, then adding back the parents' 20 points multiplied by the .5 coefficient. If we started out knowing that one parent's IQ was 120 but the other parent's IQ was unknown, our best bet would be a child's IQ of 108 (because in this case we would be multiplying the 20 points by a correlation coefficient of .4).

All these calculations assume that the mean toward which we are regressing is the population mean—an IQ of 100. Sometimes, however, it seems appropriate to pick another mean. It would be reasonable to use the broad population average when you are focusing on individuals whose ancestors can be thought of as coming out of the population as a whole. But if you are wondering about families clearly tied to particular gene pools—Koreans, blacks, Sephardic Jews, members of the British aristocracy—it would make sense to use means for the relevant group (assuming you could get the data). If the group's mean was over 100, for example, the estimate for the child would be raised accordingly.

Thus far we have been talking only about the single best estimate of the child's IQ. But, of course, very few children hit this bull's-eye. Most will have test scores scattered around it, so the more important question addresses the *range of possibilities* for the child. How much dispersion would there be around this mean?

The usual measure of variability in such calculations is the standard deviation (SD). In the population as a whole, the mean IQ is 100 and the SD, as measured on the Wechsler test, is 15 points. As elaborated in our prefatory note on statistics, this means that 68 percent of the population is within 15 points of the mean and 95 percent of the population is within 30 points—that is, between 70 and 130.

Because parent-child IQ correlations are positive, we would expect less dispersion around the children's mean scores. It turns out, however, that there is still plenty of dispersion. The SD for the child's possible scores is reduced only from 15 points to 13.[39] Which means that there is a 68 percent chance of the child's being within 13 points of 110 and a 95 percent chance of his being within 26 points—that is, between 84 and 136.

It seems pertinent, in eyeballing these figures, to invoke the famous "law of large numbers." This principle, central to the insurance business, tells us that when probabilistic events are repeated endlessly, we can make extremely accurate predictions about average outcomes, even if we are hopelessly uncertain about the outcome of a single event. We can state with a high degree of confidence that couples with an IQ midpoint of 120 will on average have children with IQs of 110. But we cannot be terribly confident about the score of any particular child.

Will he score higher than his parents? There is a 22 percent chance of his doing so. But there is also a 22 percent chance of his scoring below the population average of 100. Anything—well, almost anything—is possible in a particular family. Siblings raised in the same household differ from one another, on average, by about 12 IQ points. That is less, to be sure, than differences in the population as a whole. (Average difference among two individuals selected at random from the population: about 18 points.) Still, the fact of a highly heritable IQ does not guarantee high IQs to all the progeny of high-IQ families.

8

The View From Twin City

Twins are endlessly fascinating, and they offer a unique opportunity to study human nature. This is especially true of monozygotic (i.e., identical) twins, the so-called MZs. No one has pursued and studied MZs more relentlessly than a team of scholars based at the University of Minnesota. Since the late seventies, they have tested more than 100 sets of twins raised apart, and more than fifty of them were identical twins (MZAs). Most of the twins have come from the United States and Great Britain, but a few of those tested came from as far off as China and Australia.[1]

Studies of twins have rather consistently shown that, on average, they have lower IQs than singletons—typically lower by around 5 points. Several reasons for the twin-singleton gap have been adduced. One is that twins are more likely to suffer from intrauterine overcrowding, with the result that one or both will receive insufficient nutrients in the prenatal environment. It is well established that when twins differ markedly in birth weight, the one with the lower weight—the presumably less well nourished one—will have a lower IQ in later life. Since twins in general weigh less than singletons at birth, it seems reasonable to infer that some part of that 5-point gap, or maybe all of it, reflects these prenatal hazards.[2]

Another hypothesis relates the lower IQs of twins at least in part to twin psychology. This proposition, which refers mainly to the MZs, is that twins are less driven to excel than are singletons. They are thought to lack a certain amount of ego: Seeing themselves not exactly as individuals but as members of a "team," they are less inclined to seek to stand out in different spheres, including the sphere of mental ability. This hypothesis is somewhat conjectural; however, it is difficult to think of identical twins down through history who have attained any fame for intellectual distinction. A volume called *Three Hundred Eminent Personalities,* published in 1978, notes that "twins ...clearly...are underrepresented among the eminent."[3] In the modern world, the closest I can get to an example is the Medvedev brothers. Roy Medvedev is a Russian political scientist who was a prominent member of the Congress of People's Deputies when that institution was onstage in the final months of the Soviet Union. His MZ twin is Zhores Medvedev, a distinguished biologist who was driven into exile in the Brezhnev years and established a new life in London.

The Minnesota studies show that MZAs are far more similar than anyone had anticipated, and the similarities concern a lot more than IQ. The similarities range over an enormous number of traits and repeatedly deliver the same message: Individuals who are genetically identical respond to their genes far more than to their social and economic environments. The twins turn out to be alike in ways that were unanticipated by even the most committed hereditarians and that are still far from being understood.[4]

Viewing the incredible "coincidences" in the lives of

separated identical twins, some scholars have tried to make a case that their adoptive circumstances must have been similar. The case has not been made successfully, however. To the extent that the adoptive environments can be captured by standard social-science data—for example, data on the education and socioeconomic status of the adoptive parents—the data suggest only very weak environmental effects on the MZA similarities.[5]

To be sure, some critics of the studies have suggested that the twins' adoptive environments may have been similar in subtle ways not captured in the data. In effect, the critics are positing an "X Factor," somewhat like the one often invoked by scholars arguing that all black-white IQ differences must be environmental in origin (see chapter 12). Prof. Thomas Bouchard, prime mover behind the Minnesota studies, says he has been hearing for many years about this mysterious environmental factor, said to make identical twins more alike. The factor remains unidentified, even though it would presumably have been visible to the social workers and other adoption officials who are said to have arranged for the similar environments.

In fact, Bouchard has argued, "many of the MZA pairs were...reared under what appeared to us to be significantly different circumstances." He mentions the case of a pair of British women seemingly out of *Pygmalion*: "One twin had a distinct Cockney accent while the other spoke like the Queen." The former had been brought up by working-class parents and dropped out of school at sixteen; her sister was educated in a posh private school. Yet their IQs differed by only one point.[6]

The IQ similarities of the MZAs is the feature that has attracted the most attention. As we have seen (in chapter 7), the MZAs correlate about .75 in IQ. But in many respects, the most startling findings of the Minnesota studies concerned their similarities on other traits. "On multiple measures of personality and temperament, occupational and leisure-time interests, and social attitudes, monozy-gotic twins reared apart are about as similar as are monozy-gotic twins reared together," said Bouchard, reporting on his studies in *Science*.[7] In other words, the personalities and attitudes of identical twins are essentially unaffected by whether or not they grew up with their natural parents. Those who were raised apart and presumed by themselves (in most cases) to be singletons nevertheless turned out, repeatedly, to be leading lives eerily like those of their twins. "During their lives as supposed singletons," Bouchard has written, "they had worked at similar jobs, had similar hobbies, given their pets and children similar names, developed similar fears, likes, and dislikes, similar habits..."[8]

The Minnesota Study of Twins Reared Apart goes back to 1979, when Bouchard read an Associated Press story about a pair of identical twins, separated in the first few weeks of life, who had recently discovered each other. The "Jim twins"—Jim Springer and Jim Lewis—established early on a pattern of spooky coincidences that seem to mark the lives of separated MZs.

I will confess that when I first started reading about these coincidences, I was suspicious that they represented what students of statistics have sometimes called "data mining." The thought behind that phrase is that you can always find a certain number of arresting or oddball patterns if only you have enough data to dig through. Stock-market analysts, for example, are notorious data miners. They are forever coming up with such insights as the fact that for seventeen years in a row the market has risen on balance in the three trading days preceding Labor Day (to cite a finding solemnly reported by a Dean Witter analyst some years back).[9] With 365 days in the year and thousands of possible intervals to look at in the period before each of those days, it is hardly surprising that an enterprising data miner managed to fasten on one interval in which prices always seemed to rise.

Might the coincidences in the lives of separated identical twins be another example of data mining? Given the enormous number of human traits and preferences one can examine—I told myself—it would hardly seem surprising that somebody who set out looking for similarities between two humans could find a fair number of them: similarities in their preferences for brands of toothpaste, in their choice of hobbies, and everything in between. I must say, however, that my concerns about data mining broke down fairly fast when I started hovering over some of the stories about twin coincidences. The stories simply overwhelm you.

Take the Jim twins. They were thirty-nine when reunited. Both had earlier married women named Linda, then got divorced, then married women named Betty. Both had served as sheriff's deputies in their respective Ohio towns. Without ever meeting each other, both had vacationed at the same beach resort on the Gulf Coast of Florida. Both liked working with wood and had similar basement workshops. One had a son named James Alan, the other a son named James Allan. The detail I found most stunning of all: Each had built a circumarboreal bench around a tree in his yard (i.e., the benches were built so as to wrap around the tree trunks). In each case, the bench was painted white. Both Jims drank Miller Lite, chain-smoked Salems, liked stock-car racing, and did not like baseball. Both were delighted to be invited to the University of Minnesota (with their wives) for a week of testing. On many different measures, Bouchard later reported, their test scores were about as close as those you would expect from the same individual taking a test twice.[10]

The testing procedure that has evolved at Minnesota is dauntingly detailed. Typically, the twins arrive in Minneapolis on a Saturday. On Sunday they get a briefing on the schedule they will follow in the ensuing week and begin completing questionnaires. During the week ending the following Saturday—when they would typically leave—

they get tested from 8:00 A.M. to 5:30 P.M.

The testing begins with an exhaustive medical exam, courtesy of the University of Minnesota School of Medicine, that would cost many thousands of dollars if one tried to replicate it in the private sector. Testees also get a detailed "psychophysiological assessment," involving measurements of brain waves, heart patterns, galvanic skin responses, and reaction time (RT). Their "psychomotor" skills, such as eye-hand coordination, are measured. They fill out a detailed questionnaire, and undergo an interview, about their sexual preferences and practices. They get several different intelligence tests, including the WAIS. To avoid any possibility of "examiner bias"—the bias that the tester might show if he started out expecting the second twin to score about the same as the first—the twins are tested simultaneously by different examiners in different rooms. In addition to the WAIS, the twins take the Raven Progressive Matrices and the Mill-Hill Test (a multiple-choice test of word knowledge), both of which are administered and scored by computer.

The twins, and to some extent their spouses, also submit to extensive interviews about their lives. One interview is designed to capture the amount of stress they have undergone over the years. A videotaped interview about "social life history" is intended to capture something of each individual's personal style. The twins also undergo a battery of tests designed to measure their interests and values.[11]

It is the interests and values that generate the eeriest of the coincidences:

• Mark Newman and Jerry Levey were MZs separated five days after birth and reunited at age thirty-one. Until the reunion, neither knew he had a twin brother. Both turned out to be volunteer firemen. Levey went to college and came out with a degree in forestry. Newman planned to go to college and study forestry but in the end took a job trimming trees in his hometown. When they were reunited, Levey had a job installing fire alarms. Newman had a job installing sprinkler systems. Both are bachelors. Both do a lot of hunting and fishing. Both like old John Wayne movies and Chinese food.[12]

• Among the MZ twins understandably receiving special attention were "the Nazi and the Jew," as a number of journalists have labeled them. The two were separated when their parents divorced soon after their birth in 1932. Their father was Jewish, but one of the twins, Oscar Stohr, ended up living with his maternal grandmother in the Sudetenland—the German-speaking area of Czechoslovakia—and as a child was taught to be a good Nazi. His brother, Jack Yufe, lived with the father, a merchant who ended up in Port-au-Prince in Trinidad, where Jack attended a synagogue. The twins had a brief, tense encounter in their early twenties, then were reunited a quarter century later in a meeting at the Minneapolis airport, en route to Bouchard's laboratories. At the meeting, both men were wearing rectangular wire-rimmed glasses. Both wore blue shirts. Both shirts had epaulets and two breast pockets. Both men had short, clipped mustaches. It later turned out that they were similar in more bizarre ways. Both always flushed urinals and toilets before using them. Both thought it was funny to sneeze loudly in situations calling for quiet—in elevators, for example. Both had a habit of stretching rubber bands around their wrists. Both dipped buttered toast into their coffee.[13]

• A fair number of the twins turning up in Minneapolis are British women—typically women who were initially separated, and sent to remote areas of the British Isles, during the Luftwaffe's blitz over London and other large cities early in World War II. One pair who were reunited at the University of Minnesota are Bridget Harrison and Dorothy Lowe (their married names). Both proved to be housewives, with finely manicured hands. Each wore four rings on one hand, three on the other. Bridget has a son named

Richard Andrew and Dorothy has a son named Andrew Richard. Bridget has a daughter named Catherine Louise and Dorothy has a daughter named Karen Louise. Bouchard says he finds this coinidence especially mind-bending in that the naming of children is always presumably a joint decision of the two parents.[14]

• Another pair of once-separated British women who made it to Minneapolis are Barbara Herbert and Daphne Goodship (their married names), widely identified in news stories as "the giggle sisters." It seems that they giggle a lot, endlessly setting one another off whenever they get together. Critical detail: The families that raised them as girls did not include any gigglers. Another arresting detail: At age fifteen, both had accidents in which they fell down a flight of stairs, and ever since then both clutch banisters whenever moving on stairs. Each one had a miscarriage, then each had two boys and a girl—in that order. Despite the women having been brought up separately, their handwriting looks almost identical.[15]

What is one to make of these wild coincidences? Perhaps the main and most obvious point to emerge from them is that your genetic constitution powerfully predisposes you to cetain kinds of behavior that will inevitably help to shape your larger environment.

The mechanism by which genes would have produced some of the coincidences remains mysterious. But then, we are still a long way from having identified the genes involved in behavioral traits, much less the manner in which they might interact. David Lykken, who is another principal in the Minnesota twin studies and who has served as president of the Society for Psychophysiological Research (SPR), has expressed some preliminary thoughts about what may be happening. Take, for example, that astounding detail about the separated twin sisters, each of whom wore seven rings on her fingers. Lykken ruminated about them as follows in his 1981 presidential address to the SPR:

> I am inclined to think that [such] coincidences could be understood in terms of the interaction or confluence of independent traits, each...under genetic control. Having long-fingered, good-looking hands, a somewhat extroverted personality, an attraction to glitter and a taste for adornment, the ability to achieve enough material success to allow the purchase of jewelry—all these are presumably independent traits, each possibly subject to genetic influence, which might interact so as to incline the woman who possessess all of them to wear mulitiple rings.[16]

It is doubtless not surprising that the anecdotal reports on eerie coincidences have attracted more attention from the media than have the University of Minnesota's aggregated data on personal traits. But many of these data are ultimately more fascinating than the anecdotes.

Take, for example, the data relating genes and political beliefs. I confess to being among the many kibitzers of American politics who have long wondered about a possible link between political views and psychological propensities. The rhetoric of American politics, which features "bleeding heart liberals" and "flinty conservatives," often seems to assume that there is some such link.

Furthermore, there seems to be in American politics a rather durable "gender gap" that leaves women looking somewhat more liberal than men. Could it be because (as Carol Gilligan and other psychologists have argued) women are genuinely more caring and empathetic than men?[17] I had always assumed it might well be so; also, that within the two sexes personality to some extent predicted political belief.

But until I caught up with the research by Bouchard and his colleagues, it had never occurred to me that the connections might be via genes. In the SPR address,

Lykken takes note of the surface implausibility of this proposition, then hammers home what he views as the stunning reality:

> One might be inclined to doubt that conservatism—the tendency to endorse traditional values—has any genetic basis at all.... Our sample of MZA twins, however, suggests that the genetic influence actually is considerable; perhaps William Buckley Jr. and I. F. Stone Jr. owe their positions on the political spectrum as much to their genomes as to the example set by their parents. If someone has a high (or low) score on conservatism, we can predict not only his political views but also his attitude toward established religion, toward racial differences, capital punishment, abortion...; we can predict his views on gun control, welfare, the MX missile, and so on and on.... These correlated attitudes [are] all influenced perhaps by some genetic inclination to march to the music of the same big drum.... [18]

The "score on conservatism" mentioned by Lykken was based on responses to a Multidimensional Personality Questionnaire, one of whose scales measures conservative attitudes, defined, in Lykken's summary, as "an affinity for traditional values, including strong allegiance to established authority." Evidence for the strong heritability of such attitudes lies in the fact that conservatism scores of identical twins correlate far more strongly than do those of fraternal twins. Among twins raised apart, the correlation is .54 for identical twins, .39 for fraternal twins. Among those raised together, the correlation is .58 for identical twins, .35 for fraternal twins. Just as they were on measures of intelligence, the identical twins raised apart proved more similar on these measures of conservatism than did fraternal twins raised together. [19]

It is important to focus on just what is, and isn't, being predicted here by genetic similarities. What *isn't* being predicted is political views unrelated to notions about tradition and authority. In other words, there is no reason to believe that MZs would correlate strongly on their beliefs about supply-side economics, which in the context of the early eighties was plainly being counted as conservative doctrine—but which was quite untraditional, if not revolutionary. The same might be said about views on the minimum wage or the capital-gains tax. It is only on the "gut issues," where traditional ideas and/or established authority are being challenged, that you would expect strong correlations between the MZ pairs. To be sure, a lot of the liberal-conservative splits do seem to involve gut issues.

These genetic predispositions to certain political attitudes are apparently reinforced by "assortative mating"—the tendency of people to marry others with traits like their own. This tendency works to increase the range of differences in these traits. If, for example, there were no assortative mating for IQ—if people getting married were oblivious to the mental abilities of their spouses—then the distribution of IQs would keep getting pulled toward the center. In fact, assortative mating for IQ is extremely strong. As observed in our introductory note on statistics, the correlation between husbands' and wives' IQs is even stronger (.45) than is the correlation for their heights (.30), and this works to increase the number of very high and very low IQs.

Bouchard reports that the correlation for political attitudes of spouses is even higher than that for IQ of spouses; on some estimates, the coefficient for political attitudes is around .60. "At equilibrium," Bouchard has observed, "assortative mating as high as .60 for conservatism will have more than doubled the population variance in this basic dimension of political attitude, abundantly renewing in each generation the polar extremes of the political Left and Right." He added, ironically, that it was somewhat unclear what evolutionary purpose was served by promoting diversity in political attitudes.[20]

It is understating matters to state that these astonishing data—on politics, circumarboreal benches, and everything in between—leave a lot of questions to be answered. The twin studies make it plain that genes influence behavior in ways not previously imagined, even by committed hereditarians. The effort to identify the genes involved and to explain how their influence is brought to bear looks to be one of the more fascinating scientific explorations of the decades ahead.

9

The Mystery of Cyril Burt

The saga of Cyril Burt is instructive on several levels. For openers, it sends a powerful message about the extent to which the IQ debate is poisonously politicized. In particular, it points up the fury engendered by an idea with which Burt was long identified: that differences in intelligence are mostly genetic in origin.

The Burt story also tells us much about the near-decisive role of the media in deciding who are the good guys, and who are the villains, when IQ is the subject. Burt has been cast as a major-league scoundrel since the late seventies, and in the early nineties, he was still getting regularly pummeled in the press—a peculiar fate indeed for a man lionized while he was still alive.

Sir Cyril Burt, a titan of IQ studies, died in 1971 at the age of eighty-eight. A man of awesome intelligence, vast erudition, and boundless energy, he had thoroughly dominated Britain's psychology establishment for half a century. His influence was worldwide: His disciples and fervent admirers were running academic psychology departments and research projects all over the Western world.[1] Just before his death, the American Psychological Association gave him the prestigious Edward Lee Thorndike Award (never before given to a foreigner).[2] In a posthumous collection of essays published in his honor, he was called "dean of the world's psychologists."[3]

Against that background, it does seem remarkable that after his death, scholars around the world were arguing about whether Burt was a charlatan who had faked his data.

The story of his fraud, or alleged fraud, has taken a number of serpentine turns. When Burt died in 1971, he had many enemies in the world of British psychology, but his scholarly stature was unquestioned. When the charges of fraud surfaced in 1976, they were at first dismissed or explained away by many members of the psychological establishment. By 1979, however, belief in his guilt was nearly unanimous. Even those who had admired him during his life, and continued to support his basic views about a heritable IQ, were now unhappily concluding that he was obviously guilty as charged—that the "research" underpinning his ideas was in large measure made up.

What came next seemed even more astonishing. Two British scholars, working independently and without knowledge of each other, went back and reexamined the evidence on which the fraud charges rested. By the late eighties, both had produced books arguing persuasively that the case against him had been inspired by the vindictiveness of political leftists determined to discredit his hereditarian ideas. Neither book decisively proved him innocent of fraud, but both left you thinking—well, they left me thinking—that the case against him was far from proven.

A final, incredible detail: Both of the books supporting Burt were ignored by the mainstream media. The books were reviewed respectfully in several scientific jour-nals, including *Nature, Science,* and *Behavior Genetics;* but nei-ther book had its existence acknowledged by the *New York Times,* the *Washington Post,* the major newsmagazines, or any of the other publications that routinely take on the task of helping Americans make up their minds about major matters.

It is true, of course, that many books go unreviewed, including some that seem quite meritorious. But it does appear odd that the media, which had repeatedly run news stories and articles about the significance of Burt's fraud, never got around to mentioning the substantial new evi-dence suggesting that there had never been one.

The performance of the *New York Times* was typical. In the period when Burt's guilt was widely assumed, the *Times* had run seven or eight articles about the meaning of the case. The moral usually drawn in the articles was that he-reditarian ideas could now be viewed as false; sometimes the articles' authors went on to reflect on the damage done by those ideas in the past. Fred Hechinger, long the educa-tion editor of the *Times,* wrote in 1979 that the exposure of Burt's fabrications "gives new validity to warnings against the use of sociological and psychological data to make pol-icy decisions about what can or should be done with or for groups of people."[4] You might view Hechinger's point as ultimately absurd—are educators supposed to ignore the data when they make policy decisions?—but you would be entitled to wonder how, having published such arguments, the paper could ignore the emerging possibility that there had never been a fabrication.

Burt's influence had indeed been enormous. His pro-digious data collection—especially the data on identical twins reared apart—and powerfully marshaled arguments had contributed significantly to the case for a heritable in-telligence. He had also been among the first to demon-strate significant class differences in average IQ. He supported a two-track system in the schools, with IQ tests used to identify those who would and would not benefit from a broad academic education; at the same time, he had worked hard to ensure that the tests would be used to identify lower-class students deserving scholarships. In time, his ideas became policy. When he was knighted in 1946, the Labour party's minister of education, Ellen Wilkinson, quite appropriately wrote to him: "So much of the work in which you have been a pioneer is now playing an increasingly important part in education."[5]

Whether Burt was a fraud or not, he was incontestably a genius. Although he never had any special training in mathematics, he made major contributions to factor analysis.[6] At University College in London, his base of operations for most of his professional career, he was legendary as a lecturer. Here, from the biography of Burt by L. S. Hearnshaw, is a student's recollection of him from the thirties:

> Burt was the best of the forty or fifty lecturers I heard at various times during my five years at London University.... He spoke with great fluency, never hesitating for words and never using unusual or technical language unless it was impossible to convey the meaning accurately [without it]. His lectures appeared to be spontaneous ... he referred to notes only to produce references or cite data.... He drew upon an immensely wide background of knowledge, but he carried his learning lightly.... After hearing Burt once, I never missed one of his lectures avoidably.[7]

A quarter century later, in 1957, Arthur Jensen (then a young graduate student) also heard Burt deliver a lecture and came away bearing the same impression of effortless brilliance. The brilliance did not desert Burt even in his last years. By this time, Jensen knew him fairly well. In his 1972 obituary, he offers this portrait of the man in old age: "One would be rather hard put to characterize Sir Cyril,

even in his late eighties, as 'mild' or as a 'grand old man.'
Nor would he have liked such an image. He had a keenly
critical disposition and was quick to point out one's intellectual lapses and to relentlessly pursue an argument.
Those who disagreed with him were not let off easily."[8] Jensen liked and admired Burt, but he admits to being put off
by the man's enormous vanity.

Public attacks on Burt's integrity began with an article
about him that appeared in London's *Sunday Times* on October 24, 1976. The article had this portentous lead: "The
most sensational charge of scientific fraud this century is
being leveled against the late Sir Cyril Burt. Leading scientists are convinced that Burt published false data and invented crucial facts to support his controversial theory that
intelligence is largely inherited."

The article was written by Oliver Gillie, a journalist
specializing in medical and scientific reporting. Gillie obviously disagreed with Burt and was outraged by the idea of a
heritable intelligence, so it was not hard to cast him
as a prejudiced observer. On the other hand, his article appeared to have some highly damaging information.

For one thing, there was the matter of the missing
women. In the fifties and sixties, Burt's published papers
had repeatedly listed as coauthors a Miss Margaret Howard
and a Miss Jane Conway. In addition, Gillie noted that Burt
had arranged for publication of some of his writings under
the name of Miss Conway alone. The two women were
identified as having done much of the spadework—such as
tracking down separated twins and administering IQ
tests—that buttressed his research efforts.

And now, incredibly, Gillie was claiming that the
women did not exist. He had worked hard to track them
down, at one point advertising in the "personal" columns
of the *Times*,[9] and basically got nowhere. No trace of them
could be found, he said.

Nor was that all. Gillie had also enlisted the support of

Dr. Anne M. Clarke and Prof. A. D. B. Clarke, two psychologists (married to each other) based at the University of Hull. The Clarkes, both of whom were former students of Burt's, had long been suspicious of his data. Without charging fraud, they had earlier published commentaries on Burt's calculations that talked of "surprisingly high intercorrelations" and "suspiciously perfect" results.[10]

The charge of suspiciously perfect results was made not only by the Clarkes, and it seemed especially damaging. The charge referred to the fact that over the years Burt kept publishing data in which the IQs of identical twins reared apart (the MZAs) were invariably correlated at .77. The figure itself was not particularly surprising; indeed, it was in line with many other estimates. What was hard to explain was the consistency of Burt's results. You would expect that adding new sets of twins to his data base would result in repeated minor changes in the correlation coefficient. The figure is, after all, an estimate, reflecting some average degree of similarity in the twins being studied. The degree would be expected to vary somewhat from one set of twins to another. And so the fact that the estimate never changed fortified the idea that Burt's data were being faked.

Still, the evidence in 1976 was not by itself enough to overturn Burt's lifework and daunting reputation. Far more damaging was L. S. Hearnshaw's 1979 biography, *Cyril Burt, Psychologist*. It was written by a scholar of unimpeachable credentials—Hearnshaw was emeritus professor of psychology at the University of Liverpool. His severe judgment of Burt seemed to end the argument, for several reasons.

For one thing, he had earlier been an admirer of Burt's; in fact, he had been selected to deliver the eulogy at Burt's funeral in 1971.[11] "Furthermore, Hearnshaw had unparalleled access to the documents. Impressed by his devotion to her brother, Burt's sister asked Hearnshaw to undertake a biography of Sir Cyril. When he agreed, she turned over all of Burt's papers to him.[12] Or at least all those still in existence: A substantial number were lost in the wartime blitz.[13] And, in an utterly bizarre episode (to which we shall return below), many of Burt's other records were destroyed by his housekeeper a few days after his death.

Hearnshaw's judgment was taken seriously for another reason. Among the documents he received from Burt's sister was a long-running diary, said to be filled with all sorts of minutiae. For example, it would mention when Burt got a haircut or had tea in the garden. Yet there was nothing in the diary about the research on twins that was presumably at the center of his intellectual life. Which gave further support to the critics, now in full cry, insisting that the twin data had been made up.

Hearnshaw was already deep into his research on Burt when the *Sunday Times* article appeared. Obviously jolted by the attacks on his subject, he switched gears quite rapidly, and on many of the points at issue, he crossed over to the enemy camp.

He concluded that Burt must indeed have falsified data in several areas, beginning with those contentious twin data. In 1966, Burt had written an article in the *British Journal of Psychology* showing sizable increases in the numbers of identical twins he had studied since 1955. Hearnshaw concluded that there had been no post-1955 studies and wrote, evidently with great sadness:

> On this issue the evidence from the diaries is decisive. ... We can be sure that Burt himself did not collect any data on twins, or any other topic, during those years and that he was never visited either by Miss Howard, or Miss Conway, or any other assistant actively working for him.... We are forced ... to the conclusion that the accounts given in Burt's published papers were false, and that a measure of deception was certainly involved.[14]

In trying to explicate the meaning of the whole affair, Hearnshaw zeroed in on several questions. Among them: Why did Burt do it? When did he start doing it? How does the evidence of his fraud affect our beliefs about heritability and the other issues on which he weighed in so heavily?

Hearnshaw offers an essentially psychiatric explanation of the frauds. Specifically, Burt's frauds reflected a "progressive personality breakdown...suffered as a result of various setbacks...."[15] The setbacks had come thick and fast as he grew older. They included the loss of much of his research during air raids in 1941, the breakup of his marriage, his forced retirement from the university, his loss of control over a journal of psychological statistics that he had founded and edited for many years; finally, many of the government programs he had promoted (including two-track education) were being reversed in the sixties. His diaries were said to convey his anguish over these and other defeats. Having closely studied the periods in which Burt was allegedly cooking the data and having also looked to see what else was going on in the man's life in those periods, Hearnshaw speculated that his subject suffered a mild form of paranoia that surfaced in times of trouble.[16]

As to when Burt first "went wrong," Hearnshaw says his best guess is that it happened in the last quarter century of his life. He added: "If Burt had died at the age of sixty ...his reputation would have been unblemished, and...he would have been regarded, and rightly regarded, as an honorable pioneer in British psychology....The tragedy was his subsequent collapse."[17]

As the formulation above suggests, Hearnshaw thought much of Burt's earlier work might still be valuable. He also argued, persuasively, that the deceptions and falsifications in Burt's later work had not ultimately changed the views of scholars. Addressing a special meeting of the British Psychological Society (BPS) in 1980—the meeting was called to consider the impact of the Burt affair—

Hearnshaw put it this way: "Science is a continuing, self-correcting exercise, and Burt's delinquencies could never have deflected the course of truth more than momentarily."[18]

In any case, Burt's data on twins were scarcely the only prop under the heritability estimates psychometricians had been using. By the time Burt died, you could point to three other major studies of identical twins reared apart (see chapter 7). One, based on data for American twins, had been published in 1937; another, a British study in which Burt played no part, was published in 1962; the third study, published in 1965, was done in Denmark. Taken as a group, they showed heritability estimates of over .70—that is, their message was that over 70 percent of the variability in IQ is attributable to genetic factors. So Burt's estimate of .77 was on the high side, but not by much.

The counterattack by Burt's defenders materialized quite suddenly, a decade after the Hearnshaw biography appeared. The defense came in two books: *The Burt Affair* (1989), by Robert B. Joynson, a lecturer in psychology at Nottingham University; and *Science, Ideology and the Media: The Cyril Burt Scandal* (1991), by Ronald Fletcher, emeritus professor of sociology at Britain's Reading University. I shall not attempt a full-blown recapitulation of their wide-ranging arguments, but this much needs to be said:

• Fletcher has effectively shot down the diaries as evidence of fraud; in fact, he leaves you thinking that "diaries" is hardly the word for these documents. For many dates, there was no entry at all, and when there was an entry, it was more often than not utterly trivial—a note about the weather, for example. In some periods, the so-called diaries seem to have served more as appointment schedulers than as an account of major events in Burt's life. Fletcher seems quite justified in taxing Hearnshaw for suggesting that the diaries afforded decisive clues to Burt's deepest concerns.[19]

• Both Joynson and Fletcher argue persuasively that the "invariate correlations" are far less sinister than originally suspected. You come away from their discussions not being entirely sure why the correlations remain unchanged. Possibly the repetition of the coefficient (.77) was a genuine coincidence. Possibly Burt had grown sloppy in his old age. (Some of the statistical errors he committed had the effect of undermining, not supporting, the hereditarian case he was making.)[20] Indeed, there is evidence that he was guilty of repeated copying errors in carrying over material from one journal article to another.

What seems impossible is that he was deliberately trying to bamboozle the readers of his articles—to build a case for high heritability on phony calculations. A scholar with his mathematical sophistication would surely have been sensitive to a thought drilled into every beginner in statistics classes: that "perfect data" are inherently suspicious. We all know that flipped coins will on average come up heads half the time, and it would be plausible to mention that one had observed exactly five heads in an experiment consisting of ten flips. But anyone who claimed to have obtained this exact result in a dozen successive experiments would arouse suspicion. (The odds against any such sequence are over 20 million to one.) If Burt had been interested in conning his readers, he would surely have altered the coefficients enough to make his data more plausible.[21]

• The missing women have been accounted for. It remains unclear how much work they did for Burt, and precisely when they did it, but their existence seems not to have been an invention. John Cohen, a former student of Burt's who later became a professor of psychology at the University of Manchester, came forward during the dispute with a rather detailed memory of Miss Howard, referring to "her roundish face, her pleasing smile, her brown eyes and bobbed auburn hair, her slightly tinted spectacles, and her competence in mathematics."[22] Cohen's memory referred back to the thirties. Other scholars also turned up with recollections of one or both of the women, and the records of the BPS show that a Miss M. A. Howard was listed as a member in 1924.[23] Of course, both women would have been quite elderly, or dead, by the time Gillie began trying to track them down in the seventies. In addition, Burt's housekeeper had a recollection of being told that one or both of the women had long since emigrated to Australia.[24]

Next question: If the women had worked for him in the prewar years, why was Burt still signing their names to material he created in the fifties and sixties? The answer seems to be that he was still working over much of the material collected before the war—material in which he had been assisted by Miss Howard, Miss Conway, and others. Much of this material had been scattered after the war broke out in 1939, and he had never properly analyzed it. Fletcher supplies the context for this reworking of old data:

> There is no doubt that Burt was *continually* working over, more and more meticulously, the large collection of test scores accumulated from his several early surveys. All who have testified to this collection of data have agreed about the enormous quantity of it, the jumbled way in which it was heaped together, and— particularly as a result of the wartime evacuation and the unknown degree of destruction of some of it in the bombing of University College—the questionable degree of its coverage.... The packing of boxes and sacks of documents ... for the evacuation was a great muddle, with no one quite knowing what was sent where.... Several sacks were taken to Aberystwyth [in Wales] and "thrown into a damp and dirty cellar there," where they remained until the return to London, when they were emptied out into a great pile on the floor of a room in Burt's flat. It was only gradually,

after his retirement, when he was able to work more thoroughly on his accumulated material...that Miss Archer [his housekeeper] began to sort through the papers as Burt required them....[25]

Fletcher adds that many of those close to Burt in his retirement knew very well that the twin data he was now publishing and analyzing were not new but had been collected years earlier. To be sure, he often presented this material in ways that encouraged other scholars to assume it *was* new.

Why would he do this? In a long essay-review in the *Public Interest* addressing the issues in the Joynson and Fletcher books, Arthur Jensen speculates that Burt's vanity may have been a factor. "My own hunch," Jensen wrote, "is that his personal vanity made him want to appear to be more actively engaged in ongoing research in his old age than he actually was, and so he obscured the 'when and the how' of his data collection, an implicit deception which later engendered doubts about the data's authenticity."[26]

Many of the issues swirling around Burt's postretirement articles might have been resolved but for a bizarre episode just after his death. A day or so after he died, his housekeeper was visited by Dr. Liam Hudson, professor of educational psychology at the University of Edinburgh. Hudson had never known Burt personally, so his reasons for making the call are unclear. In any case, the housekeeper, Miss Gretl Archer, was eager to clean out Burt's flat and dispose of his belongings, and she asked Hudson to take a look at the packing cases containing his years of research on twins. Hudson did so and advised Miss Archer to throw them out. She immediately did so, not realizing that Hudson was an implacable enemy of Burt and his views.[27]

So what does the whole Burt episode mean? The Joynson and Fletcher books effectively dispose of the notion that he was a fraud who had gone through life faking his data—or, for that matter, that he was deliberately faking it in his later years. The two books are entirely persuasive in arguing that Burt was a victim of character assassination and that his critics were mainly motivated by ideological passions.

But the two books do not entirely exonerate Burt, either. The articles Burt was writing in his retirement years cannot be defended on all fronts. A judgment about those articles has to be nuanced and selective. While Burt was almost certainly not fabricating data, he seems to have grown more careless in his handling of it. In addition, he was encouraging readers—perhaps deliberately—to think that he was contributing more to the debate on heritability than in fact he was.

So even if the charge of fraud is rejected, Burt was guilty of a kind of contributory negligence. He left himself open, never a good idea for a scholar holding unpopular views. In Arthur Jensen's apt summary of the story line: "A talented scientist who works largely alone makes a good many personal enemies. He is sometimes careless and eccentric in his presentation of his studies. He becomes a prominent public figure. Most important, he develops politically incorrect theories on socially sensitive topics. This combination of factors gives his opponents—aided by sympathetic journalists—ample ammunition to attack his reputation."[28]

Early in 1992, a number of scholars in Great Britian made an effort to get the BPS, which had formally condemned Burt in 1979, to reverse that judgment. They did not succeed. Acknowledging that the earlier verdict now seemed inappropriate, the BPS nevertheless declined to overturn it, apparently because of the political passions any such exercise would have generated within the organization. In a somewhat wobbly statement, the BPS said: "Twelve years ago, the Society assumed that Burt was guilty of fraud. We no longer hold that view. It is not that we have looked at the evidence and come to a different conclusion.

We have decided that we ought not to be taking a corporate position at all.... The allegations concerning Burt are a matter of historical debate. It is not the job of a learned body in a free society to adjudicate on such matters...."[29]

But, of course, the learned body had taken a "corporate position," judging Burt guilty, in 1979.

Cyril Burt's tragedy is that after a life of extraordinary attainment, he ended up contributing to the destruction of his own reputation. For many participants in the IQ debate, the most maddening aspect of the story resides elsewhere: in the fact that media rendering of the Burt affair misled millions of Americans, and Britons, into thinking that the totally supportable views espoused by Sir Cyril— and especially his belief in a highly heritable intelligence— were now somehow discredited.

10

Of Japanese and Jews

I have argued at several points in this book that individuals with above-average IQs tend to do well in life. Not always, but often enough to be noticeable, their high IQs lead to high-status jobs and high incomes. Chapter 11 will look more deeply into the connection between intelligence levels and economic performance. Here I propose to look at some absorbing IQ data pertaining to two groups widely identified as economic successes. The groups to be brought onstage in this context are, first, the Japanese and other East Asians, and second, the Jews.

Comparisons of the two groups are fascinating, on several counts. First, because in many respects they are so similar. Both East Asians and Jews test above average, and both have demonstrated spectacular ability at translating braininess into economic success. Both produce inordinate numbers of individuals who seem like "born businessmen." Both also place tremendous emphasis on the importance of education. Oddly enough, however, they have distinctly different IQ profiles. Both test high, but they excel at different kinds of mental tests. And both have weaknesses—though not the same ones. As a matter of fact, they think quite differently.

We begin with the East Asians and with a proposition that would have seemed quite outlandish not too many years ago but looks increasingly plausible today. Basic proposition: The extraordinary successes of the Pacific Rim economies—those of Japan, Taiwan, South Korea, Singapore, and Hong Kong—reflect the high level of mental ability among the populations involved. The hypothesis is that one major reason for their superior economic performance is that, in plain terms, they are smarter than Caucasians.

There should at least be no doubt about the economic show that has been put on in East Asia. All five of the Pacific Rim economies have had outsize growth rates for three decades now. None of them have had a severe recession in that period, and all can point to staggering increases in living standards. The standard measure of economic growth is increase in real (i.e., inflation-adjusted) gross national product (GNP). In the years between 1960 and 1990, real GNP grew at a shade over 3 percent in both the United States and West Germany. In Japan over those years, it grew at 6 percent. In Korea and Singapore, economic growth averaged around 8 percent in the same period.[1]

Most American commentary on the Pacific Rim economies has centered on their outsize contributions to U.S. trade deficits. In this context, American executives increasingly bemoan the apparent superiority of the Japanese and other East Asian labor forces; they have also taken to issuing calls for some kind of transformation that will upgrade the products of American schools. Blaming the schools is very much the fashion in business these days. Why do Japanese children notoriously outperform their American counterparts by many different measures? The standard explanation is the one advanced in *Winning the Brain Race*, by David T. Kearns (then chairman of Xerox, now deputy secretary of education) and Dennis P. Doyle (a scholar based at the Hudson Institute); the book was endorsed by Secretary of Education Lauro F. Cavazos. Its explanation goes this way: "Japanese students do so well on international comparisons because they go to school for a longer day than Americans and a longer year. . . . A majority of American youngsters attend school 180 days a year, while the Japanese goes for 240. The typical American student has an hour or less of homework; the Japanese student two-and-one-half hours or more."[2]

There is little doubt that the Japanese educational system is extraordinarily effective; it does seem to extract a high level of performance from the kids it educates. But it clearly does not explain most of the East-West performance gap. For one thing, other East Asian countries have school systems far less rigorous than the daunting Japanese model[3] (and the Hong Kong schools are still British-run). Yet the record all across the Pacific Rim is one of superior academic achievement. In the recently completed international assessment of mathematics and science, thirteen-year-olds from nine different populations were studied by the U.S.-based Educational Testing Service. In math, the Korean kids—the only East Asian group in the study—came in first and the American kids last.[4] In science, the Koreans came in second, a shade behind kids from British Columbia, and the Americans again were last.[5]

In any case, the superior talents of Japanese children cannot be entirely the product of Japanese schools, since some of the superiority is already observable in kindergarten. Support for this proposition is available in the February 1986 issue of *Science*, which carried a detailed report on a study led by Prof. Harold W. Stevenson of the University of Michigan. The article described the results of an ambitious comparison of Japanese, Taiwanese, and American children in kindergarten, first grade, and fifth grade. A basic finding: American kids in kindergarten are about equal to the Taiwanese kids in mathematical understanding, but both are far behind the Japanese. By the fifth grade, the Taiwanese are much closer to the Japanese, and the Americans trail far behind both.[6]

IQ comparisons between East Asians and other populations present one maddening difficulty: comparing verbal skills across cultures whose languages are so different. The researchers have handled this difficulty in a variety of ways. In some cases, their data are based on Chinese and Japanese versions of standard Western tests (usually the WAIS or WISC). Another solution has been to compare the two populations on tests like the Raven Progressive Matrices, a nonverbal IQ test that measures abstract reasoning ability.

The first reports of high East Asian IQs began appearing in the West in the late seventies. In most cases the author of the report turned out to be Richard Lynn, a British psychometrician based at the University of Ulster in Coleraine. Lynn, then forty-seven, says he happened to read in 1976 that versions of the WAIS and WISC tests were becoming available in Japan. He wrote off for the Japanese test manuals, had them translated into English, and then began collecting and analyzing test results; before long he had a unique network of Far Eastern psychologists reporting regularly to Coleraine. More recently, he has been getting some data from mainland China.

These Chinese data are quite astonishing. Based on examinations using the Raven Progressive Matrices, the data show mainland children with IQs averaging 101 on a scale where Americans are at 100.[7] A one-point group differential would not ordinarily be worth mentioning. But IQs are powerfully correlated with several different indicators of material well-being. Scholars generally believe that something like 20–50 percent of variability in IQ is attributable to environmental factors. And in this case, the one-point advantage is exhibited by a group living in abysmal poverty. (Mainland income levels run to perhaps 5 percent of those in the United States.) The plain implication of those Raven scores is that Chinese IQs are potentially a fair amount higher than those of Americans—also that a China liberated from communism has a dazzling economic future.

One of Lynn's earliest reports dealt with a 1977 study in Singapore comparing the IQs of thirteen-year-olds in the Chinese and Malay populations. The study, based on the Raven Progressive Matrices, showed the Chinese averaging 110, the Malays 96, on a scale where British children averaged 100.[8] Lynn has also written in some detail about two 1982 studies of Chinese children in Hong Kong. One, based on Cattell's Culture Fair Test (which also emphasizes reasoning ability), showed a representative group of Chinese nine-year-olds averaging 106.7 in relation to a norm of 100 for American children of the same age.[9] The other Hong Kong study looked at Chinese children of different ages and used the Raven plus a couple of other tests, including one vocabulary test. (A measure of verbal fluency and recall, it asked the kids to write down the names of as many animals as they could think of in two minutes.) Lynn found that these data gave him an average of 109.8 for the Chinese, with that figure normed against a mean of 100 for British children.[10]

His most recent studies, which are heavily centered on Japanese test data, put a somewhat different spin on the basic message. Lynn still says that these East Asian populations have higher overall IQs than Westerners. But he now insists on a technical adjustment of the data that results in a gap of only three or four points.[11] (The nature of this adjustment need not detain us here, but it is perhaps worth mentioning that many of Lynn's colleagues dispute the need for it.)[12] In any case, he argues that the more important message of the test data is about the *structure* of this

East Asian intelligence.[13] The model used by Lynn in writing about structure is a familiar one (see chapter 2) featuring a three-layered hierarchy of abilities.

1. Sitting atop the hierarchy is g, the general factor in intelligence. In large measure, g is synonymous with reasoning ability. It is responsible for the positive intercorrelations between the specific factors, all viewed as affected by reasoning, although not to the same degree.

2. In the second layer of the hierarchy, the general factor is divided into two broad group factors, roughly characterized as verbal and visuospatial. Some mathematical and mechanical skills are powerfully influenced by the visuospatial abilities (e.g., the ability to imagine what an object would look like after being rotated in space).

3. In the third layer is a long list—as noted earlier, it keeps lengthening—of primary abilities. Some of these are thought of as particular forms of the broad verbal and visuospatial talents, but some others, like a memory for musical rhythms, are viewed as separate.

Back to the East-West differences. Beginning at the top of the hierarchy. Lynn's first finding is that Japanese children are distinctly superior in g. At least they are superior beginning around age six. At earlier ages, they fall short in g, apparently because they mature more slowly than Caucasian children. (The slower rate of maturation is in any case well documented.) But after catching up, they pull steadily ahead; and on a scale where average American white children have g scores averaging 100, the Japanese score around 104 in the years between ten and sixteen.[14]

In the second layer of the hierarchy, the picture is mixed. In the verbal portion of the general factor, Japanese children are no standouts. They again start out behind their American counterparts in the very early years, but this time they do not catch up until around age nine or ten; furthermore, they do not then proceed to pull ahead of American children, but instead continue to score around

100 on average.[15] Lynn believes that they are actually less accomplished verbally than American kids. Many of the verbal skills can be raised by intensive study, so the apparent parity after age nine probably reflects the superiority of the Japanese educational system rather than truly equal verbal ability.[16]

In the visuospatial portion of the general factor—the area governing a broad range of mathematical skills—Japanese superiority is discernible as early as age 4½. With white Americans again normed at 100, the Japanese kids score around 105 in the years between ten and sixteen.[17]

In the third layer, the specific skills break down about as you might expect. The Japanese kids are relatively weak on most verbal tests. But they are generally outstanding on tests measuring drawing ability, speed of perception, and thinking about objects being moved around in space. In case you are wondering, they do about as well as Americans on musical rhythm.[18]

Lynn's summary of the data:

> Japanese differ from American Caucasoids in four respects, namely that they have higher . . . g, low verbal ability (from the ages of 2½ to 9 but not thereafter), high visuospatial ability, and a developmental trend in which all abilities increase in strength over the years of early childhood. . . . These characteristics are also present among Mongoloids in the United States and, so far as the evidence goes, in the three Far East nations of Hong Kong, Singapore, and Taiwan.[19]

The general rule, then, is that the East Asians excel at the visuospatial tasks associated with math and science but are much weaker in the verbal sphere. Footnote to the rule: Lynn's Mongoloid-Caucasoid differences are somewhat analogous to (although greater than)[20] male-female differences in Western societies—where men on average do far better than women in math and science, while women generally test better in verbal skills. Further footnote: American men seem about as good at the visuospatial tasks as East Asian women.[21]

Where did these East-West differences come from? Since so many of the ability differences are discernible in very young children, it is just about impossible to serve up a purely environmental answer to that question. Lynn himself believes in a mostly genetic answer and has proposed an imaginative evolutionary explanation of East Asians' unique genetic heritage.

Severely compressed, his explanation goes about like this: Some 60,000 years ago, when the Ice Age descended on the Northern Hemisphere, the Mongoloid populations faced uniquely hostile "selection pressure" for greater intelligence. Northeast Asia during the Ice Age was the coldest part of the world inhabited by man. Survival required major advances in hunting skills. Lynn's 1987 paper refers to "the ability to isolate slight variations in visual stimulation from a relatively featureless landscape, such as the movement of a white Arctic hare against a background of snow and ice; to recall visual landmarks on long hunting expeditions away from home and to develop a good spatial map of an extensive terrain." These, Lynn believes, were the pressures that ulitmately produced the world's best visuospatial abilities.

What about the relative weakness of Mongoloid verbal skills? In approaching this question, Lynn notes the familiar male-female ability differences. Like most scholars, he believes that these arose from evolutionary pressures in which men needed more visuospatial skills for hunting and women needed verbal skills for child rearing. The Mongoloids, Lynn believes, took this process a step further. Living on the frigid Siberian steppes, they survived only via an evolutionary tradeoff in which verbal skills were sacrificed still further in order to gain the requisite visuospatial skills. Verbal skills are, of course, centered in the brain's left hemisphere. Lynn hypothesizes that among Mongoloids, the cortex in the left hemisphere was invaded and made to take on more visuospatial processing. There is some evidence to support this view of a different neurological structure for East Asians, although the case is admittedly not closed.[22]

We have previously (chapter 7) noted that brain size is positively correlated with IQ. It therefore seems germane to mention that East Asian brains are somewhat larger, that is, relative to body size, than those of Caucasians. J. Philippe Rushton of the University of Western Ontario has cited data to support this view. He concedes that the absolute cranial capacity of Mongoloids is smaller than that of Caucasians but argues that the relative capacity is larger:

> That Caucasoids are three standard deviations above the Mongoloid mean in body weight, but only two standard deviations higher in cranial capacity shows unequivocally that Caucasoids have relatively smaller brains than Mongoloids. It translates into a *relative* cranial capacity advantage for Mongoloids of 1,460 [cubic centimeters] versus 1,446 [cubic centimeters] when body-size variables are controlled . . . thus, at any given weight, and on average, Mongoloids have 14 [cubic centimeters] more brain volume than Caucasoids.[23]

The verbal-visuospatial difference is not the only one that distinguishes Western and Mongoloid IQ patterns. The two populations also differ in the variability of their scores. A representative sample of Americans or Europeans will show more variability than will an East Asian sample. In the familiar bell-shaped distribution curve, the bell is much narrower for the Japanese, that is, their scores are more bunched around the mean—which is what one would expect from such a homogeneous population.

This difference in the distribution of IQs is a major matter, and it is worth focusing hard on the data. Just about all Western populations report a standard deviation (SD) of 15 IQ points. (See the statistical note on page xii.) But the SD for the Japanese and other East Asian populations appears to be a shade under 13 IQ points.[24] That difference does not sound like a big deal; in fact, it does not change things in the center of the distribution. But the smaller SD, combined with the higher average IQ, has one important implication for the quality of the Japanese labor force. It means that Japan has relatively few low-IQ workers. In the United States, about 25 percent of all workers have IQs below 90 (versus only about 15 percent in Japan). For IQs below 80, the comparable figures would be around 10 percent for the United States, around 3 percent for Japan.[25]

In sum, the IQ data are serving up an explanation—or a partial explanation—for the manifest superiority of the Japanese labor force. Japan has a labor force that is overwhelmingly equipped to work efficiently in a modern industrial economy. The U.S. labor force is mostly, but much less overwhelmingly, capable of comparable performance. The bottom 10 percent of the American IQ distribution is a group that is hard to train and hard to work with effectively. As we shall see in chapter 15, the U.S. Armed Forces reject this bottom 10 percent precisely because it is difficult to train effectively. So it makes a real difference that only 3 percent of the Japanese labor force shows up in this "problem" area.

Data on Jewish IQs are less comprehensive than those on the East Asians, but there is no doubt about the basic picture. Given the conspicuous overrepresentation of American and European Jews in so many different fields calling for brainpower, it would be astounding if their IQs turned out to be below average or even average. Although the Jewish population is generally put at something like 2 percent[26] of the U.S. total, 10 percent of the Terman Gifted Group were Jewish.[27] Some 30 percent of the Nobel Prizes awarded in science have gone to Jews.[28]

Jews are superachievers by other measures, too. One is

occupational status. Christopher Jencks and his colleagues cite studies indicating that "Jews [enjoy] occupational statuses about a third of a standard deviation higher than those of other white males with the same schooling and parental education."[29] Jews are dramatically overrepresented among well-to-do Americans. Nathaniel Weyl analyzed the ethnic backgrounds of the 400 individuals represented on the 1986 *Forbes* listing of the richest Americans. He found that 92 of the 400 were Jewish.[30]

The subject of Jewish IQs is a sensitive one. I could not help noticing, when I told various friends that I was thinking of incorporating a chapter on the subject in this book, that most of them—including Jews and non-Jews—started out by wincing. I also noticed, however, that they had some trouble stating clearly what the problem was about developing these data. They were, in fact, quite keen to hear what the data show.

The subject is contentious in another way as well. In discussing Jewish IQs with others, I find that a fair number of individuals have been profoundly impressed by some often-repeated tales about Jews in past years who tested quite low. These stories center on tests given to Jewish immigrants who arrived at Ellis Island during World War I and scored very badly on IQ tests administered by the Immigration Department. The stories, endlessly repeated by critics of IQ testing, have been used to make two points about the tests: first, that the test data are essentially worthless, and second, that test scores have often been used to discriminate against minorities. On the assumption that many readers will have heard some variant of the tale, I shall preface this report on Jewish IQs with a recapitulation of what is known about the Ellis Island *cause célèbre*.

The story about the Jewish immigrants spread rapidly after publication of *The Science and Politics of IQ*, by psychologist Leon Kamin of Princeton (he is now at Northeastern), a tireless critic of testing. As Kamin told the tale, Immigration Department psychologist Henry H. Goddard found that immigrants in general scored badly. Perhaps "badly" puts the case too mildly. Based on his test scores, Goddard was said to have rated "feebleminded" 83 percent of the Jews, 80 percent of the Hungarians, 79 percent of the Italians, and 87 percent of the Russians.[31]

It is not hard to see why a judgment of this sort would trigger a certain amount of indignation. Biologist Peter Medawar said that the test findings represented "extremities of folly . . . which . . . may never be surpassed."[32] In *The Mismeasure of Man,* IQ critic Stephen Jay Gould of Harvard added the additional discrediting thought that Goddard's test scores, and testing in general, were responsible for 1924 legislation making it harder for Jews (and certain other groups) to enter the country. Gould added that testing could therefore be blamed for magnifying the toll of those lost in the Holocaust.[33]

So far as I know, the only systematic backtalk to this assault on Goddard is an article that appeared in the *American Psychologist* in September 1983. It was written by Harvard psychologist Richard J. Herrnstein and Mark Snyderman, then a graduate student in psychology. The article was not primarily concerned with those Jewish test scores; its main focus was on a larger issue: whether IQ test data had in fact played a role in the 1924 Immigration Act. Herrnstein and Snyderman argued persuasively that it had not. Along the way, however, they disposed of the myth that Henry H. Goddard had found 83 percent of Jewish immigrants to be feebleminded.

Going back to Goddard's original reports, they noted a critical detail not mentioned by his critics: Goddard was not purporting to have tested a representative sample of Jewish (or any other group's) immigrants. He was testing only a relatively small number of prospective immigrants, all of them steerage passengers, whom he *suspected* of being mentally defective. In performing the test, his main interest was to prove the usefulness of his own adaptation of the Binet intelligence test; more than anything, Goddard wanted to demonstrate that his adaptation could successfully discriminate between individuals who were somewhat below average and those who were truly mentally defective.

Herrnstein and Snyderman tell us that his test was not particularly good at making such distinctions. For our purposes, however, the more relevant fact is that he was not even attempting to test Jews in general. The article in the *American Psychologist* quotes him as stating that his study "makes no attempt to determine the percentage of feebleminded among immigrants in general or even of the special groups named—Jews, Hungarians, Italians, and Russians."[34] The insistent representation to the contrary has to be viewed as an intellectual fraud.

As noted above, Jews and Japanese have quite different sets of abilities. Perhaps the most immediate and striking fact about the Jewish data is that they show an IQ "profile" almost exactly opposite that of the East Asians. On an IQ test like the Wechsler Adult Intelligence Scale, the East Asian profile will be one registering enormous superiority on the "performance" subtests—which generally emphasize visuospatial abilities—and average or even below-average scores on the verbal subtests. The Jewish profile is the reverse: very high verbal scores accompanied by poor performance results. Jewish testees tend to do better on the Stanford-Binet than on any of the Wechsler tests, apparently because the Wechsler incorporates more of the performance items.

Jewish verbal superiority appears unmatched in any other ethnic group. An often-quoted 1970 study performed at the Ann Arbor Institute for Social Research shows Jewish tenth-grade boys with an average verbal IQ equivalent of 112.8 (on the Stanford-Binet metric), about three-quarters of a standard deviation above the average for non-Jewish white boys.[35]

Miles D. Storfer, who is president of the Foundation for Brain Research, has gone further than anyone else I am aware of in assembling studies of Jewish IQs in the United States and other countries; the results are summarized in an absorbing chapter in his *Intelligence and Giftedness.*[36]

He notes, for example, a study showing that Orthodox Jewish children applying to Hebrew day schools in New York City in the 1950s averaged 114.9. Over two thousand children were represented in the study. Less than one in seven had a score below 100.[37] Other studies cited by Storfer show similar patterns, with IQs usually in the 110 to 115 range.[38] Says Storfer: "Jewish children's scores on the Stanford-Binet will average about a full standard deviation above test norms."[39] Some studies show *rising* verbal scores as the Jewish children pass through school, but the reasons for this increase are unclear. Some scholars view it as a maturational change, that is, the group is genetically programmed to improve its already superior verbal skills with age.[40]

Arresting detail also cited by Storfer: Jewish children are terrible at drawing, even though drawing is generally correlated quite strongly with IQ. Consistent with their poor scores on the performance subtests of the Wechsler, a 1972 study shows New York Hebrew day-school children scored well below average on the Goodenough Draw-a-Person Test. (The test is not designed to measure real artistic ability, but only the child's knowledge of human physical characteristics.)[41]

These studies of children in Orthodox schools are not, of course, indicative of American Jewish children in general. The best available proxy for a representative sample is Project Talent, a wide-ranging survey, conducted in the early sixties, of white high school students. The students were given an exhaustive battery of tests (forty-nine in all!) when they were in the ninth grade, then tested again (though not on all forty-nine) in the twelfth grade. The Project Talent data include results for 1,236 Jewish students.

Here is Storfer's summary of the results:

Mathematics. The scores of the Jewish boys averaged almost a full standard deviation above those of the non-Jewish boys, and the Jewish girls' scores exceeded those of their non-Jewish counterparts by a nearly equivalent degree (0.75 standard deviations); because boys substantially outperform girls on this test, *the average score of the Jewish boys was in the top 1 percent of all test takers.*
Verbal knowledge. The Jewish boys' scores averaged 0.7 standard deviations higher than those of the non-Jewish boys, and the Jewish girls outperformed their non-Jewish Caucasian counterparts by slightly more than half a standard deviation.
Perceptual speed and accuracy. The non-Jewish students' scores were on a par with the Jewish students in this test of visual-motor coordination under speeded conditions, as well as on a test of grammar and language usage.
Reasoning with spatial forms. The Jewish students scored significantly less well on this test (half a standard deviation lower than the non-Jewish sample) and also performed poorly on a measure of short-term recall of sequences of nonword letter strings (scoring 0.3 standard deviations below the non-Jewish sample).[42]

At this point, let me anticipate an objection. In writing about the structure of intelligence among Asians, I had indicated that their outstanding performance in mathematics was linked to their superior visuospatial abililites. Yet now I am serving up data indicating that Jews, who lack these abilities, nevertheless often turn out to be preeminent in math (as indeed they would have to be to recurrently win Nobel Prizes in physics and economics).

This apparent contradiction can be resolved as follows: First, it needs to be said that mathematics is a discipline that different people approach in different ways.

Some mathematicians might be thought of as geometricians, some as algebraists. The Asians tend to be geometricians, meaning that they solve mathematical problems via a process wherein they "see" the solution spatially, in their minds' eyes. In contrast, Jews (and other Westerners) are more likely to be algebraists who attack the problems in a process heavily dependent on verbal reasoning.[43]

The distinction between the visualizers and the "reasoners" seems to be related to extraordinarily high Jewish g levels—g being mainly a matter of reasoning skills. You will recall that Asians tended to do substantially better than Caucasians in g. Japanese children, for example, have g scores about 4 points higher than their Caucasian counterparts. But Jews outscore the Asians in g, apparently by even more than the Asian-Caucasian gap.

So where do these unique Jewish mental abilities come from? *Why* are Jews so verbally gifted and so richly endowed in g? And why are they so poor in other areas?

Miles Storfer's explanation is severely environmental. He emphasizes two factors: (1) a Jewish child-rearing tradition in which infants get an extraordinary amount of feedback and mental stimulation from their parents, especially their mothers, in their earliest months and years and (2) a Jewish culture whose prayer rituals and broad emphasis on religious training encourage speech and require exposure to ideas at an early age. Storfer's summary: "The areas of cognitive strength exhibited by the Jewish people conform closely with the maternal and educational emphases provided in traditional Jewish homes."[44]

Storfer's is probably a minority opinion, however. It competes with at least two other hypotheses about superior Jewish intelligence, both explored at length over the years by Nathaniel Weyl, most recently in his *Geography of American Achievement.*

One is the idea of "winnowing through persecu-

erage, were the survivors. The idea is intuitively quite plausible. It is well established that political refugees have above-average IQs, and we all have the sense that many of them are extraordinary people. The Pilgrims who fled persecution and settled in New England seem to have been a remarkable group. In modern times, the Cuban refugees from Castro's regime have done far better in the United States than have other Hispanic groups.[45] In the thirties, the Jews who came to this country from Germany appeared to include disproportionate numbers of quite brilliant individuals, beginning with Albert Einstein.

The historian Irvin A. Agus, who did much to develop the "winnowing" hypothesis, has argued that the process can be traced back to the million or so Jews living in the Roman Empire. This Jewish population was whittled down by losses attributable to plagues or barbarian invasions or conversion to Christianity. The survivors were the wealthiest and most learned; and, Agus argued, they were the ancestors of the East European Ashkenazi Jews from whom the great majority of the world's Jewish population today is descended.[46]

Winnowing is said to have continued relentlessly throughout the Middle Ages, when pressures to convert were overwhelming in much of Europe. In Weyl's summary of the argument:

> Since religion embraced at the time almost all learning and whatever passed for science, willingness to sacrifice everything for one's faith was a hallmark of intelligence and moral fiber. History tells us of many similar situations in which religious persecution winnowed out the weaklings and left a hard core of men and women of character, willpower, courage, firm ethical convictions, and superior intelligence.[47]

Weyl views the winnowing hypothesis as having a certain amount of genuine explanatory power—but as not ultimately sufficient to explain the form that Jewish intelligence has taken. Far more important, he believes, is a phenomenon he calls "selective breeding for mind."

Weyl first laid out his case for this phenomenon in a 1966 book, *The Creative Elite in America,* in which he wrote that "Jewish intellectual eminence can be regarded as the end result of seventeen centuries of selective breeding for scholars."[48] Severely compressed, his argument goes somewhat as follows:

For generation after generation, the brightest and most verbally gifted Jewish boys were encouraged to become rabbis, and rabbis—the center of the community— were expected to marry and have large families. Given the prestige and influence of rabbis and other religious scholars, wealthier Jews competed in efforts to marry into their families, which gave these families the survival advantages that money could buy when faced with plagues and persecutions. The process was one in which the Jewish population was protecting and augmenting the supply of intellectual talent.

In Christendom, meanwhile, an opposite phenomenon was observable. Many of the most verbally gifted Christian boys were steered into the clergy, where the tradition of clerical celibacy—even if not always observed to the letter—materially reduced the staying power of verbal genes.

In short, there are both hereditarian and environmental hypotheses competing to explain the phenomenon of high Jewish IQs. Which one is right? I confess to being attracted most by Weyl's perspective, possibly because I find the hereditarian case compelling in other contexts. But his case is a long way from being proved, and you can count on many more years of argumentation about the reasons for high Jewish IQs and the peculiar structure of Jewish intelligence.

11

IQ and Productivity

We begin with a cautionary tale from the files of New York City's police department (NYPD).[1] The time is April 1939. The long depression is still very much in place, and good jobs are hard to get. *Any* jobs are hard to get. So there is a huge turnout when the department announces civil service exams that will result in the hiring of several hundred policemen. More than 29,000 men take the written exam, which is essentially just an intelligence test. By normal police standards, a sizable number of the testees are absurdly "overqualified."

In the circumstances, the NYPD set its standards high. It announced that the physical exam for cops would be administered only to the top 3,700 scorers on the written test. After the physical tests, there was more winnowing: It resulted in a new list of the top 1,400 prospects (whose rankings reflected a 70 percent weighting for written scores and 30 percent for physical scores). Going down this list, the department next offered patrolmen's jobs to 350 or so of the top candidates. In the end, 300 of them—roughly 1 percent of those who had been competing for the jobs—ended up in the class of 1940.

The 300 were plainly smart cops. If you assume that the initial 29,000 test takers were roughly representative of the country's overall IQ distribution, then you could estimate that the average IQ of the 300 was something like 130.

Fifty years later, a group of Harvard psychologists—Prof. Richard J. Herrnstein and two graduate students, Terry Belke and James Taylor—went back to the NYPD records to see what had become of the brainy class of 1940. Questionnaires were sent to the 192 men then still alive, and more than three-quarters of them responded.

Analysis of the survey data demonstrate yet again that high-IQ people do well in the world. The group had on average stayed with the police department for 24.7 years and rose high in the ranks: 43 percent reached the rank of lieutenant or captain, and 18 percent became inspectors of one kind or another. The class of 1940 also produced one police commissioner, four police chiefs, four deputy commissioners, one chief inspector, two chiefs of personnel, one director of the city's Waterfront Commission, one chief assistant district attorney, one director of the New York State Identification and Intelligence System, and one director of the New York Regional Office of the Law Enforcement Assistance Administration.

The majority who left the police world behind at retirement also did well. In their "second careers," their occupational status tended to be well above average. Peak incomes in their second careers were $2^1/4$ times the median male income (i.e., the median in the year they hit the peak), and for about 20 percent of the men the figure was three times the median. The Herrnstein group reports a strong correlation between 1940 test scores and these multiples of median income.

Even *within* the group, we learn, success in life was positively correlated with test scores. Says the Harvard report: "Rank in the police force, income, and social status were among the variables correlated with test scores. Neither background, family status nor the individual's own educational history was as predictive of success as the score earned on a 3½-hour test taken over half a century earlier."

It is curious that economists have not done more with IQ data—that, indeed, they have shown no interest to speak of in the connection between economic performance and levels of intelligence. It is especially curious given their increased interest in "human capital." The human capital school of economics emphasizes the centrality of investments in people and argues that it is ultimately as important as investments in physical capital stock. But in measuring the value of such investments, the human-capital economists never seem to get beyond education and training.[2] In a brilliant essay published in 1983, in a volume called *Intelligence and National Achievement,* Barbara Lerner chided them for being blind to the much superior measures provided by IQ and other test scores. Dr. Lerner, a psychologist and lawyer, was herself one of the first to write about the connection between IQ and national economics.[3]

This connection can be approached from several directions, but let us begin with this hard fact: People with high IQs tend to do well in life. The police data above are telling the same tale as the data on the Terman Gifted Group (see chapter 2), who earned above-average incomes, worked in prestigious occupations, and had high socioeconomic status (SES). The connection between IQ and material success is pervasive in American society and apparently in all others. There is, or should be, no real controversy about these statements: On average, the rich are more intelligent than the middle class. And the middle class is more intelligent than the poor.

To be sure, you can always pick up a certain amount of

static about what's causing what in these relationships. Do people become well off because they are smart? Or are they smart because they started off with the kinds of advantages that well-to-do people pass along to their kids? The answer is that (a) the causation flows in both directions but (b) the former effect seems much more powerful: The main reason smart people are well off is that modern market economies tend to reward people roughly in proportion to their productive skills, and these skills are closely linked to IQ. If you pick a boy at random out of the teenage population, your best predictor of his adult "success" is not his family background (as measured, say, by his father's occupational status) but his present level of intelligence (as measured by his IQ). Correlation between a boy's teenage IQ and his adult occupational status: a potent .65.[4] Between his father's occupational status and his own at middle age: a relatively modest .35 or .40.[5] Corresponding figures for girls are, alas, hard to come by.

The dollar value of IQ differences has been pointed up in a sizable number of studies. A Census Bureau study of veterans tested in 1964, when the men were in their early thirties, showed that a 15-point IQ difference had translated into an 11 percent earnings difference.[6] One famous study examined the careers of brothers who grew up together in Kalamazoo, Michigan, and had similar educational levels. Kalamazoo, which has kept records of public-school IQs since 1928, has been a treasure trove for generations of sociologists.

Brother studies are illuminating because the boys have common family backgrounds but dissimilar IQs; on average, brothers' IQs differ by about 12 points.[7] The Kalamazoo data show that an adolescent IQ difference of 15 points was associated with a 14 percent average difference in earnings at ages 35–39, even when the brothers had the same amount of education.[8]

I have some evidence of my own about the top

achievers in American business: chief executive officers (CEOs) of large corporations. I spent some forty years as a writer and editor on *Fortune* magazine and during that time met hundreds of CEOs. Not all of them proved entirely lovable, and some of them were not particularly interesting when asked for opinions on social or political issues remote from their business concerns. But I cannot recall ever meeting a CEO who did not come across as highly intelligent.

Which is understandable: To get the job, executives must have tackled a fair number of complex business problems in the early and middle years of their careers and demonstrated an ability to think strategically about those problems. They must have avoided the screwups that inevitably overtake the not-so-smart. Executives also tend to need verbal reasoning skills. It helps in particular to have the ability to dominate the argument in meetings with peers and colleagues, something not possible if you keep getting your facts wrong and your logic muddled.

In talking with acquaintances about IQs and careers, I note that many of them instantly gravitate toward a distinction. They accept that many prestigious and high-paying occupations—judges, research scientists, senior executives—must obviously be filled by people of superior mental ability; but they do not accept at all that IQ has anything to do with what they see as the ordinary run of jobs. In making this distinction, my friends are not alone. Many industrial psychologists, many sociologists, and most corporate personnel departments will tell you that intelligence is nice but not necessary. The conventional wisdom about this matter says that in filling employment openings, what you mainly need to know is the applicant's knowledge of the job, which you can typically infer from his experience, training, and formal education. You might also be interested (the conventional wisdom continues) in certain psychological traits of the applicant, like honesty and motivation; however, you have no reason to care about his intelligence, since the worker will absorb everything he needs to know through experience and on-the-job training.[9] An extreme form of this view was a quite serious suggestion put forward by sociologist Randall Collins in his book *The Credential Society*. Arguing that anybody could become a doctor, Collins proposed that we create our doctors by letting young people start out as hospital orderlies and gradually work their way up the medical career ladder.[10]

The durability of the intelligence-doesn't-matter perspective is somewhat amazing, given the massive evidence to the contrary. One compelling mass of evidence comes from the U.S. armed services, which inevitably do a lot of testing, if only because most of those applying to come aboard do not have meaningful job histories. Prospective recruits take a battery of vocational-aptitude tests, collectively identified as the Armed Services Vocational Aptitude Battery (ASVAB). Four of the tests—those measuring work knowledge, paragraph comprehension, arithmetic reasoning, and knowledge of mathematics—are combined into the Armed Forces Qualification Test (AFQT). The AFQT may be thought of as a kind of rough-and-ready IQ test, and the services use it as a screening device.

By law, the lowest 10 percent of the population (roughly those with IQs below 80) are not allowed to enlist. In the early 1990s, with the armed forces cutting back in size, the group between the 10th and 30th percentiles was also pretty much screened out. The result was a substantial increase in the quality of recruits. Says a 1989 Defense Department report: "Service members with high scores on the AFQT and with high-school diplomas display behaviors that benefit the Armed Forces. . . . People with high AFQT scores are likely to achieve skill proficiency earlier in their first enlistment than those with low scores."[11] Charts accompanying the report indicate that in addition to learning their tasks faster, the high-scoring group continues throughout a three-year enlistment cycle to do better than the low scorers on detailed measures of "hands-on performance."

AFQT scores translate quite directly into the kinds of skills called for on the battlefield. The 1989 report cites this example:

> AFQT scores have been found to predict the success rate of soldiers performing operator maintenance on the TOW launcher, a wire-guided missile system. . . . In a tank gunnery test . . . soldiers in AFQT Categories I and II [which roughly translates into IQs above 105] hit 67 percent of their targets, while soldiers in Category IV [roughly IQs between 80 and 92] hit only 53 percent of the targets. . . . Category I teams scored 75 percent more tank equivalent kills using the M-60 tank than did the Category IV teams. . . .[12]

And so on.

The intelligence-doesn't-matter perspective has been undermined in a variety of ways. First by studies demonstrating that in fact most occupations are filled within identifiable IQ ranges. Second, and more important, the conventional wisdom has been done in by data indicating that in most occupations the best predictor of performance is not job experience or formal education or any combination of the two. The best predictor is intelligence, especially intelligence defined as *g*, the common factor in IQ tests. For generating some of these studies and pointing me to others, I am indebted to Robert A. Gordon of Johns Hopkins University and Linda S. Gottfredson of the University of Delaware, who together run the Project for the Study of Intelligence and Society.

The studies relating particular occupations to specified IQ ranges were developed principally by Professor Gottfredson and lean hard on data generated by the U.S. Employment Service (USES). The USES has for many years provided the state services with a so-called General Aptitude Test Battery (GATB)—a series of tests taken by job applicants, typically in situations where local employers are asking the state services for help in recruiting. Although the USES is not eager to emphasize the point, the GATB is a kind of disguised intelligence test. Herewith some of the IQ ranges (equivalent to scores on the WAIS) that Gottfredson came up with based on analysis of the GATB data.

Physician, engineer: 114 or more.
High school teacher, real-estate sales agent: 108–134.
Fire fighter, police officer, electrician: 91–117.
Truck driver, meat cutter: 86–112.[13]

You will note that the IQ ranges associated with each occupation are fairly wide. However, the great bulk of the jobs are filled near the midpoint of the ranges, so it is reasonable to think of each occupation as basically associated with a particular layer in the IQ pyramid. Or, to state the same thought in a possibly more provocative way, the occupational hierarchy is in large measure an intelligence hierarchy.

That thought was developed explicitly in a 1985 paper presented by Gottfredson to the Personnel Testing Council of Southern California. She wrote:

The occupational hierarchy has evolved naturally and is sustained over time because enduring differences in intelligence among workers create pressures for segregating work *tasks* into different occupations by intellectual complexity and by the criticality of their good performance to the employing organization. . . . In other words, more *g*-loaded and more critical tasks have become clustered together to create the more intellectually demanding occupations [and] less *g*-loaded tasks have become clustered into jobs that are likely to be adequately performed by less intelligent workers. . . .

My analyses provide . . . evidence that *g* is the major aptitude gradient by which tasks become segregated, over time, to create the current occupational division of labor. . . . The occupational prestige hierarchy that is of such great interest in the . . . debate over social inequality is actually a *g* factor among occupations.[14]

As the foregoing powerfully suggests, general intelligence is a superior predictor of job performance. The case for *g* as a predictor has been buttressed by an avalanche of empirical studies, centered on three huge data bases. One was put together by the late E. E. Ghiselli, a psychologist who was based at the University of California at Berkeley and spent a quarter century (1949–73) of his professional life collecting and analyzing job-aptitude test records. A second data base consists of 515 studies performed over the years by the USES in the course of checking on the validity and predictive power of its GATB. The third set of studies has been generated by the U.S. Armed Forces in connection with their never-ending efforts to ascertain which kinds of warriors should be assigned to which kinds of tasks.

In studies of these data bases, intelligence-test scores did best at predicting job performance when jobs had a high measure of complexity. But the predictions were still useful even for relatively unskilled jobs. Writing in the December 1986 *Journal of Vocational Behavior*, industrial psychologist John E. Hunter of Michigan State (a major participant in the studies) reported that performance in high-complexity jobs correlated .58 with test scores. For the lowest-level tasks, the correlation shrank to .23. "This value is high enough to yield considerable utility," Hunter wrote. He added that there were no jobs at all for which tests of intelligence are not useful predictors of performance. To be sure, there are some low-complexity jobs for which they are less useful than tests of psychomotor ability.[15]

Next question: How much do these predictions matter? Alternate form of the question: Are workers in any given job different enough in ability to justify a lot of testing? The evidence suggests that they are. Or so you would conclude from a series of studies performed by Hunter and industrial psychologists Frank L. Schmidt and Michael K. Judiesch of the University of Iowa. They found that the differences between workers (as captured in objective measures of performance) were greatest in the more complex jobs but were significant at every level.

In a cluster of jobs that they ranked as "low complexity" (unskilled and semiskilled blue-collar workers), the top 1 percent of workers were about 50 percent more productive than the average worker and three times as productive as the bottom 1 percent. In "medium complexity" occupations (technicians and supervisors, for example), the top 1 percent was 85 percent above the average and twelve times better than the bottom 1 percent. In the "high complexity" area (managers, professionals, and some technical workers), the top 1 percent was 127 percent better than the average; statistical complications made it impossible to quantify results for the lowest 1 percent. In a study of professional budget analysts, Hunter, Schmidt, and Judiesch estimated that the "dollar value productivity" of superior performers (defined in this case as the top 15 percent) was $23,000 a year greater than that of the low performers (the bottom 15 percent).[16]

These data have some large implications. One is that companies able to identify good workers in advance will be in a position to raise the organization's productivity. This is precisely the claim being made for *g* testing: that at every level of complexity, it outperforms both "credentialism" and tests designed to measure specific job knowledge. Another moral of the data is that you get the biggest payoff of all when you make superior predictions about high-complexity jobs. Fortunately, this is where *g* testing does best. Hunter and Schmidt estimate that the payoff—that is, the productivity gain associated with a shift to *g* testing— would be about 2½ times as great in high-complexity as in low-complexity jobs. But even in the latter, you get significant measurable gains.[17]

The link between *g* and occupational performance has one devastating implication. As we shall see in the next chapter, tests of mental ability consistently show black Americans testing lower on average than whites; furthermore, the black-white gap is greatest in tests with the highest *g* loadings. Taken together, the data on *g* as a predictor of job performance and the data on black-white *g* differences inescapably raise some questions: Is it possible that black underrepresentation in many different occupations—and especially those offering higher pay and greater prestige—reflects something beyond the racism and discrimination traditionally invoked? Is it possible that discrimination by whites explains less than do racial differences in *g*?

The answer appears to be yes. Linda Gottfredson tackled this question in the same issue of the *Journal of Vocational Behavior* to which Hunter contributed, and served up an analysis based on a four-step research project. First, as described above, she identified the IQ ranges associated with nine occupations employing sizable numbers of American men. The second step was to identify the proportions of blacks and whites one would expect to find in each of these overlapping ranges. Third, she computed black-white "estimated ratios," that is, the proportion of blacks to whites you would expect to find in each occupation if hiring reflected nothing but the mental ability of job applicants. A ratio of 1.0 would mean the two races were equally eligible for work in the occupation; a ratio of .5 would mean that only half as many blacks as whites were eligible. Not surprisingly, the estimated ratios were extremely low in the high-IQ realms of doctors and engineers but approached parity in a number of different blue-collar and service jobs.

Finally, Ms. Gottfredson compared these estimated ratios with data on actual black and white employment in the nine occupations in 1970 and 1980. Her basic finding: The IQ ranges reflected in those estimated ratios are pretty good predictors of black employment levels in the occupations. If anything, blacks are somewhat "overrepresented" in the jobs studied. That is, they hold more of the jobs than they would be expected to hold in a world where employers were blind to race but insisted on maintaining specified levels of mental ability.[18]

In the end, the analysis leaves you with two thoughts: (1) General intelligence is a quite superior predictor of the occupations in which most people end up, and (2) when it comes to explaining the subpar job performance of American minorities, the "discrimination" model has much less explanatory power than generally assumed.

How much might the U.S. economy as a whole benefit from a broad shift to testing? A USES team led by John E. Hunter had a swing at that question several years ago and came up with an estimate of nationwide productivity gains worth around $80 billion in 1980 prices.[19] This estimate was evaluated critically in 1989 by a National Research Council (NRC) panel.[20] Its scholars agreed that many individual companies would benefit from testing, especially for high-skill, high-productivity jobs. But the NRC panel dissented from the view that the country as a whole could get gains of the magnitude estimated by Hunter.

In thinking about the national economy, they observed, you run up against the awkward fact that it is ultimately expected to employ just about everybody. And if the bad workers will end up getting hired anyway, the gains from universal employment testing will perforce be limited. They would be centered on whatever economic benefits were attainable via better matching of workers to jobs.

How extensive might these benefits be? The NRC report mentions a number of calculations and seems to find it plausible that benefits could reach 1 percent of GNP (which would be around $50 billion in 1992 prices). The panel ultimately concludes, however, that realistic dollar estimates are simply not possible given the present state of knowledge about testing.[21]

The ultimate problem, said the NRC, is that "use of the . . . GATB will not improve the quality of the labor force as a whole."[22]

The panel did not add "and bring it up to Japanese standards."

12

Black-White IQ Differences

The IQ controversy, I have argued at several points in this book, is largely an expression of America's unease about the idea of group differences in mental ability. The unease is most acute when the groups in question are blacks and whites. Depending on which IQ test you are talking about, American blacks on average score 15–18 points lower than American whites.

It is worth emphasizing that these are *average* differences, and there are sizable overlaps in the two populations. More than 5 million American blacks score above the white average, and more than 30 million whites score below the black average.[1] Note also that the difference between the two groups—the 15- or 18-point gap—is far smaller than the differences within each group. There appear to be major regional differences in black IQs, with blacks in the rural South scoring at disastrously low levels, while blacks in some northern states appear to be close to the white average. (A 1968 armed forces study showed Wisconsin with the highest black average, an IQ of 95.)[2] The evidence suggests that the entire spectrum of intellectual abilities is represented in the black race. Black scores as high as 200 have been reported.[3]

In any case, a difference of 15 or 18 points is not in itself a big deal. Two individuals separated by some such number of IQ points would not generally come across as distinctly different. Indeed, many families have siblings separated by that much, and the parents will typically have no sense that one child is more clever than the other. Indeed, the *average* difference between siblings growing up together is 11 or 12 points. In many cases, the two would qualify for the same kinds of jobs. (To be sure, the one with the higher IQ would be likely to have a higher income.) Note also that the average difference between whites and blacks is significantly less than the 21-point difference between twenty-five-year-olds (with WAIS raw scores of 114) and sixty-year-olds (raw scores of 93).[4]

Still, there is no getting around certain large and troubling implications of black-white differences. The implications seem most troubling when you turn from the average differences and focus instead on the differences at the extremes—when you contrast the two overlapping bell-shaped distribution curves and look at the proportions in each group scoring above and below certain levels. If you tell yourself that the top professional and managerial jobs in this country require an IQ of at least 115 or thereabouts, then you also have to tell yourself that only about $2\frac{1}{2}$ percent of blacks appear able to compete for those jobs. The comparable figure for whites would be about 16 percent. (See the previous chapter for some indications that the zone around 115 is, in fact, a reasonable cutoff.) Total black population with IQs over 115: about 800,000. Comparable figure for whites: about 30 million.[5] If blacks had the same IQ distribution as whites, the black total would be over 5 million.

The data are even more depressing on the downside. An IQ in the 70–75 range, which many psychologists would label "borderline retarded," implies a life that is guaranteed to be short of opportunities. Very few students in that range will absorb much of what elementary schools teach, and virtually none will graduate from high school; few will succeed in finding and keeping good jobs. None will be admitted into the armed forces (required by law to screen out the lowest 10 percent of the distribution). The bad news is that a substantial minority—apparently more than one in five—of American blacks have IQs below 75. Around one in twenty whites are below 75.[6]

Most educated Americans find such data painful to contemplate and excruciatingly difficult to discuss. In the academic world, many psychologists refuse to study the gap. A significant minority of academic psychologists would like to ban all research on black-white IQ differences. The 1986 convention of the American Psychological Association featured a formal debate on whether such research should be permitted. Several reasons for a ban have been adduced. We have noted elsewhere the Marxist perspective, which sees the research as part of a larger effort by the ruling class to keep the poor in their place. Others argue that dwelling on the IQ gap is in any case pointless, since the data have no policy implications: They will not— in any case should not—affect the way black and white individuals are treated by American society. Finally, some academics contend that the data work to undermine the already fragile self-esteem of blacks. (An argument within this argument is whether black self-esteem is in fact low. Viktor Gecas, a sociologist based at Washington State University, surveyed the literature on this subject in a 1982 study published in the *Annual Review of Sociology* and concluded: "With regard to race, current research has found either no difference between the self-esteem levels of blacks and whites, or that blacks have slightly higher self-esteem than whites."[7])

In this chapter, I propose to undertake two tasks: (1) to describe the black-white IQ differences and (2) to elaborate several hypotheses about their origins. In the final chapter of this book, I will also argue that research into these issues is useful and probably inevitable—and has large policy implications.

The black-white IQ gap is 15 points when measured on the Wechsler tests, 18 on the Stanford-Binet. Both tests are, of course, normed so as to produce an average of 100 for the American population, but the white average is a bit higher. On the Wechsler metric, whites and blacks average 102 and 87, respectively. On both tests, the gap between the races is almost exactly 1 SD (standard deviation). The gap of 1 SD has been observed since the earliest days of intelligence testing.[8]

There are also significant black-white differences in the *structure* of mental abilities. The test-score patterns show that the two groups are good at different things. On average, whites do better on all the subtests, but their margin of superiority varies considerably from one subtest to another. Or look at it this way: If you took a sample of black and white children, all of whom had scored around 100 on the WISC-R—that is, the black kids in the sample were above the black average—you would expect to find significant black-white differences on six of the thirteen subtests. The average black kid would do better on Arithmetic and Digit Span; the average white kid would do better on Comprehension, Block Design, Object Assembly, and Mazes.[9] (The last-named subtest, not included on the adult Wechsler test described in chapter 1, requires a child to track his way through a maze with a pencil. The Mazes subtest measures the child's ability to see ahead.)[10]

These subtest differences have one common theme, and its name is g. The tests on which the gap is greatest are those with the most g loading—which means, in general, those that call most heavily on reasoning and problem-solving abilities. The June 1985 issue of *The Behavioral and Brain Sciences* carries a long report by Arthur Jensen analyzing eleven sizable studies of black-white IQ differences. The underlying data had been collected by different researchers at different times (but none before 1970). All the studies had several things in common: All were based on large population samples, all measured a broad range of mental abilities, and all included black-white breakdowns of their various subtests.

In all eleven studies, Jensen found consistently strong positive correlations between the size of the black-white gap on subtests and the extent to which the subtests called on *g*. The same issue of *Behaviorial and Brain Sciences* carried commentaries on these data by twenty-nine other scholars, including both supporters and critics of Jensen's analysis. Some of the critics argued that it was wrong even to be discussing the gap. A few argued that *g* was a meaningless abstraction. But most accepted that there was indeed a strong and meaningful statistical relationship between *g* and the gap. The correlation coefficient, after appropriate adjustments, appears to be well above .60.[11]

In other words, the black-white IQ gap is in large measure a reflection of differences in reasoning and problem-solving ability.

This was not exactly news in 1985. Long before Jensen set out to quantify the "*g* effect" in black-white differences, it was generally well known that the differences were greatest in measures of abstract reasoning, not so great in measures of verbal skill, smallest of all in memory and rote learning.[12]

Well, where did these differences come from? *Why* do blacks and whites exhibit divergent test-score patterns? Three kinds of answers have been proposed.

One answer is "cultural bias." This is the answer that an intelligent layman is most likely to have heard all his life: Blacks score poorly because the tests were designed with middle-class white kids in mind. This explanation of low black scores seems intuitively plausible to many Americans, and it has been a major theme in media coverage of IQ-related issues. In *The IQ Controversy*, Mark Snyderman and Stanley Rothman report on their exhaustive "content analysis" of IQ stories in major American media. In one part of the analysis, they sent coders looking for both positive and negative treatment of this thought: "Intelligence tests are culturally biased (are largely a measure of exposure to white middle-class culture)." For the fifteen-year period beginning in 1969, the coders found that thought treated positively on twenty-four occasions in the *New York Times*, twelve in the *Washington Post*, three in the *Wall Street Journal*, fifteen in the newsmagazines, and nine in television coverage—a total of sixty-three news and feature stories making a case for cultural bias. In contrast, they found only three articles shooting down the case. (They also found twenty stories that evenhandedly reported both perspectives.)[13]

Some academics have also promoted the cultural-bias explanation. One was David C. McClelland of Harvard, who developed this theme in an enormously influential 1973 article ("Testing for Competence Rather Than 'Intelligence'") in the *American Psychologist*. Said the article: "Tests have served as a very efficient device for screening out black, Spanish-speaking, and other minority applicants to colleges."[14] McClelland added that IQ-like tests were "clearly discriminatory against those who have not been exposed to the culture, entrance to which is guarded by the tests."[15]

The cultural-bias explanation will not fly. It simply does not conform to certain observable facts. As noted above, it collides with the fact that blacks do relatively well on the culturally loaded verbal sections of IQ tests; it is the subtests that are virtually devoid of cultural content—those emphasizing abstract reasoning ability—on which blacks do worst.

In gravitating to cultural bias as an explanation of the gap, many people confound two separate questions: (1) Do blacks who take the tests come to them with the same cultural advantages as whites? (2) Do the tests predict performance equally well for whites and blacks? The answer to question number 1 is: No, obviously. Blacks on average are indeed disadvantaged relative to whites (just as poor whites are disadvantaged relative to middle-class whites). On average, black (and poor white) kids grow up in households with fewer well-educated parents, they attend worse schools, they have fewer books at home, etc. But these cultural disadvantages, which help to *explain* lower black test scores, do not mean that the tests are biased against blacks.

The acid test on bias is the test's predictive power. The critical question is not number 1 but number 2. An IQ test would have a serious problem of bias if it generated scores that meant different things for different groups. In fact, this does not happen. IQ tests in general do about equally well at predicting the performance of blacks and whites, and any given score predicts about the same outcome for each race. If anything, the tests show a slight bias in *favor* of blacks; that is, their performance is marginally overpredicted.

This overprediction was noted in a 1982 study by the National Research Council (NRC). The council—an arm of the National Academy of Sciences—looked closely at the issue of test bias against blacks and basically concluded that there is no bias. (That conclusion applies to a broad range of mental tests, including but not limited to formal IQ tests.) Writing of the equations used to convert test scores into predictions of performance, the NRC stated:

> At the undergraduate college level, the equation for white students has usually been found to result either in predicted grades for blacks that tend to be about equal to the grades they actually achieve or . . . somewhat better than the grades they actually achieve. The

tendency for predicted grades to be higher than actual grades is somewhat higher for black students with
high test scores. . . . The results of studies at law
schools are generally consistent with those at the undergraduate level.[16]

The council found a similar pattern when it turned to
mental-ability tests used to predict performance in private
employment and in the air force. Bottom line: "The results
do not support the notion that the traditional use of test
scores in a prediction equation yields predictions for
blacks that systematically underestimate their actual performance. If anything, there is some indication of the con-
verse. . . ."[17]

At this point, we come to an intriguing morsel of information. The Snyderman-Rothman experts were asked
whether they thought the black-white IQ gap involved cultural bias. The question made it clear that bias was being
related to the test's predictive power: "To what extent does
an average American black's score underrepresent his or
her actual level of those abilities the test purports to measure?" The experts were asked to pick a number from 1 to
4, with a response of 1 signifying that the tests were believed to be "not at all or insignificantly biased," a 2 meaning that they were "somewhat biased," a 3 meaning that
they were "moderately biased," and a 4 meaning that they
were "extremely biased." The average of the experts' answers was 2.12. In other words, "somewhat biased."[18]

To be sure, "somewhat biased" is not a total rejection
of the tests. It is a long way from the extreme condemna-
tions of IQ tests routinely proffered by uninformed kibitzers on the IQ debate. Still, the judgment raises questions.
How could a significant number of experts have (apparently) concluded that the tests do not predict performance
for blacks as well as whites? In an academic environment
swarming with researchers who would give an arm to prove
test bias and with nobody finding it—and with the Na-

tional Academy of Sciences having shot it down in the 1982 study—why would so many experts vote for "somewhat biased"?

Snyderman and Rothman themselves were evidently somewhat puzzled by this survey response. They note, however, that the judgment on cultural bias had a political component to it. On most of the questions the experts tackled, their political perspectives (as revealed in responses to a battery of questions about social values) seem not to have influenced their conclusions. But on several of the most politically sensitive questions, especially those involving group differences, there were measurable dissimilarities in the responses of the liberal and conservative experts. Snyderman and Rothman seem to believe that when all is said and done, the liberal experts put their politics ahead of the evidence. Their own formulation: "Our hypothesis is that expert opinions on all the questions concerning group differences are related to the political perspective of the respondents. The dilemma . . . between the data on group differences and political belief faced by a liberal psychologist must be greater than that faced by a conservative, who might be more inclined to value efficiency over equality of outcome."[19]

In short: The more liberal experts felt obliged to override the evidence that the National Academy of Sciences scholars found so compelling.

None of this is meant to suggest that cultural bias is a nonproblem. The problem does in fact recur insistently in IQ testing—but it is centered on testees from non-English-speaking homes. There are many well-documented cases of kids from Chinese and Hispanic families whose IQ scores rose substantially when they were either tested in their own languages or moved from the WISC, say, to some "culture-fair" test like the Raven Progressive Matrices. The Raven is a test requiring essentially no language skills. (It calls for solutions to reasoning problems based on abstract figures and designs.)

Black children do not improve their scores when switched over to culture-fair tests; if anything, they usually do worse on such tests. Some psychologists have hypothesized that blacks would benefit from testing in "black English," especially in those portions of the tests requiring a fair amount of verbal interaction with the tester. The hypothesis has not been supported by experiments. Test results suggest that black kids on average perform just as well when dealing with standard English as with the dialects and special vocabulary of black English.[20]

A second popular explanation of the black-white IQ gap is that it reflects black-white environmental differences. This explanation clearly has some validity. Although there are endless arguments about the magnitude of the effect, it is clear that IQ is affected in some degree by environment; it is also beyond dispute that blacks on average are environmentally disadvantaged relative to whites. So it is reasonable to suppose that some, maybe even all, of the black-white gap is related to that disadvantage.

One ingenious demonstration of this relationship was performed by, of all people, Arthur Jensen. I say "of all people" because Jensen is usually (and correctly) thought of as minimizing environmental contributions to IQ differences. Still, his perspective does include some environmental effects, and he set out in the late seventies to prove their existence empirically. He did it by collecting IQ data from schools in rural Georgia—an area where, it seemed clear, blacks had extra-heavy disadvantages, both economically and educationally. The mean IQ of the blacks in his sample was only 71, far below the national black average of about 85.[21]

That 14-point difference in itself proved nothing about environmental effects. In principle, the 14 points could have been explained entirely in heritable terms.

(The local black population, for example, might simply have been a subgroup without strong genetic links to blacks elsewhere.) The real environmental effect lay elsewhere in the data: in the difference between younger and older siblings in Jensen's sample of blacks. The younger siblings had significantly higher IQs than their older brothers and sisters. The average difference was 3.31 IQ points. This could only mean that as the black kids grew older, they incurred a "cumulative deficit" in mental ability. They were being dragged down by extreme poverty and inferior schools. There was no comparable deficit for the white siblings in the sample. And, Jensen observed, he had failed in earlier efforts to detect any significant cumulative deficit among better-off blacks attending relatively good schools in California.

So the environmental effects are real. Measurable social differences must explain some of the black-white IQ gap. But they do not, apparently, explain most of it.

Here we come to some dismaying math. There is broad agreement about the environmental advantages of whites over blacks. Whites on average grow up in families with higher incomes and have parents who had better educations and worked in more prestigious occupations. It turns out, however, that these advantages account for only a small part of the IQ gap. When you eliminate them from the picture—that is, when you look at blacks and whites who are statistically similar on such measures—you reduce the gap only from 15 points (on the Wechsler scale) to 10 or 12 points.[22]

Another discouraging perspective: The broadest measure of environmental effects is SES; most of the other differences listed above are in fact subsumed under SES. But tests of black and white kids at different levels have shown rather regularly that low-SES white kids score as high as high-SES black kids.[23]

A similar portrait emerges from Scholastic Aptitude

Test (SAT) data. The data for 1992 (based on breakdowns made available by the Educational Testing Service) indicate that black students at the highest family income level (over $70,000) scored somewhat lower than white students at the lowest income level (below $20,000). Combining the verbal and math scores of the two groups, those high-income black students had a median of 862; the median for the low-income white students was 869. Black students with a parent who had graduated from college had a median of 786; white students whose parents had not graduated from high school had a median of 794.[24]

These details do not quite end the argument about environmental effects, however, In principle, it would still be possible that all or most of the black-white gap was attributable to other kinds of environmental factors—to factors not being captured in standard social-science data. A kind of last-ditch argument for the environment is sometimes made by positing an "X" factor. The X factor is something that nobody knows how to quantify or even describe very clearly, but—the argument goes—it comes with the experience of being black in America; it makes that experience unique and utterly noncomparable to the lives led by whites. In the process, it undermines the relevance of all those correlation coefficients that seem to show only limited environmental contributions to the gap. And in some way that nobody can quite make clear, the X factor works to suppress mental abilities.

Might there really be an X factor that explains the gap? Many, perhaps most, scholars find the proposition excessively mysterious and have, accordingly, gravitated to a third possible explanation of the gap: one that includes a genetic effect.

The possibility that the black-white IQ gap might have a genetic component is difficult to talk about in public. In an age when pressures for "political correctness" are increasingly hard to resist—and especially hard in academic settings, where a lot of the experts reside—the suggestion that some of the gap might be explained genetically is about as politically incorrect a statement as one could make. Still, at least this much has to be said: While the issue cannot be settled definitively, the statement has a lot of support (as we shall see).

In principle, the issue of a genetic contribution to the black-white IQ gap could be settled. Suppose that some superbeings from another planet landed on earth and imposed as much control over human beings as human scientists now impose over laboratory rats. As long as we are being fanciful, suppose also that these superbeings got interested in the roots of the black-white IQ gap. They would have no difficulty designing experiments to get at the truth of the matter. They could take randomly selected groups of whites and blacks. They could tightly control the environments of both groups. They would arrange for experimental breeding within each group and between the two groups, then examine the IQs of the three groups of offspring—in all, no more difficult than breeding rats that are good (or bad) at finding their ways through mazes, which human psychologists do all the time. Luckily, the superbeings are not expected to land anytime soon.

Possibly some readers are wondering why it has taken us so long to get to the possibility of a genetic contribution to the black-white IQ gap, since we had already established (in chapter 7) that just about everyone agrees there is some heritable component in IQ differences. But that broad agreement applies only to heritability *within* groups. The regression equations used to demonstrate the IQ effects of changes in income, education, etc., require that other environmental effects be held constant. The equations cannot be used when there is a chance of some huge noncomparability like an X effect. Bottom line: Nobody knows how to measure heritability between groups whose background environments may be noncomparable.

This does not mean there is no genetic contribution to the black-white IQ gap—only that it cannot be demonstrated via the usual methods. A plurality (45 percent) of the experts surveyed by Snyderman and Rothman, and a slender majority of those expressing an opinion on the issue (52 percent), said they believed the black-white gap does have some heritable component. (They were not asked to estimate its size.) Only 15 percent of those with an opinion believed the gap was entirely environmental in origin. One percent said it was entirely genetic, and the remainder of those who answered said they just did not believe there were enough data to support any reasonable opinion.[25] Snyderman and Rothman commented on these data with a certain wonderment. They observed: "That a majority of experts who respond to this question believe genetic determinants to be important in the black-white IQ difference is remarkable in light of the overwhelmingly negative reaction from both the academic and public spheres that met Jensen's statement of the same hypotheses. Either expert opinion has changed dramatically since 1969 [when Jensen's original statement was published] or the psychological and educational communities are not making their opinions known to the general public."

It is not hard to think of some reasons for the majority's belief in a genetic contribution to the black-white IQ gap. One reason is that the black-white gap is observable at very early ages, when, presumably, environmental effects have not fully taken hold. The 15-point gap on the WISC-R is in place by age five.[26]

But perhaps the major reason for the experts' collective judgment has been the failure of the gap to shrink in the age of desegregation. At least it appears not to have shrunk. If in reality it has not, we would seem to have evidence that the environmental effects on IQ differences have been much overrated. Whatever one thinks about the depth of racism and prejudice in America today, it would be hard to maintain that they are still flourishing at the levels of the 1940s and 1950s. Black environments have plainly improved relative to those of whites. Fifty years ago, American blacks were not free to work or live where they chose, mostly lived in rural poverty, and were condemned to separate and inferior schools. Yet there are no clear-cut signs of a narrowing IQ gap as these handicaps were reduced or eliminated.

To be sure, statements about the trend of the black-white gap are necessarily somewhat imprecise. Not all the data are as recent as one would like, and not all point in the same direction.

One large, relatively recent representative national sample was provided by the 1980 "profile of American youth" administered by the National Opinion Research Center of the University of Chicago. The sample consisted of 12,000 young people, fifteen to twenty-three, who were tested on the Armed Services Vocational Aptitude Battery (ASVAB). The results were reported in *Advantage and Disadvantage: A Profile of American Youth*, by R. Darrell Bock of the University of Chicago and Elsie G. J. Moore of Arizona State University. The authors note with evident dismay and puzzlement—"in view of the considerable amount of time, energy, and resources focused on the problem"—that black test scores still lag white scores by as much as they had in 1966, that is, by about one standard deviation.[27]

On the other hand, the black-white SAT gap plainly *has* shrunk in recent years. During 1978–92 the gap in verbal-math scores combined fell from 245 to 196 points, a decline of 20 percent.[28] The black SAT gains have been occurring in a period when the number of black testees has been rising, both in absolute numbers and as a proportion of all testees. The rise suggests forcefully that the higher black scores are "real," that is, not just the result of the black test population becoming more selective.

What can one make of these divergent findings? One possible interpretation: The black middle class—whose kids are most heavily represented among the blacks taking SATs—has truly benefited from desegregation, but the overall black record is still being dragged down by the still-swelling black underclass.

Uneasy to begin with about the existence of a black-white IQ gap, Americans tend to be doubly disturbed by the thought that it might have a genetic basis. They equate it with another thought: that blacks are "innately inferior," a formulation they identify as racist and understandably feel they cannot live with.

In fact, a genetic explanation for the gap (or, more realistically, for some part of it) does not imply that black-white differences are foreordained. The thought behind the genetic hypothesis is that any racial group—any gene pool—will inevitably raise or lower its average IQ in the way it mates. If the higher-IQ members of the group have a disproportionate share of the children, then the group average will rise over time, and vice versa. If it were firmly established that the black-white IQ gap had a heritable component, this would imply only that in past generations whites on average had a more favorable ratio of high-IQ births to low-IQ births than did blacks. In principle these patterns might someday be reversed; there is nothing in the genetic hypothesis to preclude eventual IQ parity for the black and white races—or, for that matter, eventual superiority for blacks.

Alas, there are no signs in current population data of a genetically driven rise in black IQs. Among both blacks and whites in America, fertility is inversely correlated with IQ, and the correlations are if anything more negative for blacks. Daniel Vining, Jr., a demographer based at the University of Pennsylvania Population Research Center, has published (in the journal *Intelligence*) estimates of the relevant correlations between IQ and live births for American women during the seventies. For young white women between twenty-five and thirty-four, the correlation coefficient was −.18. For black women in the same age zone, it was −.20.[29]

Returning now to a question raised earlier: Should scholars study such questions? In a way, it is astonishing that the quesion has to be taken seriously. Not long ago, the tradition of free inquiry seemed unassailable on the campuses. The faculty credo of the New School for Social Research contains a statement that scholars everywhere once accepted as received wisdom: "No man can teach well, nor should he be permitted to teach at all, unless he is prepared 'to follow the truth of scholarship wherever it may lead.'" I should confess that I came across that passage in listening to the American Psychological Association debate on the propriety of discussing black-white IQ differences. One of the participants, Robert Proctor of the New School, opposed all such discussion. Another participant, Robert A. Gordon of Johns Hopkins, quoted the credo at him.[30]

I suggested above that I thought the study of black-white differences was useful and, probably, impossible to bar. Underlying that thought is a fairly simple question: How can you *not* study issues inextricably linked to great questions of public policy?

13

Are We Getting Smarter?

I have argued elsewhere in this volume that national intelligence levels are a critical determinant of national performance. Obvious next question: Are American intelligence levels rising or falling?

As previously indicated, the heavyweights of the psychometric profession very much disagree as to the direction of national (and for that matter worldwide) intelligence trends. The disagreements have reflected large anomalies in the data: Some of the data have pointed to rising intelligence levels, while other data seem to signal a disastrous national "dumbing down" process. Below we shall consider some ingenious recent solutions to these riddles about the trend of IQ. But first it will pay to focus on the anomalous data.

Begin with some well-advertised bad news. Average scores on the Scholastic Aptitude Test (SAT) are still significantly below the average of the sixties. Between 1967 and 1992, average verbal scores on the SAT fell from 466 to 423, average math scores from 492 to 476.[1] The SATs are in effect intelligence tests (they correlate about .80 with the Wechsler Adult Intelligence Scale), so the decline in these scores would seem to represent truly bad news about the IQ trend.

To be sure, some part of the decline is attributable to the "democratization" of the SAT: The million-odd students taking the test now are a less elite group than those taking it in the fifties and sixties. Beginning in that period, more and more poor and minority students joined the ranks of college-bound seniors who took the SAT. The proportion of minority students rose from perhaps 3 percent in 1963 to 28 percent in the early nineties. Clearly, poor and minority students contributed to the decline in average scores. Much of the commentary on this decline implies that it was actually a rather healthy phenomenon: It signified not a loss of intelligence among high school seniors but a more democratic society, one in which the benefits of a college education were no longer reserved for a relatively small elite.

But this buoyant and understandably popular view of the case does not stand up to analysis. It was effectively shot down by Charles Murray and R.J. Herrnstein, who put a quite different spin on the data in an article in the *Public Interest* that appeared early in 1992.[2] The authors argue persuasively that the elite group itself has shown real slippage. They make several devastating points.

First, if you ignore the increased representation for minority students and focus only on white students taking the SATs, you run into instant bad news. Scores for white SAT students declined significantly between 1963 and the early 1990s. In 1963, to be sure, the College Board did not give ethnic breakdowns of the test population. However, it was then almost entirely white, and it is possible to estimate scores for whites only that year. Murray and Herrnstein calculate that white students then had verbal scores averaging around 478 to 482 and math scores averaging around 502 to 505. (SAT scores range from 200 to 800.) These 1963 verbal scores are about 40 points higher, and the math scores perhaps 12 points higher, than the comparable figures for white students in 1991.

And there are reasons for thinking that even those figures understate the true decline. One reason is that the great bulk of the decline took place in a period when the tests were actually becoming easier (a point conceded by the Educational Testing Service). Tests at the beginning and end of that period were not entirely comparable. The Murray-Herrnstein judgment: "SAT scales got easier during 1963 to 1967 by about 8 to 13 points on the verbal and perhaps 10 to 17 points on the math. . . . The same person would, in other words, have earned a higher score on the later SATs than the earlier ones, owing purely to changes in the test scales themselves."[3] Adjusting the slippage for white students to reflect these incomparabilities, we now find ourselves looking at declines of around 50 points in the verbal test and something like 25 or 30 points in the math.

Possibly some readers are wondering at this point about the possibility of "democratization" *within* the pool of white testees. It is, in fact, widely believed that the base-broadening phenomenon was not just a matter of more minorities taking the SATs but also reflected major increases in the number of less privileged whites going on to college. Might the decline in white scores reflect this broader white base?

The answer is no. Murray and Herrnstein look closely at this possible explanation of the decline in white scores and rule it out. The expansion in the white SAT population occurred in the fifties, not the sixties, that is, the base of white students was broadened well *before* the white scores started declining. In fact, the white group was becoming more elite, not less, in the period when scores were head-ing south. Says the *Public Interest* article: "Our net estimate is that from 1963 to 1972, the proportion of white seniors taking the SAT dropped from 33 percent to less than 28 percent of the white senior population, with a smaller continued drop between 1972 and 1976."[4]

Which means that even the adjusted decline in SAT scores mentioned above—50 points on the verbal test, 25 or 30 points in math—understate the ability declines of white students. Murray and Herrnstein have not attempted to translate the increasing "exclusivity" of the white test takers into additional points one might take off the group's scores. But clearly, the decline has been substantial. It is very hard to look at the figures and not conclude that intelligence was slipping in a universe that surely includes most of the country's best students.

Fascinating footnote to the above: When you look at "the brightest of the brightest," as Murray and Herrnstein also did, you stumble across an odd phenomenon. Students scoring at the highest levels are exhibiting divergent trends in the verbal and math scores. The proportion of students scoring over 700 on the math test has increased quite substantially in recent years. Among white students, the proportion has risen from under 3 percent in the early eighties to over 4 percent in the early nineties. But this pattern is reversed on the verbal front, where only 1 percent now score above 700; the figure was a shade higher in the early eighties and higher still (close to 2 percent) in the early seventies.

This divergent performance on the verbal and math tests is interesting on several counts. The verbal portion of the SAT is more "*g* loaded," so the attrition there might be viewed as one more datum translatable into evidence of slipping intelligence. Murray and Herrnstein suggest that it may also reflect a systematic "dumbing down" of such verbal-oriented studies as history, civics, and literature, where standards were compromised in order to make courses easier. They add that there are limits to how much you can dumb down calculus.

To be sure, the SATs and other college admissions tests are given to an unrepresentative group of young Americans—the half or so of high school kids who are college-bound. But many of the data for lower-school children are also depressing. A persistent theme in recent reports from the National Assessment of Educational Progress (NAEP) is the decline in children's thinking ability. Summarizing NAEP data that spanned two decades, the Educational Testing Service reported in the fall of 1990: "The NAEP results indicate a remarkable consistency across subject areas—students are learning facts and skills, but few show the capacity for complex reasoning and problem solving. . . . Most of the gains appear to have occurred in lower-level skills and basic concepts. . . . In contrast, most of the declines have occurred in the area of higher-level applications."[5]

For those who took these data to mean that American thinking skills were in retreat, there was no shortage of explanations for the decline. The boob tube was an obvious candidate. Declining standards in the schools was another. Also available were some solid-looking "dysgenic" reasons, that is, explanations based on data showing above-average birthrates in the low-IQ population. Given the high heritability of IQ, dysgenic data would afford a convincing explanation of declines in thinking.

Daniel Vining, Jr., a demographer based at the University of Pennsylvania Population Research Center, has been a major source of such data. Looking at a broad nationwide sample in the late seventies, Vining found that Americans with IQs of 70 had .6 to 1.2 more children, on average, than did Americans with IQs of 130.[6] Among both black and white women, fertility rates and IQs were negatively correlated (as noted in the last chapter). In the eighties, Vining was still reporting "dysgenic" trends. In a 1983 paper published in *Personality and Individual Differences,* he added the thought that these trends are not just a reflection of social-class differences in fertility. "The negative relationship between IQ and fertility is not simply the oft observed inverse relationship between class and fertility," he commented. "It persists after controlling for family background, as indexed by father's education. . . . On average, the higher the IQ, the more years of formal schooling . . . the smaller the family, both now and in the future when family size will have been completed." Vining calculated that the dysgenic trends he was writing about implied overall IQ losses averaging somewhere in the zone between .6 and 1.5 IQ points per generation.[7]

All of which would seem to help explain the decline in intelligence implied by all those gloomy data from the College Board and the NAEP.

This brings us to a rather awesome anomaly: IQ scores are apparently *not* falling. There is, in fact, considerable evidence to suggest that they are rising. An avalanche of data shows that in recent years American children—indeed children around the world—have rather consistently scored higher on old IQ tests (from the thirties and forties) than did the kids who originally took them. James Flynn, a scholar based at Otago University in New Zealand, has done much to assemble these data, has aggressively promoted the idea that test scores are in a sustained secular rise, and has pretty much won over those academics who once resisted this proposition.

Nor are the gains confined to children. In the Netherlands, Belgium, and Norway, there were huge gains for military recruits (i.e., contrasted with recruits of a generation earlier), demonstrating that whatever is happening has a certain amount of staying power. Here is Flynn's summary of the main evidence:

Young adults in 1980 outscored the young adults of 1950 by about 18 points on Raven's [the Progressive

Matrices], 15 points on Wechsler . . . and 11 points on purely verbal tests. These trends hold for every nation for which we have data, fourteen nations originally but now Denmark, Sweden, Brazil, Israel, Scotland, and perhaps China have joined the list to make a total of 20. The best data come from the Netherlands and show a 20-point gain on Raven's.[8]

Today it is widely conceded that test scores are in a slow, long-term rise. The gains have been greater for visuospatial than for verbal skills; on tests like the Wechsler Adult Intelligence Scale (the one I took), the gains seem to have been far greater for the "performance" parts of the test than for the verbal parts. Still, gains have been clear and measurable in both areas. Overall, test scores have been increasing at a rate that seems to average around .3 IQ points per year, which translates into some 15 points during the past half century.[9] An interesting implication of that figure: The difference between us and our grandparents is roughly equivalent to the current black-white difference in America (also around 15 points).

The data are puzzling, to put it mildly. If intelligence is in some broad secular rise of the kind showing up in IQ scores, how do we account for the decline in SAT scores? In a world with rising IQ scores, we would expect to see far more geniuses, colleges bursting with young prodigies, lower schools with far higher proportions of gifted kids. But educators report no such phenomena. They are still besieged by demands for remedial reading courses, and we are still looking at the dismal SAT scores and disappointing NAEP findings. Vining's data on dysgenic population trends remain convincing. What, then, is producing those higher test scores?

The reports of higher scores at first led many scholars to assume that the new test results represented some transient effect in children's lives. Programs like *Sesame Street*, for example, might be helping youngsters to read earlier and othewise stimulating their thought processes. Perhaps television in general, for all the rampant mindlessness of much programming, might at least bring young children into awareness of the world around them much sooner, enlarging their vocabularies and their stock of information. If these were the phenomena responsible for boosting the IQs of six-year-olds, it would be reasonable to expect that the gains would be transitory and could be reconciled with the gloomy bulletins from the SAT front. But, as we have seen, substantial gains over prior generations are still observable when the kids are old enough to be military recruits.

Flynn was especially intrigued by the anomaly of higher test scores unaccompanied by observable increases in prodigies and geniuses—or, indeed, in academic achievement among ordinary students. "Why do these skills [the kinds measured by standard IQ tests] not translate into real-world intelligent behavior?" he asked in a 1990 article, adding:

> What profit is there in producing massive problem-solving gains if these pay so few dividends in creativity, inventions, vocabulary, and do not result even in enhanced academic achievement? The present situation is truly baffling. It is as if we suddenly discovered a dramatic escalation in juggling skills and yet there was no carry-over to socially significant sport—no one seemed to have better timing or coordination when playing football or basketball or cricket.[10]

Several approaches to these conundrums have been proposed. Some scholars have hypothesized that the purported rise in IQ is mainly an artifact of greater test sophistication among students today. Flynn, who is resisting this hypothesis, has cited a number of scholars pushing it in private correspondence with him.[11] Arthur Jensen says he finds it somewhat persuasive.[12]

Flynn himself has concluded that the anomalies reflect

deficiencies in the IQ tests. In general, he believes, the tests are far more limited in their utility than we (and he) once thought. He believes not that people are genuinely becoming more intelligent but that the tests are unable to provide meaningful comparisons across generations. "IQ tests," he judges, "cannot bridge the cultural distance that separates one generation from another."[13] The import of this position is that each generation has its own learning, reasoning, and problem-solving challenges and that it would be absurd to view Thomas Jefferson as less intelligent than the average Virginian in 1991 simply because a magically resurrected Jefferson might score low on the Wechsler Adult Intelligence Scale. (He would surely have trouble with Information, Vocabulary, and Comprehension, all with deep roots in twentieth-century culture.)

Flynn does not stop with this transgenerational point. Having made the point, he proceeds to argue that the tests must also be viewed as suspect when they are used to compare individuals growing up in totally different cultures—Americans, for example, and natives of the Pacific Rim countries. Flynn also seems suspicious of IQ comparisons between blacks and whites, even between men and women. In short, he resolves the riddle—the mismatch between higher test scores and lower levels of achievement by other measures—by telling us that IQ tests cannot be used to compare different groups. He does not deal with findings of the National Research Council (see page 155) and others, indicating that IQ scores have essentially the same predictive power for blacks as for whites.[14]

Flynn is not the only scholar arguing that IQ tests cannot be used to compare groups with different cultural backgrounds. "IQ simply cannot be used to compare individuals who have grown up in different eras," says Charles Locurto, a psychologist based at the College of the Holy Cross in Worcester, Massachusetts. Like Flynn, Locurto suggests this may mean that "perhaps it [the IQ test] cannot be used even to compare individuals living within the same generation who may nonetheless have experienced different cultural milieus."[15]

Still, why did IQ scores go up while academic achievement went down? In addressing this question, Locurto differs somewhat from Flynn. Locurto believes that intelligence probably was rising in the sixties and seventies but that the rise was largely or entirely offset by failures in the educational system. "It might be the case that while general cultural sophistication has increased IQ scores slightly during that period of time, the decline in the effectiveness of schools has entirely negated the impact of those improvements on tests of scholastic success."[16]

Summary of the case thus far: Flynn and Locurto agree that intergenerational comparisons are highly problematic but disagree as to whether intelligence is actually rising out there in the real world. Flynn is skeptical of real gains. Locurto inclines to the view that there have been real gains in intelligence but that they have been masked or offset by failures in the educational system.

Our next witness is Richard Lynn, previously onstage in this book for his work on East Asian IQs. Here again, Lynn's findings are extraordinarily compelling. He believes with Locurto that there have indeed been long-term gains in average intelligence and that these gains are being somewhat muffled by poorer teaching (and also, perhaps, by students less motivated to learn). What is most interesting about Lynn's contribution is his explanation for the rise in intelligence. He attributes it almost entirely to superior nutrition.[17]

How does improved nutrition affect intelligence? Perhaps the most direct effect is on brain size. As noted earlier (chapter 7), intelligence is linked to both the size and complexity of the brain's neurological tissue. Lynn starts you off by pointing to many different studies demonstrating a worldwide increase in brain size. Among British one-year-olds, for example, average head circumference has increased by about 1½ centimeters (about six-tenths of an inch) during the past half century; at age seven, the increase is 2 centimeters.

The increase in head size implies an increase in brain size. And, in fact, autopsies of older men quite consistently show brains growing in weight over the decades. A study of 7,000 brains autopsied at the London Hospital over an eighty-year period shows brain weight increasing by around 6 grams (about one-fifth of an ounce) during these years. Comparable gains have been reported in many other studies.

The link between nutrition and head size is also well established. Children suffering severe malnutrition have smaller heads and brains. The effect of malnutrition is especially striking in the cases of identical twins. It sometimes happens that because of their positioning in the womb, one twin will receive fewer nutrients and will therefore be born smaller than the other, and with a smaller head. Studies of such twin pairs have demonstrated quite consistently that this prenatal malnutrition affects IQs years later; the twin with the larger head at birth tests higher in the teen years, even though the two are genetically indistinguishable and have typically grown up in the same household. Pointing to these and other studies, Lynn states: "It is difficult to see how the results can be plausibly explained except in terms of a permanently adverse effect of poor nutrition in infancy on subsequent intelligence."

While early malnutrition does seem to confer some permanent disadvantages, a number of studies show that the IQ shortfall can be reduced when severely underfed infants get nutritional supplements. Indeed, IQ gains have been reported among older children. Lynn mentions one British study in which verbal gains averaging nine points were scored by poorly fed twelve- and thirteen-year-old children who received vitamin and mineral supplements over an eight-month period—a finding that seems particu-

larly astonishing in that it involved verbal skills. Most studies of nutritional effects show them doing far more for
visuospatial than for verbal abilities.

Next Lynn addresses a large and rather obvious difficulty for any scholar postulating a secular rise in IQ. Anyone focusing on a half-century gain of 15 points will
naturally begin to muse about gains still further back in
time. IQ tests were not of course available 100 years ago.
But if they had been, would we now be looking at data
suggesting a gain of *30 points* for the century?

Gains of that magnitude seem highly counterintuitive.
They would require us to believe that, by today's standards,
the average IQ in the 1880s was only 70—a score now
sometimes equated with "retarded" status. It is hard to accept that our great-great-grandparents could really have
been so retrograde. But it is also hard to think of reasons
why the nutrition-based gains driving the rise in IQ would
have started only in the 1930s or thereabouts. After all,
economies were growing and living standards rising quite
substantially between the 1880s and the 1930s. Why would
the nutritional gains begin only in the 1930s?

It turns out that Lynn has an answer to this question.
Or, rather, two answers. One is somewhat speculative: He
suggests that the long transition from hunting-farming societies to more urbanized societies may have left increasingly high fractions of the population chronically
underfed and that only when humankind was well into the
twentieth century did it become possible for economic and
scientific advances to reverse this nutritional slide. This
has a ring of armchair argument about it, and many readers will doubtless find it unsatisfactory.

But Lynn does leave you thinking that, whatever the
reasons, nutritional gains did in fact begin sometime
around the 1930s. His evidence centers on the fact that our
species suddenly began getting taller in this period, after
many centuries in which height had apparently remained

fairly stable. Data for Europe, North America, and Japan show rather steady gains in height since the 1930s—gains averaging around 1.2 centimeters (almost half an inch) per decade. Paralleling the gain in IQ during this period, the gain in height works out to just about 1 standard deviation. It is well established that height, like head and brain size, is affected by nutrition.

The nutritional hypothesis has one other implication: It requires us to think differently about environmental effects on IQ. As noted earlier, there is a widespread tendency to equate "the environment" with cultural-educational effects—better schools, more reading, more *Sesame Street*s (and less *Looney Tunes*) in children's lives. There is clearly a great yearning to believe that the higher test scores reflect some such environmental factors.

But the yearning bumps into two large facts, both readily accommodated by Lynn's hypothesis. Fact number 1 is the absence of all the young geniuses. Fact number 2 is the far greater gain for visuospatial ability than for verbal ability. If test scores were rising because of *Sesame Street*, then clearly verbal skills would be showing the greatest gains.

Like many others who reacted to Lynn's hypothesis— real gains in intelligence, driven mainly by superior nutrition—I found his evidence at once surprising and compelling. It is especially compelling in that it implicitly accounts for the dearth of geniuses that have bothered so many scholars contemplating those higher IQ scores. You would naturally expect that nutrition-based gains would disproportionately benefit the low-IQ population suffering from poverty; the gains would have only marginal effects on the so-called right tail of the distribution curve, where the high IQs reside.

Lynn does in fact believe that the intergenerational IQ gains were mostly occurring in the lower half of the IQ distribution. He believes that earlier generations included much higher proportions of uneducated, malnourished, and generally retarded individuals with IQs around 60 or 70. Today, Lynn argues, the IQ distribution is much less variable than it was in past generations, a proposition implying that the standard deviation (a measure of variability) of test scores has declined somewhat. He also believes that the nutrition-based gains in IQ have not yet run their course, meaning that variability in IQ is still declining.

Lynn's perspective on the IQ gains—and especially his view that they mainly benefited the lower half of the distribution—is reasonably consistent with some other data. The Murray-Herrnstein study of SAT scores also point to gains in the lower half. As observed above, the college-bound SAT population is concentrated in the upper half of the distribution. It turns out, however, that there are SAT data covering just about the entire high school population (and not only those going on to college).

These data are not well known and are seldom invoked in the wrangling over SATs. They are based on "national norms studies," conducted every seven or eight years by the Educational Testing Service.[18] The students in this case are high school juniors taking an exam called the Preliminary Scholastic Aptitude Test (PSAT). Results of these tests can be adjusted to derive an estimate of what the testees would have scored in the standard SAT. In effect, the adjusted PSAT data give us a reading on the test that applies to the entire high school population. (Well, almost entire: the tests are, of course, not taken by students who drop out before their junior year.)

The results are instructive. They show that while SAT scores of the college-bound students have slipped and never fully recovered, scores for high school kids as a whole have held up well. Summarizing the data, Murray and Herrnstein tell us: "Conservatively, high school students *as a whole* seem to be as well prepared in math and verbal skills as they were at the beginning of the sixties.

They may be better prepared than they have ever been."[19]

If the students at the top have been slipping but students overall are doing as well as ever (or better than ever), it stands to reason that students at the bottom have made real gains. This is evidently what is happening: a broad convergence toward the middle by students at each end of the distribution. Murray and Herrnstein call the process "mediocritization." While they are, of course, looking at a smaller universe and narrower time frame than Richard Lynn has been describing—Lynn's hypothesis refers essentially to the entire developed world over the past five decades—their presentation seems basically consistent with his.

Richard Herrnstein of Harvard says his own hunch is that the rising IQ scores may be a onetime gain, concentrated in the lower half of the IQ distribution and reflecting (a) mass education in developed countries and (b) the emergence of a much more pervasive media. The idea is that because of a and b, children today get far more intellectual stimulation than they would have received earlier in this century, but not the kind of stimulation that translates into higher-level reasoning abilities (which, remember, the NAEP studies find to be in decline).

Taking Lynn and Murray-Herrnstein together, we get a resolution of the anomalies that does not exactly constitute good news about the direction of intelligence. It would have been nice to believe that the slowly rising tide of IQ scores truly signified a "smarter society." The reality seems to be much less wonderful—a society in which IQs are becoming less variable, more clustered around the mean. It is certainly good news that the lower half of the IQ distribution is doing better; it is just as certainly bad news that the gains were partly offset by slippage at the top.

At first blush, that might suggest society as a whole is breaking even on this deal, but this may not be the case at all. Society may be worse off on balance. The contributions

made by the best and the brightest are incalculably important. Slippage at the top will have rub-off effects on science
and the arts and the general level of intellectual discourse.
For educated Americans, at least, "mediocritization" might
mean a much less interesting life.

14

Thinking About Eugenics

It is hard to believe, nowadays, that eugenics was once a "progressive" cause. The term itself, coined by Francis Galton in 1883, refers to systematic efforts to improve national well-being by encouraging people with the most desirable traits—which would, of course, include intelligence—to have the most children. This seemed an obviously sensible idea to Galton, who was committed to hereditarian principles. In the early years of this century, government action to advance eugenic programs was urged by numerous eminent thinkers identified as humane and high-minded. In Great Britain, they included Karl Pearson, a socialist and disciple of Galton's. (He was also an outstanding mathematician who did much to develop the correlation coefficient.) Other prominent eugenicists included Sidney and Beatrice Webb, H. G. Wells, and George Bernard Shaw. An authentic Amercian hero, Supreme Court Justice Oliver Wendell Holmes urged eugenic principles in one of his best-known opinions.

At the turn of the twentieth century, the eugenics movement was unapologetic about its program. Pearson proposed "the sterilization of failures."[1] Wells wrote a utopian novel, *Anticipations,* whose purpose, as lyrically characterized by Beatrice Webb, was "to favor the procreation of what is fine and efficient and beautiful in humanity— beautiful and strong bodies, clear and powerful minds, and a growing body of knowledge—and to check the procreation of base and servile types, of fear-driven and cowardly souls, of all that is mean and ugly and bestial in the souls, bodies, or habits of men."[2] In the preface to his *Man and Superman,* Shaw registered concern about democracy's survival in a world whose voters were a "swinish multitude" (a phrase he borrowed from Edmund Burke).[3] The "superman" of his title was to be the product of eugenics, and he would make possible an enlightened democracy. In *The Revolutionist's Handbook,* printed as a supplement to *Man and Superman,* Shaw speculated that it might be a good idea to improve the breed in Britain via a State Department of Evolution, with a seat in the cabinet. The department would "provide inducements to private persons to achieve successful results,"[4] with "success" measured, of course, by the number of intelligent and healthy babies produced. It was all very clear and logical, and eugenics was widely identified as a major theme in progressive politics.

Times have changed. Today the name most commonly associated with eugenics is Adolf Hitler, and any effort to address the concerns of the eugenics movement is guaranteed to face a barrage of cheap shots featuring references to the Nazis. Doubtless because the term evokes such instant hostility, the American Eugenics Society in 1972 changed its name to the Society for the Study of Social Biology, a mouthful that would seem to effectively camouflage the organization's purpose.[5] If you want to find a political figure in modern times who has openly espoused eugenic principles, you would have to go to Singapore. In 1983, Prime Minister Lee Kuan Yew bemoaned the relative infertility of the highly educated classes, warning that "levels of competence will decline, our economy will falter, our administration will suffer, and the society will decline...."[6] Lee is no longer prime minister, but the administration of his successor, Goh Chok Tong, continues to take eugenic principles seriously. Singapore does not have Shaw's State Department of Evolution, but it has a near equivalent—a Ministry of Finance with a dating and marriage-encouragement service. It is available to all single college graduates over twenty-one.[7]

Justice Holmes, an American intellectual hero who has been lionized in just about every other context, is invariably pilloried for his eugenic views. These surfaced most famously in a 1927 Supreme Court decision (*Buck v. Bell*) he wrote upholding the right of the state of Virginia to sterilize individuals with very low IQs. Said the opinion: "It is better for all the world, if instead of waiting to execute degenerate offspring for crime, or to let them starve for imbecility, society can prevent those who are manifestly unfit from continuing their kind. The principle that sustains vaccination is broad enough to cover cutting the Fallopian tubes...." The passage then ends with a line that has been quoted against Holmes for decades: "Three generations of imbeciles are enough." Not helping the great jurist's reputation, it has been reported that some of the Nazi defendants at Nuremberg cited this opinion in attempting to justify their own racial sterilization programs.[8]

Despite its problematic public relations, the eugenics movement has some stubborn facts and considerable logic going for it. On a purely logical level, it is a more formidable case today than it was in its turn-of-the-century heyday. The case for eugenics can be summarized about as follows: We know far more than Wells and Shaw did about the role of genetic factors in mental-ability differences. We know, by several different indicators, that people with high IQs tend to be superior citizens. As children, they are above-average students in school. As workers, later in life, they tend to be above average in productiveness. If they enter the armed forces, they tend to be above-average recruits. Their careers tend to feature above-average incomes, they apparently live longer (as evidenced by the Terman Gifted Group), and there is abundant evidence that they have happier lives. So in principle, we can assume that the America of 2050 would be a better place to live if, between now and then, the high-IQ population had more kids than the low-IQ population.

We also know that this is not what usually happens in advanced industrial societies. The basic rule among demographers is that industrialization first brings a decline in mortality rates, then a decline in birthrates. But something else happens during this "demographic transition." Before industrialization, the highest-status women have the highest birthrates. After industrialization, high-status women suddenly turn out to have the *lowest* birthrates. The rule in advanced societies continues to be that the rich get richer and the poor get children. An interesting exception to this rule will be noted below.

These demographic effects are, of course, undesirable from a eugenic point of view. Note that they would be undesirable even if, as Richard Lynn and some other scholars believe (see the previous chapter), average IQ is in a long secular rise. Lynn's data leave you thinking that even if he is right, the rise in IQ is concentrated mainly in the low end of the distribution—that is, the higher average levels would reflect fewer problems at the bottom rather than substantial gains at the top. At any average level of IQ, however, we would presumably want as many supersmart and creative people as we can get. To be sure, the eugenic case would seem even more compelling if it turns out, as other scholars believe, that average IQ is actually falling.

Whatever the long-term trend, it is possible right now to point to government policies that are in several respects *dysgenic,* that is, they have the effect of increasing the pro-

portion of births chalked up by the low-scoring population. This is not to argue that dysgenic policies are
wrongheaded in every case—only to suggest that their putative benefits should be seen as tradeoffs against the costs
associated with lower IQs. Among the more obviously dysgenic policies now in place:

• Restrictions on abortion at both the state and federal
levels are almost certainly dysgenic in effect. Middle-class
women of ordinary intelligence generally have no trouble
terminating unwanted pregnancies in the United States today. Today and in the foreseeable future, it is mainly the
poor and ignorant who end up having unwanted children.
• The federal program of Aid to Families with Dependent Children and other welfare measures are massively
dysgenic. They encourage low-income women who have no
husbands and no means of support—an overwhelmingly
low-IQ population—to nevertheless have children.
• Affirmative-action programs for professional
women would seem to be dysgenic. When the U.S. Department of Labor encourages federal contractors (a category
including just about every large company and university in
the land) to increase the proportion of women in top jobs,
it is presumably also encouraging highly educated married
women to invest more heavily in their careers and less
heavily in raising families. It is hard to quantify the effect
of such policies—which are not, of course, the only reason
for educated women being in the work force—but instructive to contrast the United States and Japan in this regard.

Japan, it happens, is the big exception to the rules
above about the workings of the demographic transition.
In unliberated Japan, the rich, too, beget children. High-
status women in this superindustrialized country have just
as many kids as poor women. R. J. Herrnstein of Harvard
put the case this way several years ago: "The Japanese population has a higher average IQ than the American. In pub-

lic discussion, this IQ differential is usually attributed to the superiority of Japanese schools, but...the superior IQ scores of the Japanese population may be to some extent yet another consequence of the demographic transition, which...has had less of a differential effect in Japan than it has had here."[9]

Anyone brooding over the examples above of dysgenic policy should have no trouble figuring out why eugenic arguments would instantly be in trouble in the political arena. Their main and obvious problem: Eugenic principles would tend disproportionately to reduce births among low-income minority-group members and increase births among middle-class whites. In a world where organizations like Planned Parenthood are already being accused of "genocide" for helping blacks obtain abortions,[10] it is hard to envision many congressmen identifying themselves with legislation that would have a disparate impact on black births.

Some years back, the late William Shockley, a Nobel laureate in physics (for his work in developing the transistor) and a knowledgeable participant in IQ-related debates, proposed a much-publicized scheme to further eugenic principles. It was centered on a "voluntary sterilization bonus plan," in which government would pay low-IQ individuals to accept sterility. The payment would be $1,000 for each IQ point below 100. (There would also be sterilization payments to victims of such genetically transmitted diseases as sickle-cell anemia and hemophilia.) So far as I can ascertain, not a single politician ever spoke kindly of the proposal, and it was routinely denounced and ridiculed in the press. Although Shockley's proposed program was voluntary, it was widely compared to Nazi sterilization of "inferior races." The *Atlanta Constitution* ran an article stating that "the Shockley program was tried out in Germany during World War II." Shockley sued the paper for libel. He won the case at trial, but the jury awarded him only one dollar in damages.[11]

In part because of the way Shockley promoted it—he had a genius for negative public relations and often seemed more interested in provocation than persuasion—the sterilization program never had a chance. In any case, it also had some large intrinsic problems. In some measure, it was offensive precisely because it *was* voluntary and would therfore have required participants to humiliate themselves by declaring their own "dumbness" in order to collect.

A program that seems to make more sense but is more modest in its objectives is based on the Repository for Germinal Choice (RGC), an institution established in 1963 and heavily influenced by the ideas of Hermann J. Muller, an eminent geneticist and also a Nobel laureate. Muller had an extraordinary history. A committed Marxist, he had left a position at the University of Texas, moved to Soviet Russia, and become first a leading figure in Soviet genetics and then a suspect when Stalin began his campaign against hereditarian principles (see chapter 7). He prudently fled to the West at this point and set up the RGC together with a scientist named Robert K. Graham, the developer of the modern hard-resin spectacle lens.[12]

The RGC, operational since 1980, is a resource for husband-wife families in which the husband is sterile. It stores germinal material under liquid nitrogen and offers prospective users detailed information about the traits (but not the names) of the donors, who are screened to ensure they have no genetic defects. Many of the donors were distinguished scientists, and a few (including Shockley) were Nobel laureates. As of mid-1992, more than 150 children have been born to the families using the service, and more than 100 have the genes of distinguished scientists. All the kids are said to be bright and healthy.[13] The program seems positive in every respect, but its modest size and special purpose leave it not exactly looking like a national eugenics program.

Is there any expectation at all for the emergence of eugenic trends in the United States? It is hard to see much hope for programs coming out of the political process. It is possible, however, to envision profound eugenic effects flowing from some new technologies that may one day enable individuals all along the IQ spectrum to produce more intelligent children.

It is clear, at least, that such *possibilities* will expand enormously if the Human Genome Project pays off as it is widely expected to. The project, in which the U.S. government is investing some $3 billion (over fifteen years), represents an effort to identify and locate every gene in the human system. One early payoff from the project, almost certainly, will be the development of new genetic tests enabling parents to know the risks of their transmitting certain diseases to their children—cystic fibrosis, for example.

But eventually the project will have mapped some significant number of the genes bearing on intelligence. An absorbing article by Robert Wright in the *New Republic*[14] zeroes in on the implications of such breakthroughs and comments that they give us "the capacity for homemade eugenics: individual families deciding what kinds of kids they want to have." Why, after all, should families use this knowledge merely to avoid diseases like Down's syndrome? Why not also avoid "unexceptional intelligence"?

Which, soon enough, may be avoidable. Wright serves up a number of intriguing scenarios of families wrestling with the new capabilities. Mothers will be able to boost their production of eggs significantly (with the help of hormones). It is already possible to perform DNA analyses of eggs fertilized in vitro, and in the not too distant future individual cells from selected eggs can be tested to see whether they contain genes bearing on (among other things) intelligence. Each cell tested can be viewed as a "preembryo," which may or may not be replaced in one of the eggs.

Wright asks you to imagine this situation:

> Six preembryos await insertion in the uterus. The doctor explains that one of them carries Down's syndrome, and would probably give the child an IQ in the range of 40 to 70. The parents choose to discard it. And just out of curiosity, they ask, is there anything the doctor can say about the other children? Well, yes: assuming the child would live in a moderately rich educational environment, baby A's IQ has a 90 percent chance of falling in the 80–100 (below average but normal) range; baby B's 90 percent range is 90–110 (average); baby C's 95–115; baby D: 110–130; baby E: 120–140. Well, um, doctor, as long as we're being selective, could we toss out A and B, too?

The scenario is all too plausible (although I found myself wondering why the parents stopped at B), as are a number of others posed by genetic research. Nobody knows how the scenarios will ultimately play out. It may well be that the right of parents to make such choices will itself get to be a political issue. But it does at least seem possible that the political failures of the eugenics movement will be followed by a kind of invisible, unorganized triumph off in the private sector.

15

The Case for Testing

The case for IQ testing is simple, straightforward, and unpopular. It rests on the well-established proposition that in many different situations, decision makers can make better judgments if they have test data to help them. In the American school system, still the principal consumer of formal IQ tests, testing makes it easier to identify underachievers, to ascertain who needs remedial treatment, to decide who gets to skip a grade. In other contexts, quasi-IQ tests like the Scholastic Aptitude Tests (SATs), the Labor Department's General Aptitude Test Battery, and the Armed Services' Vocational Aptitude Battery help decision makers decide which candidates represent the best bets and which should be turned away. Listening to some of the expressed concerns about IQ tests creating classes of winners and losers in America, you could get the impression that the tests are given mainly to decide who ends up with bragging rights in the intelligence derby. In fact, the tests are given because a lot of different decision makers find them useful.

IQ research, an exercise centered on analysis of the test scores, is even less popular than testing itself. The case for performing this research begins with the fact that the research data have always been fascinating. The infinity of correlations extracted from these data have enormous explanatory power. As observed along the way in this volume, they help us understand why some people get ahead and others do not. They help us understand the nature of race, sex, and age differences in thinking. They illuminate the powerful tug of the genes on individual differences in intelligence. They leave us thinking that to an extraordinary extent, the occupational hierarchy in the United States is an IQ hierarchy. They demonstrate the connection between mental ability and productiveness, especially but not only in the "brainpower jobs" like computer programming; the data also make it plain that even in low-level jobs, general intelligence is positively correlated with performance.

To be sure, the data also remind us of the limits of IQ's predictive powers. None of those correlations are close to 1.0. The .50 correlation between IQ and income, for example, tells us that smart people start out with an edge in life but are a long way from being guaranteed winners. Your high IQ can be more than offset by your laziness, bad luck, ill health, or abrasive personality. Squaring that .50 correlation and converting it into a "coefficient of determination" (see the note on statistics at the beginning of this book), we learn that only about 25 percent of the variability in income is traceable to IQ differences. Still, a casino with a 25 percent edge at the gaming tables would regularly take its patrons (assuming it had any) to the cleaners; and the squared correlation is large enough to guarantee that high-IQ people will be enormously overrepresented among the affluent.

We have seen that IQ testing and research are unpopular for several reasons but that the heart of the matter is the profound American commitment to the ideal of equality. The tests insistently remind us that people are not equal— at least not in mental ability. On several different grounds, many Americans seem profoundly fearful of such reminders, especially when inequalities are spotted among racial groups. A curious feature of the current push for multicultural awareness on college campuses, with its attendant celebration of "diversity," is the refusal of the celebrators to acknowledge that there might actually be some diversity in mental abilities. Prof. Linda Gottfredson of the University of Delaware, a prominent figure in the IQ debate, was assailed by university officials in the late eighties for having accepted grants from the Pioneer Fund, a New York-based foundation. The problem, according to Andrew B. Kirkpatrick, Jr., chairman of the university's board of trustees, was that this foundation had sponsored research with racial implications. Kirkpatrick said that the university wished to "enhance the racial and cultural diversity of faculty, staff, and students" and that its efforts to do so would be "hampered" if its scholars accepted grants from foundations identified with the idea of group differences.[1] In the name of diversity, it seems, you are not allowed to discuss racial differences.

In a rational world, American educators would be paying a lot of attention to IQ research. The version of intelligence measured by IQ tests is something close to being synonymous with "learning ability." (When the Snyderman-Rothman scholars were asked to identify the most important elements of intelligence, 96 percent named "capacity to acquire knowledge."[2]) Since Americans have been chronically unhappy with what their children learn in school, you would think that they would want to know a lot more about the link between IQ and education. The link is a much-studied subject, with obvious implications for educational policy. The central question raised by the studies is:

What kinds of teaching are best for students at different IQ levels? You would think that the giant research bureaucracy in the U.S. Department of Education would be evidencing a continuing interest in such questions. Instead it has fled from them. Several years ago, I contacted a helpful assistant to the secretary (then William Bennett) and asked what data the department had on the relationship between IQ and academic achievement. He wrote back telling me that the answer was essentially none. He added: "Insofar as intelligence is considered a fixed limit on achievement, it may not be viewed as a high priority study," a statement I translate to mean that the department does not wish to have formal knowledge of data suggesting some students have limits.[3]

How can this be? One can only assume that the broad unpopularity of IQ research has made it impossible for the department's political leadership to focus on it.

Research on differences in mental ability is feared for another reason: the putative link between equal ability and equal rights. You sometimes hear formulations implying that the equal rights constitutionally guaranteed to Americans are somehow dependent on a consensus judgment that all people (and all ethnic groups) are truly equal in ability. Statements of this belief are often accompanied by professed concerns about democratic America lapsing into totalitarian modes of thought. Hitler stigmatized non-Aryans as inferior, then proceeded to deprive them of all human rights, and therefore—the argument goes—it is pernicious even to take note of group differences in ability.

That argument itself is pernicious. It is absurd to equate an individual's or group's below-average test scores with "inferiority." I know of no scholars involved in research on group differences who would put forward any such inhumane formulation, publicly or privately; it is only *critics* of the research who keep trying to make that equation, presumably in the hope that they are thereby helping to suppress discussion of IQ differentials.

In addition to being pernicious, the argument rests on a stunning non sequitur. Equality of rights in the United States does not depend on a belief in equal ability. Whatever Jefferson did or did not believe about all men literally being created equal, the equal protection guaranteed by the Fourteenth Amendment to the Constitution was put in place in order to protect a population—the newly liberated slaves—that was widely understood to be illiterate and uneducated.

Even if equal rights had come into the Constitution by some other route, it would be a bad idea to link the idea of equal protection to the idea of equal abilities, for reasons stated forcefully by Nobel laureate F. A. Hayek in *The Constitution of Liberty.* "Nothing...is more damaging to the demand for equal treatment," Hayek wrote, "than to base it on so obviously untrue an assumption as that of the factual equality of all men." He added:

> To rest the case for equal treatment of national or racial minorities on the assertion that they do not differ from other men is implicitly to admit that factual inequality would justify unequal treatment; and the proof that some differences do, in fact, exist would not be long in forthcoming. It is of the essence of the demand for equality before the law that people should be treated alike in spite of the fact that they are different.[4]

Some egalitarian Americans have another, quite different reason for disliking the data generated by IQ research. Their problem is that they *want* to treat people differently. They quite reasonably identify the below-par social and economic performance of American minorities as a corrosive social problem. But their explanation of the problem begins and ends with discrimination, and their solution centers on affirmative action. They are inflexibly uninterested in the message that much, perhaps most, of that subpar performance is predicted by minorities' subpar IQ scores.

One extraordinary example of resistance to this message occurs in a volume called *A Common Destiny: Blacks and American Society,* produced by a distinguished panel of scholars for the National Research Council (an arm of the American Academy of Sciences). The volume is more than six hundred pages long. It has brought together an avalanche of valuable data on the culture, education, housing, health, and economic performance of American blacks and concludes, not surprisingly, that "by almost all the ...indicators, blacks remain substanially behind whites."[5] But in explaining this lag, the scholars never get beyond discrimination. Reviewing the book in the *Public Interest,* R. J. Herrnstein of Harvard found astonishing the authors' unwillingness to look further, the more so in that other National Research Council studies had identified "tested aptitude" as a major factor in material success. Said Herrnstein: "No individual trait predicts as much about one's personal destiny in America as test scores. Given the hypothetical choice of being black with an IQ of 120 or white with an IQ of 80, one should choose the former to get ahead in America now or in the readily visible future."[6] How could this enormous project have gone forward over a span of more than five years without evidencing any interest in the IQ data? You have to tell yourself that psychological resistance to the data must have been overpowering.

Egalitarian pressures guarantee that tests of mental ability travel a rocky road in the United States these days. The tests tend to generate lawsuits on behalf of groups that score low, and the suits have often prevailed. Herewith three reports from the war on testing:

• In the California public-school system, it was until recently impermissible to give IQ tests to black children.

Other children could be tested, but not blacks. This astonishing arrangement resulted from a class-action lawsuit tried in 1977–78. The suit complained that IQ testing resulted in disproportionate numbers of black children being placed in EMR classes (for the "educable mentally retarded") and that the placements stigmatized the kids and deprived them of equal educational opportunity. The state responded that (a) the tests were unbiased and (b) the EMR classes were helping children who needed help. But Federal District Judge Robert F. Peckham found for the plaintiffs. He ordered that IQ tests no longer be administered to black children for any reason—*even if the parents requested the tests.*[7]

In September 1992, Judge Peckham relented in part, in response to a lawsuit brought by black parents who wanted their kids tested. His modified ruling said they could be tested provided that test results were never used to place the children in EMR classes or their equivalent.

• In New York State, the legislature decreed in 1987 that SAT scores could no longer be the sole basis for awarding state scholarship prizes. The new arrangement required that high school grades be used along with SATs. The legislature imposed this requirement in the wake of a lawsuit complaining that the SAT must be biased because men had been outscoring women—by something like 60 points for the verbal-and-math tests combined. The suit was brought by a coalition of feminist and antitesting activists whose cause was taken up by the legislature.[8]

Neither the judge who heard the suit nor the legislators who passed the law had a theory to explain how bias was translating into a 60-point gap. Both basically ignored the explanation provided by the College Board, which administers the SAT. The Board's explanation: Women's scores were lower on average than those for men not because the test was biased but because the women taking it were more likely than men to come from minority and low-

SES families.[9] When you adjust for socioeconomic status, the verbal gap disappears, and the math gap shrinks to 20 or 25 points.

To be sure, that leaves us still looking at a small gap. Does it mean that the SATs are just a little bit biased? A more likely interpretation of the SES-adjusted figures is that they represent the interaction of two research findings already cited in these pages. Finding number 1: At any given level of IQ, women will do better at verbal tests, men better at quantitative tests. Finding number 2: With more variable IQs, men are overrepresented at the extremes of the distribution curve. In an above-average group like the teenagers taking the SATs, you would expect men to be overrepresented at the top. (They would also be overrepresented in any group of teenage retardates.) So they overcome the male disadvantage on the verbal tests and hang on easily to their edge at math.

You will possibly not be surprised to learn that no pressure groups in New York have been pushing this analysis of SAT tests. The field has been swept by those screaming "bias."

• Throughout the United States, state employment services have been increasingly restricted in their efforts to send over the best workers when employers call for help. In deciding who is best qualified, the state services used to rely primarily on a test supplied by the U.S. Employment Service (USES): the General Aptitude Test Battery (GATB). The test, heavily g loaded, predicts job performance with a high level of accuracy (as noted in chapter 11). In the 1970s, the tests came under increasing criticism because blacks on average scored lower than Hispanics and Hispanics scored lower than whites; these disparities triggered claims of test bias and threats of litigation. Eager to preserve testing but leery of going into court, the USES agreed in 1981 to a compromise: It would instruct the state agencies to provide separate rankings for black and white workers. Each race would have its own set of scores and percentile rankings.[10]

In the spring of 1990, an anonymous government official mailed off the racial conversion tables to Robert Holland, associate editor of the *Richmond Times-Dispatch,* and he hastened to publish examples of how they worked.[11] Suppose, for example, that a white worker, a Hispanic worker, and a black worker took the test for a toolmaker's job. Suppose that all three had a raw score on the test of 300. In that case, the black job candidate would be placed in the seventy-ninth percentile, the Hispanic, in the sixty-second percentile, and the white toolmaker, in the thirty-ninth percentile. Needless to say, the black worker would get the job interview; indeed, he would have gotten it with a raw score well under 300. The "race-norming" arrangement guaranteed that black, Hispanic, and white job applicants would each get the same proportionate number of referrals. It did not, of course, guarantee that the employer would get the best applicants.

Race-norming was outlawed by the Civil Rights Act of 1991. But instead of returning to a system of simply referring applicants with the highest GATB scores, USES has announced plans to come up with a new test.

Stories like these could be multiplied endlessly. I take it that multiplication would be superfluous, as all three stories echo themes that will look familiar to any casual reader of the daily papers. The three situations described above have several things in common.

First, all involve massive, ideologically driven denials of reality. Rejecting the possibility that groups might actually differ in mental ability, all three of the stories depict a society detemined to prove that test-score differences can only reflect test bias.

These denials impose substantial costs on society—also on a certain number of identifiable individuals. One victim who first surfaced in 1987 was Mary Amaya, a mother in California, who was bothered by her son's educational progress and became infuriated upon being told that he could not be tested because he was black. Thousands of other unnamed and unknown children have also been hurt by the California ban on testing. The results of the ban were described by Rogers Elliott, a Dartmouth-based lawyer and psychologist who wrote a book (*Litigating Intelligence*) that dealt at length with the California suit. Writing in 1987, Elliott observed: "Many, perhaps half, of all children removed from EMR classes in California have been placed in regular classrooms—which means that they have been returned to the environments in which they had failed in the first place.... Since the early 1970s, thousands of children have never been placed in EMR who would have been so placed before that time."[12] It is hard to believe those kids are better off.

The Amaya story continued to make headlines early in this decade. When Mary Amaya demanded that her son be tested, she was told that this was impossible so long as he was considered to be black. State education officials proposed blandly that Mrs. Amaya, who is of Mexican descent, identify the child as Hispanic, which would make it legal for him to take an IQ test. She turned down this proposal, saying she did not want the boy to be in the position of repudiating his black father, and along with other black parents brought suit against the state for the right of their children to take IQ tests.

It was this suit that led to Judge Peckham's retreat in September 1992. But even after his new ruling, it is unclear whether IQ tests have a future in California schools. The state's education commissioner has been unrelentingly hostile to the tests, and they are now banned in the Los Angeles and San Francisco school districts.[13] It is hard to believe the state's kids will be better off as a result.

Nor is it credible that the campaign against GATB is helping American competitiveness or supporting the "search for excellence" in American business. Nobody knows how to figure the cost of the campaign, but one message built into it is that excellence is not, after all, a top priority.

It is hard to think of benefits that offset these costs. When testing is eliminated, you do not ordinarily eliminate the need to make distinctions among people—poorly performing students who might need remedial help, SAT scholarship prospects, or machinists hoping to catch on at General Electric. The first effect of eliminating formal tests is to replace them with informal or less precise or egregiously prejudiced arrangements: job interviews, for example, or teacher grades. Can anybody really anticipate that New York State has eliminated prejudice with its new criteria for determining who will win the valuable (up to $10,000) and prestigious Empire State scholarships? A guaranteed result of bringing school grades into the equation and downgrading the role of SAT scores is pressure on teachers to inflate the grades of the SAT test takers.[14]

After two decades of massive affirmative-action programs in government and just about all large corporations, many Americans find it hard even to imagine any sizable organization not committed to racial preference. It happens, however, that one extremely large and quite prominent organization does well without it; furthermore, minorities do very well in the organization—the U.S. military. For many years the armed services have been more than 20 percent black.[15]

The military has been described as a "radical meritocracy."[16] Anyone wishing to enlist in the armed services must first take the vocational aptitude test battery, several sections of which function as an IQ test equivalent. By law, the services are required to screen out prospects in the lowest 10 percent of testees, roughly those below IQ 80. Individuals accepted as recruits instantly find themselves in a regime where only "merit" matters. Said Charles Moskos in an article in the *New Republic*: "Basic training is the leveling experience par excellence. The mandatory short haircuts, the common uniform, the rigors of eight weeks of infantry training, all help to reduce pre-existing civilian advantage. For many youths from impoverished backgrounds, successful completion of basic training is the first occasion on which they can outshine those coming from privileged backgrounds."[17] The armed services offer the spectacle, all too rare in American life, of blacks exercising authority over whites without generating resistance and resentment—because everybody knows the authority was earned.

It is a regime entirely without discrimination and almost entirely without reverse discrimination. (The "almost" in that sentence refers to the fact that women and minority-group members seem to get preference for promotions in situations where the distinction between candidates is effectively too close to call.) White recruits are more likely to end up in highly technical fields; black recruits are more likely to end up in clerical work or the supply services.[18] But thousands of blacks—beginning with the 7,500 or so commissioned officers and the 80,000-odd noncoms—have found that the armed services offer opportunities superior to those available in the civilian economy. And not only in conventional career terms. As Moskos observed in the *New Republic,* the army is integrated in ways that Harvard cannot begin to emulate. Visiting an army dining facility, he was struck by "the easy mixing of races" and noted: "Black and white soldiers eat together in seemingly random fashion. The bantering that goes on across the tables seems to have no particular racial direction. What a contrast with the self-imposed segregation found in most college dining halls today."[19]

IQ tests represent a constant challenge to egalitarian social policies. Where the policies assume equal ability, the tests play the role of hated whistle-blowers.

This is notoriously true where IQ tests confront affirmative action. One of affirmative action's sustaining ideas is the proposition that minority "underrepresentation" in the labor force, and especially in the better, higher-paying jobs, is an expression of irrational bias. This idea is instantly in trouble when confronted with IQ test data, which insistently remind you (a) of lower average scores for minorities and (b) the link between test scores and job performance. It is an understatement to say that black-white IQ studies have "policy implications." A more reasonable formulation would be that the studies represent a profound and insistent challenge to affirmative action.

What of the argument that group-ability differences should not be studied or discussed—that public parading of the differences can be traumatic to low-scoring groups? The argument seems never to be accompanied by evidence of trauma. But even if such evidence were producible, I do not see how we could (a) systematically suppress evidence of group differences while (b) systematically implementing policies of group preference. My own view is that the preferential policies make the studies not only inescapable but far more sensitive than they would otherwise be. If our public policy demanded not preference but the treatment of blacks as individuals—in employment, college admissions, and everything else—then the relevance of the group data would be instantly undermined.

It is worth recalling that many well-known group differences are not at all sensitive. Poor whites, for example, score appreciably lower than middle-class whites. I have never heard anybody argue that this detail should be suppressed as too painful for the poor. But if public policy were suddenly to require employment and educational preferences for the poor—and to construe their low rates of progress as evidence of continuing bias—then the group's average performance would be a contentious and inescapable issue.

One major message of the IQ data is that groups are different. A major policy implication of the data, I would argue, is that people should not be treated as members of groups but as individuals.

Notes

STATISTICS AND THE IQ DEBATE: A HANDHOLD FOR THE DAUNTED

1. Jensen, *Bias in Mental Testing*, 319. The numerous studies relating IQ to school grades have left scholars looking at a fairly wide range of estimates, and the correlations mentioned are midpoints of ranges (.60 to .70 and .50 to .60) cited by Jensen.

2. Cohn, Cohn, and Jensen, "Myopia and Intelligence," 53–58. The article also cites a study of 2,527 California high school students in which those wearing correctional lenses for nearsightedness had IQs averaging eight points higher than those of the other students.

3. Jensen, *Straight Talk*, 90.

4. Ibid., 20.

5. Kiener and Keiper, "Some Correlates," 40–45.

6. Hartigan and Wignor, *Fairness in Employment Testing*, Table 7-2, 138. The correlation was extracted from test scores for 23,428 workers who took the Labor Department's General Aptitude Test Battery. The GATB has nine subtests, three of which (general intelligence, verbal aptitude, and numerical aptitude) are taken to be a composite measure of cognitive ability. Three other subtests (motor coordination, finger dexterity, and manual dexterity) are a composite measure of "psychomotor ability." It is these two composite measures that correlate .35.

1. WHAT IT'S LIKE TO TAKE AN IQ TEST

1. Jensen, "Speed of Information Processing," *Intelligence*, 266.
2. Aiken, *Assessment of Intellectual Functioning*, 126.
3. Matarazzo, *Wechsler's Measurement*, 236. The correlations vary some-what from one age group to another, but Information and Vocabu-lary are always at the top. In my own group (60 to 64), Information correlates .81 with full-scale IQ and Vocabulary correlates .79.

2. SEARCHING FOR INTELLIGENCE

1. Boring, "Intelligence," 35–37.
2. For an example of a scholar assailing Boring's concept of intelli-gence, see Peter H. Schönemann's essay in Mogdil and Mogdil, *Consensus and Controversy*, 313–27.
3. Wechsler, *Selected Papers*, 32.
4. Wechsler, "Intelligence Defined," 135–39.
5. Gardner, *Frames of Mind*.
6. Sternberg, *Beyond IQ;* also see his "Beyond IQ Testing" in *National Forum*.
7. See Peters, *Practical Intelligence*, 11, for a statement of the "street smarts versus school smarts" case.
8. The survey itself was conducted in the fall of 1984.
9. Snyderman and Rothman, *The IQ Controversy*, 56.
10. Ibid., 58.
11. Johnson, *Intellectuals*, 202.
12. Aiken, *Assessment of Intellectual Functioning*, 141.
13. Herrnstein, *IQ in the Meritocracy*, 106.
14. Snyderman and Rothman, *The IQ Controversy*, 71.
15. See Jensen's article on Spearman in Sternberg (ed.), *Encyclopedia of Intelligence*, to be published in 1993.
16. Matarazzo, *Wechsler's Measurement*, 237.
17. See Jensen, *Straight Talk*, 60, for the failure rate on this question. The correlations are from a telephone conversation with Jensen.
18. For example, see Lynn, "Intelligence of the Mongoloids," which states (814), "The purest measure of Spearman's *g* consists of ab-stract reasoning tests. . . . "
19. The hierarchy is elaborated, and its relationship to factor analysis lucidly explained, in Jensen, *Bias in Mental Testing*, 185–258.
20. The Educational Testing Service, which designs the Scholastic Apti-tude Test, today declines to cite an IQ correlation, but Henry Chauncey, a former president of ETS, has been quoted (in Klit-gaard, *Choosing Elites*, 92) as stating that the SAT is essentially an intelligence test. A correlation of .80 between IQ and the GATB was reported by John Hawk, a scholar based at the U.S. Employment Service, in a telephone conversation. In 1989, I interviewed a test-ing specialist in the Department of Defense, who told me that DOD had made a point of not even trying to ascertain the correlation between IQ and the ASVAB. When I mentioned that I had heard it

was around .80, he laughed and said—not for attribution—"Yeah, that's about right."

21. Brand's correlates are tabulated in his essay, "The Importance of General Intelligence," in Mogdil and Mogdil, *Consensus and Controversy*, 251–65.

22. See Jensen, "The Effects of Inbreeding," in *Personality and Individual Differences*. Vol. 4 (1983), 71–87. Evidencing the strong heritability of *g*, the article cites data on "inbreeding depression"—the tendency of genetically related parents to produce children with subpar test scores. The scores reflect the degree of the parents' genetic similarity; for example, children of first-cousin marriages are apt to be further below par than children of second-cousin marriages. Jensen's data, based on the Wechsler Intelligence Scale for Children, show that the degree of inbreeding depression correlates positively and significantly with the *g* loadings of the WISC subtests.

3. How Much Do "Street Smarts" Matter?

1. Published by Cambridge University Press in 1986.

2. Sternberg and Wagner, *Practical Intelligence*, 85.

3. Ibid., 52.

4. Published by Harper & Row in 1987.

5. Sternberg and Wagner, *Practical Intelligence*, 237.

6. Ibid., 163–82.

7. Ibid., 13–30.

8. Ibid., 54.

9. Ibid., 31–50.

10. Ibid., 307.

11. Sternberg, *Intelligence Applied*, 303.

12. Peters, *Practical Intelligence*, 92.

13. For example, see Gilligan, *In a Different Voice*.

14. Sternberg and Wagner, *Practical Intelligence*, 364. Italics in the original.

15. Nickerson, *American Journal of Psychology*, 301.

16. Rimland, "A Search for Tests," 247.

17. Riggio, Messamer, and Throckmorton, "Social and Academic Intelligence," 695.

18. Personal communication.

19. Personal communication.

20. Jensen, "Understanding *g*."

4. The Roots of the Controversy

1. Jensen, *Bias in Mental Testing*, 173, notes that teachers' ratings of children's intelligence correlate .60 to .80 with IQ scores.

2. Gilbert, *Nuremberg Diary*, 31.

3. Hauser, *Muhammad Ali*, 143.

4. Reeves, *A Question of Character,* 42.
5. Morris, *Richard Milhous Nixon,* 91.
6. Mustain and Capeci, *Mob Star,* 60.
7. Wilson and Herrnstein, *Crime and Human Nature,* 154–56.
8. Jensen, *Straight Talk,* 249, cites a ratio of 1.2 to 1 above IQ 140, but some other estimates run much higher. Eysenck, *The Intelligence Controversy,* refers to a 37 percent male advantage above IQ 132.
9. Matarazzo, *Wechsler's Measurement,* 355, shows that on the WAIS Arithmetic subtest, men on average outscore women by 10.35 to 9.25, while on the Vocabulary subtest women on average outscore men by 10.02 to 9.65. These differences are trivial or nonexistent among children, but become pronounced after puberty.
10. Jensen, *Bias in Mental Testing,* 216, notes that the most *g*-loaded subtests are Information, Similarities, and Vocabulary.
11. Oakes et al., *Multiplying Inequalities,* 45.
12. *New York Times,* December 21, 1988, B8.
13. See, for example, the *Wall Street Journal* account of the Oakes study, April 23, 1990, B1.
14. Carnegie, *Turning Points.*
15. The best available account of tendentious media coverage of these issues appears in Snyderman and Rothman, *The IQ Controversy,* especially chapter 7, 203–48.
16. See, for example, the passage complaining about "those who wish to use tests for the maintenance of social ranks and distinctions." Gould, *Mismeasure,* 155.
17. The author is here stealing quotes from an article he wrote about the Gould book in *Fortune,* December 28, 1981, 37.
18. *New York Times,* July 17, 1972, 34.
19. The *Post* article is cited (but no date given) in Spitz, *The Raising of Intelligence,* 138.
20. Heber's downfall is described in ibid., 136.
21. Ibid.
22. Garber, *The Milwaukee Project.*
23. See Jensen, "Raising IQ Without Increasing *g*," for a review of the Garber book. The review ends with these words: "Garber's full-scale report of the Milwaukee Project is an impressive work, and he deserves much credit for seeing it through. It is neither his fault nor anyone else's fault that, unfortunately, the findings offer no assurance that such extraordinarily intensive and extensive environmental intervention comes even near to being either a feasible or an effective solution to the personal and social misfortunes to which the Project was addressed with high hopes in 1966."
24. Herrnstein, "IQ Testing and the Media," 68–74.
25. Snyderman and Rothman, *The IQ Controversy.*
26. Seligman, "Measuring Intelligence," 70–72.
27. Garraty and Gay, *The Columbia History of the World,* 126, 943.

28. Jensen, "Francis Galton," in *Encyclopedia of Intelligence*. The Jensen essay tells us *en passant* that Galton, who is repeatedly stated to have invented the "nature-nurture" dichotomy, was in fact anticipated by Shakespeare in *The Tempest* (Act IV, Scene i).

29. Ibid.

30. Fancher, *The Intelligence Men*, 69–70.

31. Ibid., 70–78, for the evolution of Binet's tests between 1905 and 1911.

32. Ibid., 98–104, for Stern's contributions.

33. Ibid., 132–40, for the road to the Stanford-Binet.

34. Ibid., 149–61, for Wechsler's contributions.

35. Ibid., 141–45. Fancher mentions that Terman seemed determined to disprove the folk wisdom of early twentieth-century America, which held that child prodigies generally came to bad ends, and to show— perhaps with himself as an example—that the reverse was true. The twelfth of fourteen children in an Indiana farm family, Terman had been an academic star as a child.

36. Figures are from Terman and Oden, *The Gifted at Mid-Life*, 3–5.

37. Ibid., 7.

38. Ibid., 7.

39. Ibid., 8.

40. Ibid.

41. Ibid., 11.

42. Ibid., 8. Their spectacles would appear to confirm the positive correlation (cited in our statistical note, p. xiv) between IQ and myopia.

43. Ibid., 29.

44. Ibid., 132.

45. Ibid., 133.

46. Ibid., 74.

47. Ibid., 85.

48. Ibid., 87.

49. Ibid., 88.

50. Ibid. Since 1971, it has been called *American Men and Women of Science*.

51. Ibid., 97.

52. Ibid., 93.

5. JENSENISM

1. Except where a written source is indicated, the biographical details and comments attributed to Jensen throughout this chapter are from the 1989 interview and numerous subsequent conversations.

2. It has since been reprinted in Jensen, *Genetics and Education*, and Select Committee, *Environment, Intelligence, and Scholastic Achievement*.

3. U.S. Commission, *Racial Isolation*, 138.

4. Jensen, *Genetics and Education,* 70.
5. Ibid., 136.
6. Haldane, "Heredity," 494.
7. Fifteen years after Jensen's essay appeared, the Snyderman-Rothman survey of scholars showed that on average they believed in a heritability of around 60 percent. See *The IQ Controversy,* 95.
8. Jensen, *Genetics and Education,* 163.
9. The essay concludes on this note: "[T]he ideal of equality of educational opportunity should not be interpreted as uniformity of facilities, instructional techniques, and educational aims for all children. Diversity . . . of approaches and aims would seem to be the key to making education rewarding for children of different patterns of ability. The reality of individual differences thus need not mean educational rewards for some children and frustration and defeat for others."
10. Personal communication from Jensen.
11. *Harvard Educational Review,* Vol. 39 (1969), No. 2. The comments, and Jensen's response, were reprinted in Select Committee, *Environment, Intelligence and Scholastic Achievement,* 589–707.
12. In Jensen's response, he cited articles in *U.S. News & World Report* (March 10, 1969), *Newsweek* (March 31, 1969), *Science News* (April 5, 1969), and *Time* (April 11, 1969) as among those suggesting the commentators markedly disagreed with the main points of his original article.
13. *Harvard Educational Review,* Vol. 39 (1969), No. 3.
14. The article, in the *New York Times Magazine* of August 31, 1969, was by science writer Lee Edson.
15. Jensen, *Genetics and Education,* 14.
16. Symonds and Jensen, *From Adolescent to Adult.*
17. Jensen, "What Is the Question? What Is the Evidence?" 207.
18. Eysenck, *The Scientific Study of Personality.*
19. Jensen describes his perplexities with these data, and their relation to his studies of Level I and Level II thinking, in "What Is the Question?" 222 ff.
20. Snyderman and Rothman, *The IQ Controversy,* 71.
21. Jensen, "Speed of Elementary Cognitive Processes," 66.
22. Jensen, *Bias in Mental Testing,* 709.
23. See Vernon, "Studying Intelligence the Hard Way," 391.
24. Terman, *The Gifted Group,* 58.

6. SLIPPING: HOW INTELLIGENCE DECLINES WITH AGE

1. See, for example, Matarazzo, *Wechsler's Measurement,* 57.
2. Wechsler, *Selected Papers,* 217.
3. Matarazzo, *Wechsler's Measurement,* 511.
4. Cited in Fancher, *The Intelligence Men,* 153.
5. Salthouse, *Theoretical Perspectives,* 51.

6. Ibid.

7. See Aiken, *Assessment of Intellectual Functioning,* 136–37, for charts depicting WAIS performance at different age levels.

8. Salthouse, *Theoretical Persepectives,* 43. The author reports one study showing a correlation of –.33 between age and scores on Following Directions.

9. Ibid., 261.

10. Jensen, "Why Is Reaction Time Correlated?" 7.

11. Salthouse, *Theoretical Perspectives,* 83.

12. Wechsler, *Selected Papers,* 215.

13. Matarazzo, *Wechsler's Measurement,* 354.

14. Ibid.

15. Salthouse, *Theoretical Perspectives,* 226, describes some of the difficulties in testing long-term memory.

16. Matarazzo, *Wechsler's Measurement,* 354.

17. See their essay in West and Sinnott, eds., *Everyday Memory and Aging,* 235.

18. Ibid.

19. Ibid., 240.

20. Matarazzo, *Wechsler's Measurement,* 322–24.

7. Behind Nature and Nurture

1. A common estimate is 100,000, but nobody knows the exact number of genes in the human system. Presumably the federally funded Human Genome Project, which as of early 1992 had identified about 3,000 genes, will ultimately supply an exact count.

2. Massive uncertainties envelope this issue. One also hears estimates as low as ten.

3. Wills, *Inventing America,* 207–17.

4. Smith, 15.

5. Tocqueville, *Democracy in America,* part I. Chapter 3.

6. Muller, "The Destruction of Science," 575–92.

7. Medvedev, "The Stalin Question," 45, notes that Lysenko was not repudiated until after Khrushchev's downfall in 1964.

8. The author, a student of Hook's, recalls his making this point more than once.

9. Herrnstein, *IQ in the Meritocracy,* 197–98.

10. Personal communication.

11. Wheeler, "A Comparative Study," *Journal of Educational Psychology.*

12. Scarr and McCartney, "How People Make Environments."

13. Bouchard and McGue, "Familial Studies," 1056.

14. Glees, *The Human Brain,* 1.

15. Willerman et al. "Brain Size and Intelligence," *Intelligence,* 223–28.

16. Lewontin, Rose, and Kamin. *Not in Our Genes,* ix–x.

17. Ibid., 145.

18. Snyderman and Rothman, *The IQ Controversy*, 95. The scholars estimated white heritability at .596, black heritability at .571.

19. Eysenck and Kamin, *The Intelligence Controversy*, 126.

20. Bouchard and McGue, "Familial Studies," 1056. The article is a summary of 111 different studies on familial resemblances in measured intelligence.

21. The logic underlying such formulas is elaborated at length in Jensen, *Straight Talk*, 98 ff.

22. Lykken, "Research With Twins," 361.

23. Eysenck and Kamin, *The Intelligence Controversy*, 127.

24. Cited by Eysenck in *The Intelligence Controversy*, 164.

25. See Lykken, "Research With Twins," 368. He mentions that "DZ twins are only about half as likely as MZ twins to volunteer as experimental subjects, and the DZs who do volunteer are probably more similar within pairs than are DZ twins in general."

26. Bouchard and McGue, "Familial Studies," 1056.

27. Jensen, *Straight Talk*, 175.

28. Bouchard and McGue, "Familial Studies," 1056.

29. See Farber, *Identical Twins*, 8, for an account of the three studies.

30. Bouchard and McGue, "Familial Studies," 1056.

31. See Thomas J. Bouchard, Jr.,"The Hereditarian Research Program," *Consensus and Controversy*, 58.

32. Snyderman and Rothman, *The IQ Controversy*, 93.

33. Bouchard et al., "Sources of Human Differences," 224.

34. Ibid., 225.

35. Ibid.

36. Ibid.

37. See Robert Plomin, "Genetics of Intelligence," in Mogdil and Mogdil, *Consensus and Controversy*, 48.

38. Bouchard and McGue, "Familial Studies," 1056.

39. The author is indebted to Robert A. Gordon, professor of sociology at Johns Hopkins University, for walking him through this calculation. Here, with no effort to explain the reasoning behind it, is how that SD is derived. First, you take the square root of the parent-child correlation, giving you .25. Next you subtract this figure from 1, giving you .75. Then you take the square root of this remainder, giving you .87, and multiply this figure by the population SD of 15—which leaves you with your own family SD of 13.

8. The View From Twin City

1. Bouchard et al., "Sources of Human Differences," 223.

2. See Bouchard and Segal, "Environment and IQ," 396–97, for a discussion of possible sources of the twin IQ deficit.

3. Goertzel, Goertzel, and Goertzel, *Three Hundred Eminent Personalities*, 327.

4. In "Twins Reunited," 59, Constance Holden quotes David T. Lykken of the Minnesota twin project as stating: "What is emerging in my mind is that the most important thing to come out of this study is a strong sense that vastly more of human behavior is genetically determined or influenced than we ever supposed."

5. In *The IQ Game*, H. F. Taylor argued that the twins' similarities were explained by similar backgrounds. Bouchard appears to have effectively demolished the argument in a rejoinder in *Intelligence*, Vol. 7 (1983), 175–84.

6. Bouchard, "Nature via Nurture," 9–10.

7. Bouchard et al., "Sources of Human Differences," 223.

8. Bouchard, "Nature via Nurture," 2.

9. His name was Robert Stovall and he said it in 1978.

10. Chen, "Twins Reared Apart," offers one of many detailed accounts of the "Jim twins."

11. This account of the procedure is taken from a project description (undated) published by the University of Minnesota Department of Psychology; the account was checked with the department early in 1992.

12. For details on Levey and Newman see the AP story of June 18, 1986: "Twins Learn of Each Other Through Firefighting."

13. See Holden, "Identical Twins Reared Apart," for one account of "the Nazi and the Jew."

14. See "Uncanny Twins," a feature story in the *Sunday Times* (of London) Weekly Review, May 25, 1980.

15. Ibid..

16. Lykken, "Research With Twins," 364.

17. Gilligan, *In a Different Voice*.

18. Lykken, "Research With Twins," 370.

19. The figures here are slightly different from those in Bouchard et al., "Sources of Human Differences," and are based on later data.

20. Bouchard, "Nature via Nurture," 7.

9. THE MYSTERY OF CYRIL BURT

1. Hearnshaw, *Cyril Burt, Psychologist*, 136, mentions a long list of Burt's graduate students and notes that many of them went on to hold influential positions in Britain and abroad.

2. Ibid., 227.

3. Ibid.

4. *New York Times*, January 30, 1979.

5. Hearnshaw, *Cyril Burt, Psychologist*, 146.

6. The extent of his contributions to factor analysis is one of the subsidiary themes of the Burt controversy. See Hearnshaw, 154–81, for an argument that Burt made significant contributions and yet was guilty of fraudulently claiming too large a role. See also Joynson, *The Burt Affair*, 103–29, for an argument that Burt's claims are at least plausible.

7. Hearnshaw, *Cyril Burt, Psychologist,* 135.
8. Jensen, *Psychometrika,* Vol. 37 (1972).
9. Hearnshaw, *Cyril Burt, Psychologist,* 235.
10. Fletcher, *Science, Ideology, and the Media,* 116.
11. Hearnshaw, *Cyril Burt, Psychologist,* vii.
12. Ibid., viii.
13. Ibid., 286.
14. Ibid., 240.
15. Hearnshaw, in Beloff, *A Balance Sheet,* 4.
16. Ibid.
17. Ibid.
18. Ibid., 7.
19. Fletcher, *Science, Ideology, and the Media,* 150–52.
20. Ibid., 173.
21. Joynson, *The Burt Affair,* 130–63.
22. Fletcher, *Science, Ideology, and the Media,* 98.
23. Ibid., 99.
24. Jensen, "IQ and Science," 103.
25. Fletcher, *Science, Ideology, and the Media,* 284.
26. Jensen, "IQ and Science," 103.
27. Ibid., 97.
28. Ibid., 105.
29. Press release issued by the British Psychological Society, February 24, 1992.

10. OF JAPANESE AND JEWS

1. Data from *International Financial Statistics, Yearbook, 1991,* published by the International Monetary Fund.
2. Kearns and Doyle, *Winning the Brain Race,* 58.
3. For more on the superiority of Japanese schools, see Lynn, *Educational Achievement in Japan.*
4. Lapointe, Mead, and Phillips. *A World of Differences,* 14.
5. Ibid., 36.
6. Stevenson, Lee, and Stigler, "Mathematics Achievement," 1986.
7. Personal communication from Lynn.
8. Lynn, "The Intelligence of the Chinese and Malays," 126.
9. Lynn, Hampson, and Lee, "The Intelligence of Chinese Children," 30.
10. Lynn, Pagliari, and Chan. "Intelligence in Hong Kong," 425.
11. Lynn, "The Intelligence of the Mongoloids." Our imprecision here reflects the fact that Lynn was testing different age groups within several different populations on several different tests.
12. The dispute centers on disagreements about whether intelligence levels generally have been rising in the developed world. Lynn believes that they have (see chapter 13) and therefore also believes that the East Asian test reports, based on later data, must be ad-

justed downward to make them comparable to data on Caucasian IQs.

13. Lynn, "The Intelligence of the Mongoloids," 814, states: "The intelligence of the Mongoloids differs from that of Caucasoids more in the pattern or profile of their abilities than in the overall IQ."
14. Ibid., 816.
15. Ibid.
16. Ibid., 817.
17. Ibid., 816.
18. Ibid., 818.
19. Ibid., 825–26.
20. Ibid., 834. Lynn observes that the Mongoloid-Caucasoid difference in visuospatial ability is about four times greater than the male-female difference.
21. Suggestive detail: Men typically outscore women by around 55 points on the math part of the U.S. Scholastic Aptitude Test, but Asian-American women score at about the same level as white men.
22. See Lynn, "The Intelligence of the Mongoloids," 832–34, for a statement of this evolutionary theory.
23. Rushton, "Reply to Willerman," 365–66.
24. Vining, "Mean IQ Differences," estimates the Japanese SD at 12.8 points.
25. The figures, calculated by the author, assume that IQs are normally distributed (a proposition generally accepted by scholars), that the U.S. population has a mean of 100 and a standard deviation of 15, and that the Japanese population has a mean of 103.5 and an SD of 12.8.
26. Norden, "Counting the Jews," 41. The article cites the 1990 National Jewish Population Survey, which estimated a Jewish population of 5.5 million, some 2.2 percent of the U.S. total. The criterion for inclusion was not religious affiliation but self-identification; about 20 percent of those who identify themselves as Jewish are not religious.
27. Shurkin, *Terman's Kids,* 39.
28. Silberman, *A Certain People,* 145.
29. Jencks et al., *Who Gets Ahead?* 79.
30. Weyl, *Geography of American Achievement,* 79–90.
31. Kamin, *Science and Politics,* 16.
32. Medawar, *Advice,* 25.
33. Gould, *The Mismeasure of Man,* 233.
34. Snyderman and Herrnstein, "Intelligence Tests," 987.
35. See Bachman, *Youth in Transition,* for the description of a project in which some 3,400 boys with different religious backgrounds were given the Ammons Quick Test ("a brief, individually administered test designed to measure general intelligence"). In Gordon and Rudert, "Bad News," the Quick Test data have been converted to the Stanford-Binet equivalent cited here.

36. Storfer, *Intelligence and Giftedness,* chapter 14, 313–33.
37. Ibid., 316.
38. Ibid., 317.
39. Ibid., 320.
40. Ibid., 317.
41. Ibid., 317–18.
42. Ibid., 315.
43. I am indebted to Robert A. Gordon, professor of sociology at Johns Hopkins, for helping me to think about the paradox of Jewish non-visualizers performing well in math.
44. Storfer, *Intelligence and Giftedness,* 329.
45. See *American Demographics,* March 1992, 18, for a report entitled "Hispanic Affluence Has a Cuban Accent."
46. The argument is crisply summarized in Weyl, *Geography of American Achievement,* 139–41.
47. Ibid., 140.
48. Weyl, *Creative Elite,* 92.

11. IQ AND PRODUCTIVITY

1. Herrnstein, Belke, and Taylor, "New York City Police Department," photocopy, 1990, is the source for the tale.
2. *Economics* (twelfth edition), 620, the best-selling textbook by Paul A. Samuelson and William D. Nordhaus, defines human capital as "the stock of useful and valuable knowledge built up in the process of education or training."
3. See her "Test Scores as Measures of Human Capital and Forecasting Tools," 70–99, in Cattell, ed., *Intelligence and National Achievement.*
4. McCall, "Childhood IQs," shows IQ at sixteen correlating about .60 with adult occupational status. Waller, "Achievement and Social Mobility," examines the correlations between teenage IQ and adult occupational status for pairs of fathers and sons. The correlation for the fathers was .69. For the sons, it was only .57; however, the sons had not yet attained their highest status.
5. Duncan, Featherman, and Duncan, *Socioeconomic Background and Achievement,* 38, shows the following correlations between fathers' occupational status and the sons' when the latter were in the following age brackets: 25 to 34, .35; 35 to 44, .39; 45 to 54, .38; 55 to 64, .35.
6. Jencks et al., *Who Gets Ahead?* 120.
7. Jensen, *Straight Talk,* 195.
8. Jencks et al., *Who Gets Ahead?* 220–21.
9. See Gottfredson, "IQ vs. Training," for an explication of, and strenuous disagreement with, this "training hypothesis."
10. Collins, *The Credential Society.*
11. "Joint-Service Efforts," chapter 2, 2–3.
12. Ibid., chapter 2, 13.

13. Gottfredson, "Societal Consequences," 400–1.
14. Gottfredson, invited paper presented at a 1985 conference of the Personnel Testing Council of Southern California, on "The *g* Factor in Employment Testing," 10–11.
15. Hunter, "Cognitive Ability," 345.
16. Hunter, Schmidt, and Judiesch, "Individual Differences in Output," 36.
17. Ibid., 37.
18. Gottfredson, "Societal Consequences," 398–403.
19. U.S. Department of Labor, "Economic Benefits," *USES Test Research Report No. 47*, 1983.
20. Hartigan and Wigdor, eds. *Fairness in Employment Testing*, 235–48.
21. Ibid., 244–46.
22. Ibid., 241.

12. BLACK-WHITE IQ DIFFERENCES

1. The estimate assumes that IQs in the two populations are more or less normally distributed and that the black-white gap is about one standard deviation. On these reasonable and broadly accepted assumptions, about one-sixth of all blacks would be above the white average. The black population in 1992 was generally estimated at around 32 million.
2. Jensen, *Straight Talk*, 224.
3. Ibid., 208.
4. See the raw-score data in chapter 6, page 65.
5. Again, the estimates assume that the distribution of IQs can be roughly represented by the bell-shaped normal curve.
6. Again assuming the normal curve.
7. Gecas, *Annual Review*.
8. Shuey, *Testing of Negro Intelligence*, offers the most complete summary of pre-1965 data.
9. Jensen, "Nature of the Black-White Difference," 203–4.
10. Aiken, *Assessment of Intellectual Functioning*, 156.
11. Jensen, "Nature of the Black-White Difference," 202.
12. Jensen, "How Much Can We Boost IQ?" 81.
13. Snyderman and Rothman, *The IQ Controversy*, 216.
14. McClelland, "Testing for Competence," 1.
15. Ibid., 7.
16. Wigdor and Garner, *Ability Testing*, 77.
17. Ibid., 77.
18. Snyderman and Rothman, *The IQ Controversy*, 117.
19. Ibid., 133.
20. Jensen, *Straight Talk*, 138. He notes: "Highly verbal, individually administered tests that depend on understanding the tester, such as the Stanford-Binet IQ test, have been translated into Black English

and administered to black children by black testers who are adept in the dialect. The scores do not differ from those obtained when the test is given in Standard English."

21. This passage is taken from Jensen, "Cumulative Deficit," 184–91.
22. Reynolds and Gutkin, "A Multivariate Comparison," 178.
23. Jensen, *Straight Talk*, 191–93. His data, based on 622 black and 622 white California schoolchildren, show whites in all but the two lowest deciles scoring higher than blacks in the highest deciles.
24. Data provided to the author by the College Board.
25. Snyderman and Rothman, *The IQ Controversy*, 128.
26. Jensen, *Straight Talk*, 212.
27. Bock and Moore, *Advantage and Disadvantage*, 79.
28. The College Board, *1992 Profile of SAT and Achievement Test Takers*.
29. Vining, "Dysgenic Trend," table 3, 248.
30. Tape of the debate in author's possession.

13. ARE WE GETTING SMARTER?

1. The College Board, *1992 Profile of SAT and Achievement Test Takers*, iii.
2. Murray and Herrnstein, "Behind the SAT Decline."
3. Ibid., 38.
4. Ibid., 44.
5. Educational Testing Service, *America's Challenge*, 33.
6. Vining, "Dysgenic Trend," 247.
7. Vining, "Dysgenic Fertility," 511.
8. Flynn, "IQ Tests and Cultural Distance," 2.
9. The evidence is summarized in Flynn, "Massive IQ Gains."
10. Flynn, "IQ Tests and Cultural Distance," 2.
11. Flynn, "The Ontology of Intelligence," 28.
12. Personal communication.
13. Flynn, "IQ Tests and Cultural Distance," 2.
14. Ibid., 3–4; also see Flynn, "The Ontology of Intelligence," 26.
15. Locurto, *Sense and Nonsense*, 166.
16. Ibid., 167.
17. Lynn's argument, summarized in the following passage, is taken from "The Role of Nutrition," 273–85.
18. See Murray and Herrnstein, "Behind the SAT Decline," 36–38, for an explanation of the national norm studies.
19. Ibid., 40. Italics in the original.

14. THINKING ABOUT EUGENICS

1. Himmelfarb, *Poverty and Compassion*, 366.
2. Ibid., 366–67.
3. Shaw, "Man and Superman," 502.
4. Ibid., 725.

5. VanCourt, "Interview with Bajema," 10.
6. Quoted in the *Economist,* September 24, 1983, 34.
7. The dating service is described and extensively ridiculed in Chua, "Unstudly," 11–13.
8. Novick, *Honorable Justice,* 477, cites the Nuremberg report and refers to *Buck* as Holmes's "most notorious opinion."
9. Herrnstein, "IQ and Falling Birthrates."
10. A UPI dispatch of January 21, 1990, quotes the Rev. Joseph Dallas of Milwaukee as calling Planned Parenthood "racist" and claiming that it is practicing genocide against blacks. *USA Today* of May 8, 1990, quotes the Rev. Ron Ross of Stafford, Virginia, as equating abortion with "black genocide."
11. *Washington Post,* September 15, 1984, A2.
12. See Graham, "Combating Dysgenic Trends," 328–33, for an account of Muller's odyssey.
13. Data in this paragraph supplied by Graham.
14. Wright, "Achilles' Helix," 21–29.

15. THE CASE FOR TESTING

1. Letter of July 2, 1990, from Kirkpatrick to Pioneer Fund president Harry F. Weyher.
2. Snyderman and Rothman, *The IQ Controversy,* 56.
3. Letter dated March 25, 1988. I do not feel at liberty to disclose my correspondent's name.
4. Hayek, *The Constitution of Liberty,* 86.
5. Jaynes and Williams, eds., *A Common Destiny,* 6.
6. Herrnstein, "Still an American Dilemma," 11.
7. For an exhaustive report on the case, see Elliott, *Litigating Intelligence.*
8. *New York Times,* November 30, 1988, B6.
9. See the June 19, 1989, letter to the *New York Times* by Gretchen W. Rigol, executive director of the College Board's Admissions Testing Program, for a typical statement of the Board's case.
10. See Betz, ed., *Journal of Vocational Behavior,* for several different perspectives on this sequence of events.
11. *Richmond Times-Dispatch,* May 30, 1990.
12. Elliott, *Litigating Intelligence,* 165.
13. See the *San Francisco Chronicle,* September 2, 1992, Al, for a report on these bans.
14. The Long Island edition of the *New York Times* of May 7, 1989, LI1, reported widespread complaints because "some districts have inflated or weighted the grades of students in honors or advanced-placement courses to enhance the students' chances for scholarships. . . ." In 1991 the issue subsided when the New York legislature, facing huge budget deficits, eliminated all the scholarships.

15. In June 1992, the Department of Defense put the figure at 21 percent.
16. The phrase is attributed to sociologist Marion J. Levy, Jr., and appears in Moskos, "The Army's Racial Success Story," *New Republic*, August 5, 1991, 16.
17. Ibid., 16–17.
18. Ibid., 17.
19. Ibid., 16.

Bibliography

Aiken, Lewis R. *Assessment of Intellectual Functioning.* Boston: Allyn and Bacon, 1987.

Bachman, Jerald G. *Youth in Transition: The Impact of Family Background and Intelligence on Tenth-Grade Boys.* Ann Arbor: Institute for Social Research, 1970.

Beloff, Halla, ed. *A Balance Sheet on Burt.* Supplement to the *Bulletin of the British Psychological Society* 33 (1980).

Betz, Nancy E., ed. *Journal of Vocational Behavior* 33 (1988), no. 3.

Bock, R. Darrell, and Elsie G. J. Moore. *Advantage and Disadvantage: A Profile of American Youth.* Hillsdale, N.J.: Erlbaum, 1986.

Bouchard, Thomas J., Jr., and Matthew McGue. "Familial Studies of Intelligence: A Review." *Science* 212 (1981): 1055–59.

———. "Do Environmental Similarities Explain the Similarity in Intelligence of Identical Twins Reared Apart?" *Intelligence* 7 (1983): 175–84.

———, and Nancy L. Segal. "Environment and IQ." In Wolman, Benjamin B., ed. *Handbook of Intelligence: Theories, Measurements, and Applications.* New York: Wiley Interscience, 1985.

———, David T. Lykken, Matthew McGue, Nancy L. Segal, and Auke Tellegen. "Sources of Human Psychological Differences: The Minnesota Study of Twins Reared Apart." *Science* 250 (1990): 223–28.

———. "Nature via Nurture." Paper presented at the 1991 annual meeting of the American Association for the Advancement of Science.

Boring, Edward G. "Intelligence as the Tests Test It." *New Republic*, June 6, 1923, pp. 35–37.

Cattell, R. B., ed. *Intelligence and National Achievement*. Washington, D.C. Institute for the Study of Man, 1983.

Chen, Edward. "Twins Reared Apart: A Living Lab." *New York Times Magazine*, Dec. 9, 1979.

Chua, John. "Unstudly: Why Singapore's Smartest People Are Undersexed." *New Republic*, Jan. 27, 1992, pp. 11–13.

Cohn, Sanford J., Catherine M. G. Cohn, and Arthur R. Jensen. "Myopia and Intelligence: A Pleiotropic Relationship?" *Human Genetics* (1988), pp. 53–58.

College Board, *1992 Profile of SAT and Achievement Test Takers*. New York, 1992.

Collins, Randall. *The Credential Society: An Historical Sociology of Education and Stratification*. New York: Academic Press, 1979.

Duncan, Otis Dudley, David L. Featherman, and Beverly Duncan. *Socioeconomic Background and Achievement*. New York: Seminar Press, 1972.

Educational Testing Service. *America's Challenge: Accelerating Academic Achievement. A Summary of Findings from 20 Years of NAEP*. Princeton, N.J., 1990.

Elliott, Rogers. *Litigating Intelligence: IQ Tests, Special Education, and Social Science in the Courtroom*. Dover, Mass.: Auburn House, 1987.

Eysenck, H. J. *The Scientific Study of Personality*. London: Routledge & Kegan Paul, 1952.

———, and Leon Kamin. *The Intelligence Controversy*. New York: Wiley-Interscience, 1981.

Farber, Susan L. *Identical Twins Reared Apart: A Reanalysis*. New York: Basic Books, 1981.

Fancher, Raymond E. *The Intelligence Men: Makers of the IQ Controversy*. New York: W. W. Norton, 1985.

Farley, Reynolds, and Walter R. Allen. *The Color Line and the Quality of Life in America*. New York: Russell Sage Foundation, 1987.

Fletcher, Ronald. *Science, Ideology and the Media: The Cyril Burt Scandal*. New Brunswick, N.J.: Transaction Publishers, 1991.

Flynn, James. "The Ontology of Intelligence." In *Measurement, Realism and Objectivity*, John Forge, ed. D. Reidel Publishing Co., 1987.

———. "Massive IQ Gains in Fourteen Nations: What IQ Tests Really Measure." *Psychological Bulletin* 101 (1987): 171–91.

———. "IQ Tests and Cultural Distance." *SET: Research Information for Teachers*, no. 2 (1990), pp. 2–4.

Garber, Howard L. *The Milwaukee Project: Preventing Mental Retardation in Children at Risk*. Washington, D.C.: American Association on Mental Retardation, 1988.

Garraty, John A., and Peter Gay, eds. *The Columbia History of the World*. New York: Harper & Row, 1972.

Gecas, Viktor. *Annual Review of Sociology, 1982*. Palo Alto, Calif.: Annual Reviews, Inc., 1982.

Gilbert, G. M., Ph.D. *Nuremberg Diary.* New York: Farrar, Straus, 1947.

Gillie, Oliver. "Crucial Data Was Faked by Eminent Psychologist." London. *Sunday Times,* Oct. 24, 1976.

Gardner, Howard. *Frames of Mind: The Theory of Multiple Intelligences.* New York: Basic Books, 1983.

Gilligan, Carol. *In a Different Voice: Psychological Theory and Women's Development.* Cambridge, Mass.: Harvard University Press, 1982.

Glees, Paul. *The Human Brain.* New York: Cambridge University Press, 1988.

Goertzel, Mildred George, Victor Goertzel, and Ted George Goertzel. *Three Hundred Eminent Personalities.* San Francisco: Jossey-Bass Publishers, 1978.

Gordon, Robert A., and Eileen E. Rudert. "Bad News Concerning IQ Tests." *Sociology of Education, 1979* 52: 174–90.

Gottfredson, Linda S. "IQ vs. Training: Job Performance and Black-White Occupational Inequality." Paper presented at a symposium at the 1986 annual meeting of the American Psychological Association.

———. "Societal Consequences of the *g* Factor in Employment." *The Journal of Vocational Behavior,* Dec. 1986.

Gould, Stephen Jay. *The Mismeasure of Man.* New York: Norton, 1981.

Graham, Robert K. "Combating Dysgenic Trends in Modern Society: The Repository for Germinal Choice." *Mankind Quarterly* 27 (1987): 327–35.

Gutkin, T. B. A., and Cecil R. Reynolds. "Factorial Similarity of the WISC-R for White and Black Children from the Standardization Sample." *Journal of Educational Psychology* 73 (1981): 227–31.

Haldane, J. B. S. "Heredity." In Encyclopedia Britannica, 1944 edition, Vol. XI, 494.

Hartigan, John A., and Alexandra K. Wigdor, eds. *Fairness in Employment Testing: Validity Generalization, Minority Issues, and the General Aptitude Test Battery.* Washington, D.C.: National Academy Press, 1989.

Hauser, Thomas. *Muhammad Ali: His Life and Times.* New York: Simon & Schuster, 1991.

Hayek, F. A. *The Constitution of Liberty.* Chicago: University of Chicago Press, 1960.

Hearnshaw, L. S. *Cyril Burt, Psychologist.* Ithaca, N.Y.: Cornell University Press, 1979.

Herrnstein, R. J. *I.Q. in the Meritocracy.* Boston: Atlantic-Little, Brown, 1973.

———. "IQ Testing and the Media." *Atlantic,* August 1982.

———. "IQ and Falling Birthrates." *Atlantic,* May 1989.

———. "Still an American Dilemma." *Public Interest,* Winter 1990, 3–17.

———, Terry Belke, and James Taylor. "New York City Police Department Class of 1940: A Preliminary Report." Photocopy, 1990.

Himmelfarb, Gertrude. *Poverty and Compassion: The Moral Imagination of the Late Victorians.* New York: Knopf, 1991.

Holden, Constance. "Identical Twins Reared Apart." *Science* 207 (1980), no. 21.

———. "Twins Reunited." *Science 80,* Nov. 1980, 55–59.

Humphreys, Lloyd G. "Trends in Levels of Academic Achievement of Blacks and Other Minorities." *Intelligence* 12 (1988) no. 3.

Hunter, John E. "Cognitive Ability, Cognitive Aptitudes, Job Knowledge, and Job Performance." *Journal of Vocational Behavior,* Dec. 1986, 340–62.

———, Frank L. Schmidt, and Michael K. Judiesch. "Individual Differences in Output as a Function of Job Complexity." *Journal of Applied Psychology.* 75 (1990) no. 1, 28–42.

Itzkoff, Seymour. *The Road to Equality: Evolution and Social Reality.* New York: Praeger, 1992.

Jaynes, Gerald David, and Robin M. Williams, Jr., eds. *A Common Destiny: Blacks and American Society.* Washington, D.C.: National Academy Press, 1989.

Jencks, Christopher, and Associates. *Inequality: A Reassessment of the Effect of Family and Schooling in America.* New York: Basic Books, 1972.

———. *Who Gets Ahead? The Determinants of Economic Success in America.* New York: Basic Books, 1979.

Jensen, Arthur R. "How Much Can We Boost IQ and Scholastic Achievement?" *Harvard Educational Review* 39 (1969), no. 1, 1–123.

———. "Reducing the Heredity-Environment Uncertainty." *Harvard Educational Review* 39 (1969), no. 2, 209–43.

———. *Genetics and Education.* New York: Harper & Row, 1972.

———. "Sir Cyril Burt: Obituary." *Psychometrika* 37 (1972): 115–17.

———. "What Is the Question? What Is the Evidence?" *The Psychologists.* London: Oxford University Press, 1974.

———. "Cumulative Deficit in IQ of Blacks in the Rural South." *Developmental Psychology* 13 (1977), no. 3, 184–91.

———. *Bias in Mental Testing.* New York: Free Press, 1980.

———. *Straight Talk About Mental Tests.* New York: Free Press, 1981.

———. "The Effects of Inbreeding on Mental Ability Factors." *Personality and Individual Differences* 4 (1983): 71–87.

———. "The Nature of the Black-White Difference on Various Psychometric Tests: Spearman's Hypothesis." *Behavioral and Brain Sciences* 8 (1985), no. 2, 193–263.

———. "Understanding *g* in Terms of Information Processing." *Educational Psychology Review,* in press.

———. "Raising IQ Without Increasing *g.*" *Developmental Review* 9 (1989): 234–58.

———. "Speed of Elementary Cognitive Processes: A Chronometric Anchor for Psychometric Tests of *g.*" *Psychological Test Bulletin* 4 (1991), no. 2, 59–70.

———. "Why Is Reaction Time Correlated with Psychometric *g*?" Paper presented at a symposium on reaction time at the 1991 annual meeting of the American Psychological Association in San Francisco.

———. "IQ and Science: The Mysterious Burt Affair." In *Public Interest,* Fall 1991, pp. 93–106.

Johnson, Paul. *Intellectuals.* New York: Harper & Row, 1988.

Joynson, Robert B. *The Burt Affair.* London and New York: Routledge, 1989.

Kamin, Leon J. *The Science and Politics of IQ.* Potomac, Md.: Erlbaum, 1974.

Kearns, David T., and Denis P. Doyle. *Winning the Brain Race: A Bold Plan to Make Our Schools Competitive.* San Francisco: ICS Press, 1988.

Kiener, Von F., and E. Keiper. "Some Correlates Between Facial Cues and Intelligence." *Homo* 28: 40–45.

Klitgaard, Robert. *Choosing Elites.* New York: Basic Books, 1985.

Lapointe, Archie E., Nancy A. Mead, and Gary W. Phillips. *A World of Differences: An International Assessment of Mathematics and Science.* Princeton, N.J.: Educational Testing Service, 1989.

Lewontin, R. C., Steven Rose, and Leon Kamin. *Not in Our Genes: Biology, Ideology, and Human Nature.* New York: Pantheon, 1984.

Locurto, Charles. *Sense and Nonsense About IQ: The Case for Uniqueness.* New York: Praeger, 1991.

Loehlin, John C. "Should We Do Research on Race Differences in Intelligence?" *Intelligence* 16 (1992), no. 1, 1–4.

Lykken, David T. "Research With Twins: The Concept of Emergenesis." Presidential address to the 1981 annual meeting of the Society for Psychophysiological Research. *Psychophysiology* 19 (1981), no. 4, 361–73.

Lynn, Richard. "The Intelligence of the Chinese and Malays in Singapore." *Mankind Quarterly* 18 (1977): 125–28.

———. *Educational Achievement in Japan.* London: Macmillan, 1987.

———. "The Intelligence of the Mongoloids: A Psychometric, Evolutionary and Neurological Theory." *Personality and Individual Differences* 8 (1987), no. 6, 813–44.

———, Susan Hampson, and Margaret Lee. "The Intelligence of Chinese Children in Hong Kong." *School Psychology International* 9 (1988): 29–32.

———, Claudia Pagliari, and Jimmy Chan. "Intelligence in Hong Kong Measured for Spearman's *g* and the Visuospatial and Verbal Primaries." *Intelligence* 12 (1988), no. 4, 423–33.

———. "The Role of Nutrition in Secular Increases in Intelligence." *Personality and Individual Differences* 11 (1990), no. 3, 273–85.

Matarazzo, Joseph D. *Wechsler's Measurement and Appraisal of Adult Intelligence,* 5th ed. New York: Oxford University Press, 1972.

McCall, R. B. "Childhood IQs as Predictors of Adult Educational and Occupational Status." *Science* 197 (1977); 482–83.

McClelland, David C. "Testing for Competence Rather Than for 'Intelligence.'" *American Psychologist.* 28 (1973); 1–14.

Medawar, Peter B. *Advice to a Young Scientist.* New York: Harper & Row, 1979.

Medvedev, Roy A. "The Stalin Question." In Cohen, Stephen F., Alexander Rabinowitch, and Robert Sharlet, eds. *The Soviet Union Since Stalin.* Bloomington, Ind.: Indiana University Press, 1980, 32–49.

Modgil, Sohan, and Celia Modgil, eds. *Arthur Jensen: Consensus and Controversy.* Philadelphia: Falmer Press, 1987.

Morris, Roger. *Richard Milhous Nixon: The Rise of an American Politician.* New York: Henry Holt, 1990.

Moskos, Charles. "The Army's Racial Success Story: How They Do It." *New Republic,* August 5, 1991, 16–20.

Muller, H. J. "The Destruction of Science in the USSR." In Steinberg, Julien, ed., *Verdict of Three Decades: From the Literature of Individual Revolt Against Soviet Communism: 1917–1950.* New York: Duell, Sloan, and Pearce, 1950.

Murray, Charles, and R. J. Herrnstein. "What's Really Behind the SAT Score Decline." *Public Interest,* Winter 1992, 32–56.

Mustain, Gene, and Jerry Capeci. *Mob Star: The Story of John Gotti.* New York: Franklin Watts, 1988.

Nickerson, Raymond S. Untitled review of *Practical Intelligence,* Sternberg and Wagner, eds. *American Journal of Psychology* 101 (1988), no. 2, pp. 293–302.

Norden, Edward. "Counting the Jews." *Commentary,* October 1991, 36–43.

Novick, Sheldon M. *Honorable Justice: The Life of Oliver Wendell Holmes.* Boston: Little, Brown, 1989.

Oakes, Jeannie, with Tor Ormseth, Robert Bell, and Patricia Camp. *Multiplying Inequalities: The Effects of Race, Social Class, and Tracking on Opportunities to Learn Mathematics and Science.* Santa Monica, Calif.: Rand Corporation, 1990.

Osborne, R. Travis, Clyde E. Noble, and Nathaniel Weyl, eds. *Human Variation: The Biopsychology of Age, Race, and Sex.* New York: Academic Press, 1978.

Peters, Roger. *Practical Intelligence: Working Smarter in Business and the Professions.* New York. Harper & Row, 1987.

Poon, Leonard W., David C. Rubin, and Barbara A. Wilson, eds. *Everyday Cognition in Adulthood and Late Life.* Cambridge: Cambridge University Press, 1989.

Reeves, Thomas C. *A Question of Character: A Life of John F. Kennedy.* New York: Free Press, 1991.

Reynolds, Cecil R., and T. B. A. Gutkin. "A Multivariate Comparison of the Intellectual Performance of Blacks and Whites Matched on Four Demographic Variables." *Personality and Individual Differences* 2 (1981): 175–80.

Reynolds, Cecil R., and Robert T. Brown, eds. *Perspectives on Bias in Mental Testing.* New York: Plenum Press, 1984.

Riggio, Ronald E., Jack Messamer, and Barbara Throckmorton. "Social and Academic Intelligence: Conceptually Distinct but Overlapping Constructs." *Personality and Individual Differences* 12 (1991), no. 7.

Rimland, Bernard. "A Search for Tests of Practical Intelligence." In *Mental Tests and Cultural Adaptation*, Cronbach, L. J., and P. J. D. Drenth, eds., pp. 245–50. The Hague: Mouton, 1972.

Rushton, J. Philippe. "Reply to Willerman on Mongoloid-Caucasoid Differences in Brain Size." *Intelligence* 15 (1991): 365–67.

Salthouse, Timothy A. *Theoretical Perspectives on Cognitive Aging*. Hillsdale, N.J.: Lawrence Erlbaum Associates, 1991.

Scarr, Sandra, and Kathleen McCartney. "How People Make Their Own Environments: A Theory of Genotype-Environment Effects." *Child Development* 54: 424–35.

Select Committee on Equal Educational Opportunity, United States Senate, *Environment, Intelligence, and Scholastic Achievement*. Washington, D.C.: U.S. Government Printing Office, 1972.

Seligman, Daniel. "Measuring Intelligence." *Commentary*, March 1989, pp. 70–72.

Shaw, Bernard. "Man and Superman." In *Nine Plays*. New York: Dodd, Mead, 1948.

Shuey, Audrey M. *The Testing of Negro Intelligence*, 2nd ed. New York: Social Science Press, 1966.

Shurkin, Joel N. *Terman's Kids: The Groundbreaking Study of How the Gifted Grow Up*. Boston: Little, Brown, 1992.

Silberman, Charles E. *A Certain People*. New York: Summit, 1985.

Smith, Adam. *The Wealth of Nations*. New York: Modern Library, 1937.

Snyderman, Mark, and R. J. Herrnstein. "Intelligence Tests and the Immigration Act of 1924." *American Psychologist*, Sept. 1983, pp. 986–95.

———, and Stanley Rothman. *The IQ Controversy: The Media and Public Policy*. New Brunswick, N.J.: Transaction Books, 1988.

Spitz, Herman H. *The Raising of Intelligence: A Selected History of Attempts to Raise Retarded Intelligence*. Hillsdale, N.J.: Erlbaum, 1986.

Sternberg, Robert J. *Beyond IQ: A Triarchic Theory of Human Intelligence*. Cambridge: Cambridge University Press, 1985.

———. *Intelligence Applied: Understanding and Increasing Your Intellectual Skills*. San Diego: Harcourt Brace Jovanovich, 1986.

———, and Richard K. Wagner. *Practical Intelligence: Nature and Origins of Competence in the Everyday World*. Cambridge: Cambridge University Press, 1986.

———. "Beyond IQ Testing." *National Forum (The Phi Kappa Phi Journal)*, spring 1988, pp. 8–11.

———, ed. *Encyclopedia of Intelligence*. In press.

Stevenson, Harold W., Shin-Ying Lee, and James W. Stigler. "Mathematics Achievements of Chinese, Japanese, and American Children." *Science* 231 (1986): 693–99.

Storfer, Miles D. *Intelligence and Giftedness: The Contributions of Heredity and Early Environment*. San Francisco: Jossey-Bass, 1990.

Symonds, Percival M., and Arthur R. Jensen. *From Adolescent to Adult*. New York: Columbia University Press, 1961.

Taylor, H. F. *The IQ Game: A Methodological Inquiry Into the Heredity-Environment Controversy.* New Brunswick, N.J.: Rutgers University Press, 1980.

Terman, Lewis M., and Melita H. Oden. *The Gifted Group at Mid-Life: Thirty-Five Years' Follow-Up of the Superior Child.* Stanford, Calif.: Stanford University Press, 1959.

U.S. Commission on Civil Rights. *Racial Isolation in the Public Schools,* vol. 1. Washington, D.C.: U.S. Government Printing Office, 1967.

U.S. Department of Defense, Office of the Assistant Secretary (Force Management and Personnel). "Joint-Service Efforts to Link Enlistment Standards to Job Performance: Recruit Quality and Military Readiness." *Report to the House Committee on Appropriations.* 1989.

U.S. Department of Labor, Division of Counseling and Test Development, Employment and Training Administration. "The Economic Benefits of Personnel Selection Using Ability Tests: A State of the Art Review Including a Detailed Analysis of the Dollar Benefit of U.S. Employment Service Placements and a Critique of the Low-Cutoff Method of Test Use." *USES Test Research Report No. 47,* 1983.

VanCourt, Marion. "An Interview With Carl J. Bajema." *Eugenics Bulletin,* Fall 1983, 9–16.

Vernon, Philip A., ed. *Biological Approaches to the Study of Human Intelligence.* Norwood, N.J.: Ablex, 1992.

———. "Studying Intelligence the Hard Way." *Intelligence* 15 (1991), no. 4, 389–95.

Vining, Daniel R., Jr. "On the Possibility of the Reemergence of a Dysgenic Trend With Respect to Intelligence in American Fertility Differentials." *Intelligence* 6 (1982): 261–64.

———. "Mean IQ Differences in Japan and the United States." Letter to *Nature* 301 (1983): 738.

———. "Dysgenic Fertility and Welfare: An Elementary Test." *Personality and Individual Differences* 4 (1983), no. 5, 511–18.

Waller, J. H. "Achievement and Social Mobility: Relationships Among IQ Score, Education and Occupation in Two Generations." *Social Biology* 18 (1971): 252–59.

Wechsler, David. *Selected Papers of David Wechsler.* New York: Academic Press, 1974.

———. "Intelligence Defined and Undefined." *American Psychologist* 30 (1975): 135–39.

Weisbrod, Burton A., and Peter Karpoff. "Monetary Returns to College Education, Student Ability, and College Quality." *Review of Economics and Statistics* 50 (1968), no. 4, 491–97.

West, Robert L., and Jan D. Sinnott, eds. *Everyday Memory and Aging: Current Research and Methodology.* New York: Springer-Verlag, 1992.

Weyl, Nathaniel. *The Creative Elite in America.* Washington, D.C.: Public Affairs Press, 1966.

———. *The Geography of American Achievement.* Washington, D.C.: Scott-Townsend Publishers, 1989.

Wheeler, L. R. "A Comparative Study of the Intelligence of East Tennessee Mountain Children." *Journal of Educational Psychology* 33 (1942): 321–34.

Wigdor, Alexandra K., and Wendell R. Garner, eds. *Ability Testing: Uses, Consequences, and Controversies.* Washington, D.C.: National Academy Press, 1982.

Willerman, Lee, Robert Schultz, J. Neal Rutledge, and Erin D. Bigler. *"In Vivo* Brain Size and Intelligence." *Intelligence* 15 (1991), no. 2, 223–28.

Wills, Garry. *Inventing America: Jefferson's Declaration of Independence.* New York: Vintage Books, 1979.

Wilson, James Q., and R. J. Herrnstein. *Crime and Human Nature.* New York: Simon & Schuster, 1985.

Wright, Robert. "Achilles' Helix." *New Republic,* July 9, 1990, 21–29.

Index